W9-BXP-718

SEGREGATION IN RESIDENTIAL AREAS

**Papers on Racial and Socioeconomic
Factors in Choice of Housing**

Edited by Amos H. Hawley and
Vincent P. Rock

Division of Behavioral Sciences
National Research Council

NATIONAL ACADEMY OF SCIENCES

Washington, D.C.   1973

NOTICE: The commissioned papers that constitute most of this volume were developed in the course of a study undertaken under the aegis of the National Research Council with the express approval of its Governing Board. Such approval indicated that the Board considered the problem addressed in the study to be one of national significance and that its elucidation required scientific competence that could be brought to bear through the resources of the National Research Council. The members of the Panel responsible for the study were selected for their individual scholarly competence and judgment with due consideration for the balance and breadth of disciplines. Responsibility for arranging for the commissioned papers rested with the Panel.

Available from

Printing and Publishing Office, National Academy of Sciences
2101 Constitution Avenue, N.W., Washington, D.C. 20418

LIBRARY OF CONGRESS CATALOGING IN PUBLICATION DATA

Main entry under title:

Segregation in residential areas.

    Papers originally prepared for the Social Sciences Panel brought together by the Division of Behavioral Sciences of the National Research Council.
    Includes bibliographies.
    1. Discrimination in housing—United States—Addresses, essays, lectures. 2. Negroes—Housing—Addresses, essays, lectures. I. Hawley, Amos Henry, ed. II. Rock, Vincent P., ed. III. Social Science Panel.
HD7293.S4   301.5′4   72-85593
ISBN 0-309-02042-5

Printed in the United States of America

Preface

As the American people look ahead to the remainder of this decade, they should be aware that important constructive changes in race relations have been under way for the past quarter of a century.

First, there has been a wide and apparently deep shift in the viewpoint of whites toward a more positive view of the black population. Support for equal opportunity in employment, education, housing, voting, and many other areas now marks white attitudes. To illustrate, the percentage of the white population willing to say that they are prepared to accept black neighbors has moved up from less than 40 percent to nearly 80 percent.

Second, by authority and example, the federal government has supported the removal of social inequalities between the races. All branches of government—legislative, judicial, and executive—have played significant roles in providing this support. On many fronts, the courts have acted to compel the correction and elimination of social inequalities. In the civil rights acts, as well as in other legislation, Congress has moved in the same direction. The executive branch, not only in the enforcement of particular legal requirements but by the example it has sought to set in the armed services, the civil service, and in contractual arrangements, has also provided authoritative sanction for equal treatment of minorities.

Third, the income and occupational differences between the white and black populations have been significantly reduced (although certainly not in all respects) since the end of World War II. Black family incomes have been rising more rapidly than those of the white population. More black young people than ever before are graduating from high school and going on to college.

Fourth, white awareness of the structural barriers faced by the black population has increased. Whites have become much more conscious of the impediments to equal access to employment, to education, and to housing faced by blacks, as well as to the consequences of these inequalities.

Fifth, white stereotypes of the black population have been eroded as white Americans have developed a growing capacity to view members of that minority as individuals. Objective changes in the status of blacks have helped in this regard, as have more frequent contacts in a variety of situations. Increasingly, blacks are seen as individuals differing widely in income, education, and occupational status.

Support for the reduction of racial inequities is not limited to the federal government. State and local governments are taking affirmative action that, in some instances, goes beyond the national initiatives. While these actions derive support from the major shifts in white attitudes and perceptions now under way, they also serve to endorse and undergird the continued movement toward acceptance of equal access to the full range of social, economic, and political opportunities provided by the society without regard to race.

Continued movement is vital; in many specific situations, equal access is not yet a firmly grounded reality. In some fields, existing institutional networks diffuse responsibility in a manner that permits the continuation of practices based on presumptions about public attitudes that are no longer as valid as they were a decade or two ago. For example, many real estate markets seem to be of this character. Subtle forms of discrimination continue, which seem to find support in the presumption that prejudice is as widely prevalent as it once was.

Partial success in reducing social inequities associated with race raises new issues. Having attained some access, the black population will certainly seek full equality of access to housing as well as to employment and education. Changes in white attitudes suggest a much higher degree of receptivity to this development than was present earlier. But before equal opportunity can be achieved, still further changes in the behavior of the white population will have to take place. Individually, whites may have to accept more responsibility for ensuring that the institutions of society operate in a nondiscriminatory fashion.

The papers that make up the body of this volume were originally prepared for the Social Science Panel brought together by the Division of Behavioral Sciences of the National Research Council at the request of the National Academy of Sciences–National Academy of Engineering's Advisory Committee to the U.S. Department of Housing and Urban Development. The abstracts were prepared by the staff of the Panel. The task of the Panel was to bring the existing behavioral and social science knowledge to bear on the question of the feasibility and desirability of "social mixing" in residential areas and, more particularly, in the Operation Breakthrough sites.

At the very outset of its discussion, the Panel agreed on the necessity of commissioning several papers to pull together the empirical knowledge bearing on social mixing. While sensitive to the important interrelationships between them, the Panel also agreed that racial and socioeconomic mixing could best be dealt with separately. In defining the areas to be covered in the commissioned papers, the Panel brought to bear an appreciation of the research that had been conducted and its relevance to the public policy issues faced by the U.S. Department of Housing and Urban Development. With respect to race, three areas were identified: attitudes toward race and housing, institutional and community factors that affect choice in housing, and experience in mixed residential neighborhoods. In the limited body of research bearing on socioeconomic mixing, the topic of population redistribution within metropolitan areas was identified as feasible for a state-of-the-knowledge paper. One Panel member, Cora B. Marrett, agreed to review the literature on social stratification in urban areas.

As the papers were completed, each was read and discussed by the Panel. When possible, the authors participated in these discussions. The state-of-the-knowledge papers played a critically important role in the deliberations of the Panel. Though drawn from work in several different disciplines, the papers provided a common body of empirical knowledge essential to the Panel in reaching collective judgments. In a number of instances, the papers served to correct or extend views previously derived from partial information. As a result of discussions with the authors, the issues to be addressed were sharpened and elaborated. As the papers were reviewed, they were also made available to key officials in the Department of Housing

Urban Development. In this way, they played an important part
creating an informed environment for receiving the Panel's report
l findings and the recommendations of the NAS-NAE's Advisory
mmittee to HUD, *Freedom of Choice in Housing: Opportunities
l Constraints* (Washington, D.C.: National Academy of Sciences,
72).

The papers are being made available in full both because of their
trinsic scientific interest and because of the background they pro-
de for issues that will continue to concern policy-makers and the
iblic for years to come.

The editors wish to express their appreciation to Dr. Henry David,
xecutive Secretary of the Division of Behavioral Sciences, for his
onstructive suggestions and to Dr. John Laurmann, Executive Sec-
tary of the Advisory Committee to HUD, for his cooperation.
Irs. Kay C. Harris provided indispensable administrative support
hroughout the undertaking, and Mrs. Gilda Nimer assisted in the
inal preparation of the manuscript.

AMOS H. HAWLEY
Panel Chairman

December 1972

Social Science Panel

AMOS H. HAWLEY, Kenan Professor of Sociology, University of North Carolina at Chapel Hill, *Chairman*

ARTHUR H. BRAYFIELD, Chairman, Graduate Faculty in Psychology, Claremont Graduate School

ALAN K. CAMPBELL, Dean of The Maxwell School of Citizenship and Public Affairs, Syracuse University

BENJAMIN CHINITZ, Professor of Economics, Brown University

ALEXANDER L. CLARK, Lyndon Baines Johnson School of Public Affairs, University of Texas

LAWRENCE FRIEDMAN, Professor of Law, Stanford University

ERIC LAMPARD, Professor of History, State University of New York at Stony Brook

CORA B. MARRETT, Assistant Professor of Sociology, Western Michigan University

WILBUR R. THOMPSON, Professor of Economics, Wayne State University

Contents

Introduction

The process by which scientific knowledge may be brought to bear on public policy has become a subject for systematic inquiry only in recent times. Frequently, moreover, perceptions of the process by scientists and policy-makers are neither explicit nor congruent. Although the papers in this volume are primarily intended to make a substantive contribution, their preparation and utilization illustrates one of the ways in which the scientific advisory process may be made to work with some effectiveness.

In 1969, the Department of Housing and Urban Development (HUD) entered into a contract with the National Academy of Sciences that led to the creation of a standing advisory committee to the Department. Earlier, at the Department's request, two complementary reports on research needs in the housing and urban-development area had been prepared, one by the Division of Behavioral Sciences, the other by the Division of Engineering.[1] At the out-

[1] *A Strategic Approach to Urban Research and Development: Social and Behavioral Considerations.* A report by the Committee on Social and Behavioral Urban Research, Division of Behavioral Sciences, National Research Council to the Department of Housing and Urban Development, National Academy of Sciences, Washington, D.C., 1969; *Long-Range Planning for Urban Research and Development: Technological Considerations.* A report by the Committee on Urban Technology, Division of Engineering, National Academy of Sciences, Washington, D.C., 1969.

set, however, the new standing Advisory Committee (ACHUD) was concerned primarily with the technical aspects of "Operation Breakthrough"—a major, HUD-sponsored experiment in industrialized housing.

The Department of Housing and Urban Development has been charged by the Congress to direct its various housing and urban development programs so as: (1) to provide an adequate supply of good housing and a suitable living environment for every American family; (2) to give special attention to the housing needs of lower-income groups; and (3) to assure equal access to housing for all races. As is customary, however, in stipulating these objectives the Congress left the Department the task of designing specific policies, programs, and procedures for achieving them.

The most appropriate instruments for attaining the Department's social policy objectives are far from self-evident. Operation Breakthrough, for example, was conceived as a large-scale, experimental effort to overcome some of the existing technical barriers to creating an expanded supply of mass-produced housing of good quality. Yet, the program has inevitably been concerned also with such issues as restrictive building codes, land-use problems, trade union practices, and the small scale on which many developers currently operate. Moreover, for each Breakthrough site, such questions as the effect of market factors on the economic and racial composition of the ultimate residents have had to be carefully considered.

In all its activities, the Department has tried to devise policies that are both feasible and in accord with its legislative mandates. Promoting "social mixing," including both racial and economic mixing, in residential areas is a policy whose feasibility could be examined and assessed as part of the Operation Breakthrough experiment. HUD, therefore, asked the NAS Advisory Committee for advice on ways to implement such a policy in neighborhoods of the size contemplated by the Breakthrough experiment. The Committee, in turn, asked the NRC's Division of Behavioral Sciences to establish a small panel to inquire into the contribution that the social sciences would make to the Department's understanding of the issues and opportunities involved.

Formation of the Social Science Panel was accomplished in several steps. Following its usual practice, the Division of Behavioral Sciences first identified those disciplines and fields best prepared to respond to the question at hand, namely: What is known about the feasibility and desirability of "social mixing" in residential areas? The areas identified included demography, economics, history, law, political science, psychology, and sociology. A list of possible panel members was developed for each area. In the final selection, individuals were chosen from the lists who could bring to the panel not only substantive competence but also familiarity with the policy processes associated with government housing and urban development programs.

At its first meeting, the Panel was briefed by officials of the Department of Housing and Urban Development. From the Panel's point of view, the three most important questions then and in its subsequent deliberations were the following:

1. On what specific policy questions was scientific advice being sought?
2. What was the most appropriate way to formulate those questions, so as to bring existing knowledge to bear on answering them?
3. What knowledge already available would help to answer the questions posed, and how might it best be gathered and sifted in the time available?

The Policy Context

In defining the relevant policy questions, the Panel requested and obtained the full cooperation of the Department's top staff. Individuals outside the Department concerned with, and knowledgeable about, housing and urban development policy were also interviewed. As a result, the Panel gained an understanding of the operational context in which the request for advice had been made, as well as a rich appreciation of the diversity of perspectives from which HUD's broad social policy objectives are viewed by persons and groups committed to them.

In the course of the several exchanges, it was pointed out that to meet the needs of its present and expected population, for example, the United States, between now and the year 2000, will have to build housing equivalent to that required by a community of 70,000 people *each week*. In effect, the annual level of housing production will have to be raised from about 1.5 million to 3.0 million units. To achieve the higher level, innovative approaches to various aspects of housing construction, ranging from land acquisition through industrial building technologies to marketing arrangements, will be essential.

Given the Department's estimate of present and future housing de-

mand, the catalytic role of Operation Breakthrough as a learning experience for both HUD and the housing industry becomes apparent.
Operation Breakthrough is a major research and development effort
intended to stimulate a more rapid rate of improvement and moderni-
zation of all elements of the housing-production system—technology,
design, manufacturing, marketing, land-use planning, and management.
As part of the experiment, criteria are being developed that permit
evaluation of technological innovations from the point of view of
consumer needs. State laws are being enacted to overcome the barriers that local building codes pose to the widespread use of industrialized housing technologies. A new consciousness is being stimulated among developers and government officials of the need to create
community-reinforcing environments. In its emphasis on a systems
approach to housing and residential development, Operation Breakthrough seeks to accelerate already noteworthy trends in community
planning and construction management. Moreover, changes in production technique are only part of the picture. Some authorities predict
that before the end of the present decade, industrialized housing will
dominate the market, accounting for two thirds to three fourths of
all housing production. Hence, technological innovation is likely to
be associated with, and even to require significant alterations in the
roles and functions of the many institutions presently involved in
housing production, thereby exerting a profound influence on evolv-
ing patterns of urban living.

In the Breakthrough experiment, site-selection issues have been of
considerable concern to the Department, because of the resistance encountered in some communities where sites have been proposed or
selected. Breakthrough sites range in size from 80 to 500 housing
units. In each case, the managers of the Breakthrough program have
recognized the need to establish marketing or tenant-selection criteria that ensure enforcement of the fair housing standards to which
HUD is committed, as well as help to ensure occupant satisfaction
with the total living environment. However, local opposition appears
to center around the idea of "federally subsidized housing." Although
subsidy in one form or another is implicit in a substantial portion of
new housing construction, there has been a tendency to compound
the experimental character of the program, in this case, with negative
images of "public housing."

In the course of its attempt to gain an understanding of HUD policies and programs, the Panel learned that the site-selection issues faced
by Operation Breakthrough were not unlike those faced by other pro-

grams of assisted housing. H U D's responsibilities in all such programs are not only to prevent discrimination but also to promote equal opportunity. Hence, the Department must be as much concerned with the allocation of federal funds for housing construction and services as it is with the equitable distribution of access to the existing housing supply. The two considerations are, of course, closely related, but they can also have somewhat different action implications.

Improving the quality of urban services available to people wherever they choose, or feel obliged to live, must be a complementary concern of residential policy. Urban services include education, health, transportation, and security, as well as an adequate supply of low- and moderate-income housing. However, a more equitable distribution of access to housing may also be attained by increasing the capacity of the disadvantaged or of minorities to exercise market options, for example, increasing their residential mobility. The Fair Housing Act of 1968 covers 55 million of the 70 million currently available housing units in the United States. H U D shares with the Department of Justice responsibility for vigorous implementation of the equal opportunity sections of that law. Nonetheless, as a growing number of middle-income minority families has become attracted to suburban living, and as employment opportunities have become more numerous in the urban rings of large metropolitan areas, zoning restrictions and local referenda have served to impede orderly expansion of the housing supply and, thus, to hinder the access of particular income or racial groups to housing and jobs.

H U D's responsibilities extend to the development of urban systems as a whole, but all relevant policy instruments are not under its control. It may, with its limited funds, support sites that enhance equitable access, but autonomous units of government may bar balanced development. Roads and freeways may act to facilitate or obstruct equitable access. Federal programs may be deployed to either strengthen the cohesion of metropolitan areas or reinforce their existing fragmentation, as is the case with sewerage and water systems. Orderly annexation, for example, is more likely to ensue when a city is supported in its efforts to provide sewers for the surrounding areas. Annexation, in turn, might promote more balanced attention to the need for low- and moderate-income housing. At present, such housing is frequently viewed diametrically—by the central city as an urgent need and by the suburbs as an undertaking to be avoided.

Mutual reinforcement of technology and social policy can be sought by several methods. One method would require, in order to qualify for federal support, that plans be comprehensive and take into account social as well as physical needs. Another would chip away at all the individual specific barriers to housing and dispersal and individual mobility rather than attempt to actively plan the pattern of urban development.

Despite its relative inexperience with the process of relating knowledge and policy, the Department has begun to perceive the advantages that an empirical and scientific assessment can bring to its programs. More particularly, it has begun to explore effective interface with the social sciences, which it views as underutilized and underfunded. The Office of the Assistant Secretary for Research and Technology seeks to provide a successful model for the utilization of social science knowledge in government.

HUD hoped to find microsocial engineering knowledge available in the social sciences. In the course of the Panel's work, however, it became clear that, while accumulated research can provide much information useful in formulating more effective social policy, social technology per se that is applicable to particular situations is in short supply. Thus, in responding to HUD's interest, the Panel sounded a note of caution. Science itself is intrinsically a body of fundamental knowledge. The behavioral and social sciences lack an accompanying engineering tradition.

It is also important to note that apparently discrete programmatic questions such as the feasibility of residential mixing are embedded in a larger social context, which must be taken into account. For example, the thicket of fragmented governments in metropolitan areas may have an important bearing on the feasibility of mixing in particular localities.

Policy-makers must equip themselves with people trained to search for reliable information, which they then translate into terms applicable to particular situations. The critical importance of timing in consulting the social sciences must also be stressed. For once initial policies are set, the range of feasible alternatives that might be suggested is sharply curtailed and the utility of the sciences drastically reduced.

Question Formulation

Formulating its own program of inquiry, the Panel was asked to address three questions: What is meant by the term "social mixing"?

Is it feasible and desirable? What knowledge exists in the behavioral and social sciences that bears upon these questions?

The Panel's search strategy involved five interrelated lines of inquiry and discussion. First, what ongoing trends and patterns of urban life should be taken into account? Second, viewing the Operation Breakthrough demonstration as a social rather than technological experiment, what can one learn from it? Third, what are the analytical categories from which a discussion of the primary questions can proceed? Fourth, the analytic elements must be ordered and related to policy from the standpoint of normative operational considerations. Finally, how can the conceptual framework be assessed? The need for information obtained by systematic surveys of the state of research knowledge was identified. Out of the search dynamics, an agreed-upon set of findings gradually evolved.

Trends and Patterns

National demographic data suggest that the population continues to sort itself out economically and racially by place of residence. But within metropolitan areas, how does the population redistribute itself? What significantly differentiates the central city from its suburban rings? Is it possible that both are more heterogeneous than is conventionally believed? In what critical aspects do residential distribution trends for race and those for socioeconomic class diverge? What has been the historical experience of the black minority as contrasted with that of other ethnic groups? Will new "life styles" significantly alter existing patterns? In sum, what knowledge of the broad social context should be taken into account in assessing alternative strategies of intervention?

Modern urban society is characterized by specialization and diversity. Occupations have multiplied. Patterns of family life have become more varied. Distinct new life styles are in evidence. Goods, services, and recognition are exchanged among diverse groups, this exchange providing a basic element of cohesion for the society as a whole.

The salience of status in our complex and highly differentiated urban systems has been mitigated. Yet some individuals, occupations, and communities continue to be accorded higher status than others. Perception of class distinctions associated with income and occupation, for example, is apparent in the patterns of urban residential distribution where Americans have long sifted and sorted themselves by socioeconomic class.

Similarity, not differences, characterizes residential neighborhoods. People of like income, occupation, and stage of the family life cycle tend to cluster together. As has been widely noted, families traditionally select homes in areas that will bring their children in contact with others of similar, or perhaps slightly higher, economic status. The heterogeneity of the society at large may even foster increased homogeneity in residential neighborhoods.

Historically, ethnicity and race have also played a role in shaping the pattern of residential distribution of the population. In varying degree, immigrant groups retained a sense of communal solidarity derived from a common language and culture. These groups tended to cluster together until their members were ready to disperse amid the larger society.

Historical analogies between the blacks in America and these other ethnic groups are inappropriate in several respects. Since color is visible, blacks are more effectively barred from open access to housing. Separate, identifiable black communities have persisted over a longer time and on a larger scale than those of any other ethnic group. Today, socioeconomic differences among blacks are nearly as varied as those among whites. The absolute number of poor whites is much greater, but the proportion of poor among blacks exceeds that among whites by a large margin. At the same time, the number of middle-class blacks is large and growing. Their income is rising and their occupations are becoming more diverse. Family residential requirements parallel those of whites in many respects, and status needs are similar.

Some black spokesmen seek the development of community power and the improvement of housing and other services in central city areas with large concentrations of low-income groups. Yet middle-income blacks appear to seek access to housing of their own choosing wherever it may be located. Given access to a good-quality living environment, people of similar socioeconomic status do not make choices reflecting either racial solidarity or racial prejudice.

In short, the objectives of racial mixing as contrasted with socioeconomic mixing may derive from very different motives and meet very different needs. Policies that attempt to deal simultaneously with both components may be very difficult to formulate. It also seems apparent that the institutions that must be harnessed to accomplish economic mixing are more extensive than those on which racial mixing may depend.

Operation Breakthrough Insights

Operation Breakthrough, viewed as a social rather than a technological experiment, served as a didactic model for exploring some of the practical aspects of "social mixing" questions. The experiment concretely illustrates several facets of the problem of designing an effective policy to achieve social mixing. Opposition was encountered from several communities selected for the location of Breakthrough sites. The opposition appeared to be fed by the stigma widely attached to federally supported housing. The negative image of public housing blocked perception of the differences between it and this experimental effort. Breakthrough helped to highlight the critical importance of site selection and the quality of housing in relation to social policies. Again, an examination of the location of Breakthrough sites revealed that, while some sites might be racially mixed at the outset, others might rapidly move in the direction of renewed residential segregation.

There was a play of economic forces too. Operating largely within existing financial policies, Breakthrough could only provide a relatively narrow range of housing prices, which, in turn, would confine the opportunities for economic mixing. On the other hand, the close working relation between HUD and the developers pointed to the possible importance of various kinds of managerial intervention in achieving social objectives. The experiment also provided insights into a range of possible trade-offs between the objective of increased production of quality housing, metropolitan growth policies, and racial or socioeconomically mixed residential areas.

Since almost one third of the annual production of new housing involves federal funds, the lessons to be learned from Breakthrough could have much wider significance. Systematic feedback from the Breakthrough experiment could provide valuable lessons with respect to site selection and tenant selection. Over time it could also provide information about the stability of mixed residential neighborhoods once created. Breakthrough is also a laboratory of government–developer and government–producer relations. Of course, in a broader sense, it has an influence on existing restraints on construction, on the aggregation of markets, and on project management techniques. Breakthrough may also help to illuminate the processes of technological diffusion in urban systems. As insights are acquired by government and industry, they can be applied to succeeding stages of housing-systems programs.

To capitalize on these opportunities, systematic designs, both for research and program evaluation, are necessary. Here the choice between the flexibility needed to adapt to the circumstances of a particular site and the desirability of comparability among the sites needs to be carefully weighed. Similarly, a balance must be achieved between the short-run interest of the policy-maker in improving performance of a program and the longer-run concerns of the scientist in increasing knowledge of basic social processes.

Structure of Knowledge

What are the relevant considerations in addressing the question of the feasibility or desirability of a policy of racial or socioeconomic mixing? The Panel's discussions were anchored in an understanding of the policy context, in a preliminary appreciation of ongoing trends, and in the concrete questions posed by the Operation Breakthrough experiment. Even so, the several disciplines represented on the Panel provided a multiplicity of perspectives and contributed to a spirited examination of the alternatives.

Issues of scale, stability, level, and range all enter into assessing the feasibility of residential mixing. Are there significant differences depending on whether one thinks of mixing family by family, block by block, or census tract by census tract? For example, are the implications of mixing within an elementary school area significantly different from those in a high school area? In addressing the question of scale, can the issue of optimum size in effect be ignored and all sizes encouraged? Would this in turn permit analysis of the greater acceptability of particular patterns, so available subsidies could be used to enhance preferred patterns? Currently, one problem is that most of the data relevant to racial socioeconomic mixing are at the census tract level. In small development projects, such as those of Operation Breakthrough, the question posed is the optimum pattern of family clusters within a particular neighborhood. Stability of mixed residential areas once achieved is a different, albeit related, issue. Stability is a function of housing demand and supply and is influenced by the level of prejudice and discrimination or other factors. Instability in the composition of an area technically occurs when racial or economic ratios among new residents of an area differ significantly from those of the present occupants. Presumptively, the causes of instability are complex and not well understood.

Level and range—often used to refer to the spread of housing costs in an area—are related categories. At what income or social level, one may ask, is racial mixing in residential areas most feasible? Do the various attributes associated with social level tend to compete and perhaps cancel their significance for the feasibility of social mixing? For instance, is middle-class acceptance of mixed neighborhoods offset by greater mobility potential? Since residence is a status indicator, to what extent does range reflect the feasible income or status spread? Generally, the question of feasible levels of mixing is addressed to race, while issues of feasible range focus on socioeconomic mixing.

Although mixing is frequently discussed in terms of minority movement into majority residential areas, a multiplicity of other possible patterns may be envisioned. Actual housing choice is exceedingly complex. For instance, black middle-class families may indeed seek to move into white suburbs, or they may seek out other black middle-class areas and thus form black suburban enclaves. Similar behavior may characterize the increasingly mobile blue-collar workers. Concurrently, white families may be moving back into mixed neighborhoods in the central city. Which policy more effectively promotes socioeconomic mixing: subsidizing the poor to enable them to live among those of moderate income, or subsidizing the well-to-do to induce them to move to less affluent neighborhoods? At issue in these and other alternatives are questions of relative cost and relative advantages. Clearly, there is a whole range of "mixes" to which policy might be directed. The question may not be so much "how to mix," but rather "what kind of mix is being sought." Conceivable social objectives in race mixing can extend from cultural and political dominance, on the one hand, to interactive cultural pluralism, on the other.

ATTITUDES

Prejudice obviously is a critical factor in the feasibility of racially mixed residential areas. Both in the United States and Europe, migrants have characteristically been people who were upwardly mobile and who did not, for the most part, manifest social disorganization in their communities of origin. Rural American Negroes in the cities and rural Portuguese in Paris had strikingly similar encounters with conditions for which they were not fully prepared. The task posed is to seek to understand the problems attendant on these kinds of migrations and to work to create a more constructive urban environment.

Attitudes toward desegregation have changed in recent years in
both majority and minority communities. A growing number of
blacks may perceive the advantages of a central city power base,
while at the same time an even larger number elect to live in the
suburbs. Policy formulation should take cognizance of the change
and of the distinctions among various groups of blacks: i.e., those
who want full integration, those who want no part of the dominant
social group, and those in between. What should be the government's
response, for example, to opposition to social mixing voiced by black
militants? Distinguishing between attitudes and behavior is useful. It
may be that political rhetoric has only marginal effects on voting behavior. In sum, those attitudes, both minority and majority, that affect the feasibility of alternative residential patterns need definition.

INSTITUTIONAL FACTORS

What are the institutional barriers to the growth of mixed residential
areas? A ghetto, as perceived both by the people who live in it and by
outsiders, is an area that owes its existence, in part, to impediments
to its inhabitants' moving elsewhere and, in part, to the inhabitants'
lack of the skills essential to mobility. This involuntary racial/ethnic
community, concentrated in a demarcated area, is a volatile one.
With some urgency, then, governmental efforts have moved in two
directions—facilitating movement for minority families with the
means to move and seeking to locate low- and moderate-income
housing outside the ghettos—in what has become known as the
"dispersal" policy.

Conversely, large-scale withdrawal of populations from the central
cities may not connote "flight" in the customary sense of the term.
In some jurisdictions, local laws have created a situation in which land
owners cannot rent units profitably. Housing is being abandoned primarily because of the rigidity of the price structure relative to the cost
of operating certain kinds of housing. The process of turnover from
residential to other uses has been going on for many decades. Now,
however, industry and services are moving to the outer parts of metropolitan areas, weakening the demand for more intensive land use in
the central city. But while enterprise may relocate with relative ease,
its potential employees face substantial barriers when they, in turn,
seek new residential locations.

However, the typical glacial movement outward of central city
populations may not significantly increase the number of mixed resi-

dential areas in the short run. Even when a mixed residential area achieves a degree of stability, its future stability is not assured. Transitional neighborhoods are common in urban areas. It is to be expected that each year formerly stable neighborhoods turn transitional as others achieve increasing degrees of stability. Environmental changes, such as highways, may affect neighborhood stability, but so also may the character of effective demand for residential space.

Whether homes are owned or rented may be a factor in the feasibility of social mixing. Rental properties represent the least risk to the home seeker and thus provide an easier transition for many families, assuming rental management is favorably disposed to mixing. Home ownership by minorities may be constrained not only by the resistance of present owners, but also by the reluctance of potential buyers to accept unnecessary risks. Once established, of course, communities in which ownership is high may be relatively stable. In large new developments, the marketing practices of developers may play a critical role in preventing or enhancing the establishment of mixed neighborhoods. In subsidized low- and moderate-income housing, eligible white families may balk at moving into projects with a sizable proportion of minority families. While location of such projects may facilitate integration at the project scale, the entire project is frequently resisted, through restricted zoning and other devices, by the local community.

A simulation approach may eventually prove most fruitful in examining the institutional barriers to mixed residential areas. The operation of a complex network of public and private institutions results in differential access to housing services for various racial and economic groups. But complexity itself causes responsibility for the resulting discrimination to be diffused to the point that individuals can disclaim personal involvement.

RESIDENTIAL SYSTEM

Housing, unlike services such as education, is produced and marketed primarily by the private sector of the economy. Housing transactions are mainly between a single seller and a single buyer. However, housing is negotiated within a wider institutional context. Choices of housing by individual families reflect their economic capacity and their preferences in housing and neighborhood amenities. The economic capability of an individual includes his acceptance on equal terms by the lending agencies as well as his income and savings.

Choice of housing takes account not only of the characteristics of the individual unit, but suitability of the neighborhood. Significant factors in neighborhood choice include school quality, access to employment, and the general attributes of the residents. The choice may also take into account salient characteristics of surrounding areas. For example, are the adjacent neighborhoods substantially populated by minority groups? At a given moment, supply of housing is relatively fixed. The annual increment of new units is usually a relatively small percentage of the existing stock. However, the occupancy of new units may generate several other moves creating a ripple effect.

Supply and demand in the housing field are mediated by an array of private individuals and institutions, including owners, brokers, real estate boards, lending agencies, and developers. "Effective" supply in a market depends very much on the efficiency and equity exercised by this institutional array. For example, the housing supply for minorities is significantly affected by broker willingness to bring homes in white neighborhoods to the attention of minority clients. Subtle practices implicit in the operation of the housing institution network may reduce "effective" demand. Members of the minority may be reluctant to face discriminatory practices of "institutional gate-keepers."

The role of mediating institutions differs depending on whether the housing is a rental property, an old house up for sale, or a new development. In rental properties and new developments, managerial responsibility is likely to be relatively explicit. Once a commitment to racial mixing is made, capacity to implement it is more likely to be adequate. In the case of rental properties, the management is frequently in a position to maintain stability of a mix once achieved. Moreover, rental properties may be open to a broader band of demand and represent less risk for the client than purchase. Sale of old housing is complicated and less subject to effective intervention since it is likely to involve not only an individual owner and a broker, but the multiple-listing system of a real estate board. Large-scale developers of new housing may have the greatest potential to satisfy the fair-access requirements of all groups.

In a still wider context, the supply of housing is influenced by the actions, both positive and negative, of local governments. Land-use planning, zoning, and other measures shape the pattern and character of housing development and utilization in a metropolitan area. Scarcity of suitable land for housing in the central city may compel move-

ment outward. Suburbs seeking to maintain their present status may
act to restrict the creation of moderate- and low-cost housing in their
midst. Costs of complying with local standards of rehabilitation and
maintenance may lead to abandonment of properties. And, in the ongoing process, the weakness of metropolitan government, coupled
with many parochial autonomous units, may intensify the fragmentation of the housing market, resulting in unequal distribution of the
public costs and benefits of metropolitan living.

The federal government acts within the 200-odd SMSA's (Standard
Metropolitan Statistical Areas)—each a unique constellation of forces—
not only to increase the housing supply, but also to achieve more
equitable balance in that supply and foster more equal opportunity
in access to it.

A systematic analysis of the dynamic multifaceted urban housing
system sketched above would be valuable in responding to questions
concerning the feasibility of mixing and in suggesting reliable policy
options. But policy must also be concerned with the level and scale
at which these options are sought. How important, for example, are
policies that begin to deal with specific classes of cities? And at what
scale should the emphasis be placed—the neighborhood, the local units
units of government, or the metropolitan area as a whole?

In sum, factors that may determine the feasibility and stability of
mixing include:

- Levels of tolerance and prejudice;
- Relative demand for housing among the white majorities and
the minorities;
- Supply of housing, both the actual physical supply and the
"effective" supply taking into account an array of institutional barriers to equal access;
- Local, state, and federal government policies and programs that
may impede or facilitate the creation of an adequate supply of housing and equal access to it; and
- Quality of housing and neighborhood amenities.

Normative Operational Considerations

Assuming the feasibility of racial and/or socioeconomic mixing, one
must raise questions bearing on its desirability and range. From the
separate perspectives of the minority and majority, what are the ad-

vantages and disadvantages of racially mixed residential areas? Long-run benefits might accrue to both groups. More economical use of community facilities could result. On the human level, residential contact would afford people the opportunity to judge others on individual merit rather than racial stereotypes, resulting in fuller utilization of manpower and leadership resources. In addition, reduction of prejudicial attitudes toward the minority group would provide them with benefits ranging from increased proximity to work to better-quality education, housing, and other services. Costs to both groups in the early stages could include such factors as the risk of pressure from one's group members, intergroup hostility, and loss of support of familiar institutions such as churches and schools.

Expanding the scope of concern, is it possible to estimate the social costs of various degrees of mixing? Not all costs may be reflected in actual market prices. Can they be assessed by simulations of more inclusive markets? Using simulation, can one determine whether revenue source—state, federal, or local—influences the decisions by whites to move to the suburbs? How much of the movement across jurisdictional boundaries is to escape financial and social responsibility? Are actual and perceived costs of services lower in the suburbs? If migration to the suburbs is being subsidized by the present price structure for public services, could a reverse flow to the central cities be stimulated by modifying the pattern of subsidy? Or, is it possible that the prices associated with public services and environmental amenities are not salient in the residential selection process? Perhaps urban cultural anthropologists could provide more useful insights than either demographers or economists.

The differences between integrated and segregated residential areas may be more complex than a simple dichotomy. When a place is characterized statistically as "integrated," what does that mean? It can simply mean that some statistical artifact has captured within its box some blacks along with some whites. What are the social characteristics of heterogeneity when it does in fact exist? Is a school or neighborhood "integrated" if little or no communication between the races takes place? Integrated residential areas may facilitate interracial associational contact. Is it a requirement? Clearly, where such contact arises in the pursuit of common objectives and produces positive outcomes, it is desirable. However, it may not be intrinsic to public policy. The objective may be the limited one of less racial homogeneity in the proximity of households. Even limited in this way, however, public policy may be perceived as unduly manipulative.

Housing preferences are not uniform among either the minority or the majority populations. Some blacks may choose to remain in the central city when it provides access to community power. Others, seeking the various amenities of the suburbs, may nevertheless opt to live in an ethnic enclave. Integration-minded blacks may purchase an older home in a formerly all white neighborhood only to find that similar choices by others have resulted in resegregation. Whites may seek homes elsewhere not because the area is heterogeneous, but because they anticipate eventual black homogeneity. Eligible white families may choose not to move into central city low- and moderate-income developments where there are substantial proportions of minority families. Moreover, it is unlikely that many families, black or white, move into a neighborhood because it is integrated. Rather, they seek services and amenities. Families look into the opportunities that derive from residence just as they take account of opportunities that may be associated with community power.

In light of the multiplicity of behaviors, the only tenable public policy objective would seem to be one of creating options. With respect to blacks and other minorities, actions that eliminate artificial barriers to residential choice would be of the greatest significance. Of course, the problems of discrimination will not all be resolved. Simultaneous advances will still have to be made in the occupational, educational, and other opportunity fields. The appropriate government action, whether it be even-handed, vigorous enforcement of the law, enactment of measures to improve the delivery of varied urban services, or the production and suitable location of low- and moderate-income housing, may all be assessed according to their contribution to equitable access to opportunity.

Arriving at a Consensus

When called upon to provide scientific advice for policy purposes, a responsible group soon finds that two criteria should be applied to its recommendations: truth and utility. In human affairs, there are always areas of uncertainty. Judgments on the degree of certainty will differ. The process of arriving at a consensus is subtle and complex. Yet, if scientific advice is to be effective, the effort must be made. The necessity is implicit in the process itself.

Policy-makers seek to deal with problems in a rational way. Scientists have information acquired by research and analysis. Rarely, if ever, is the fit between the two self-evident. Even if the relevance of some information seems apparent, that of other knowledge equally valid and useful may not be so self-evident.

Selection of a group to provide advice, of course, is the initial act. Typically, half a dozen or more domains of knowledge are represented. Initially, the group explores the policy context that generated the request for advice. Concommitantly, out of their own individual background and experience and by other means, they must review the research findings that may bear upon the questions posed. (The assessments presented in the state-of-the-knowledge papers prepared for the Social Science Panel played a critically important part in this review.)

An appreciation of the problem and an awareness of the relevant research provides a necessary foundation for the provision of scientific advice. But it is not sufficient. The group must also construct a common conceptual structure through which problem and knowledge can both be viewed.

Creating such a structure is seldom accomplished to the complete satisfaction of all who are involved in the process. The structures of knowledge for the separate disciplines provide rather different perceptions of significance and, indeed, of reality. Attention may be directed to different aspects of the policy context, depending on the previous experience of individuals. Similarly, the weight given to different kinds of research evidence may vary. Despite these impediments, it is necessary to arrive at a basic understanding about the structure in terms of which research knowledge and policy questions are to be related. The validity and usefulness of the advice depends, in considerable part, on the success of this transformation process.

Where advisory groups work well, this process is assumed, and all the participants are found not only searching for a common understanding of problems and research but for a common synthesis in terms of which their findings will be organized.

The search for consensus, originating in the exploratory discussions of the group, must finally be made explicit in the form of a draft report. As each participant responds to the draft, judgments are sharpened, and the supporting explanation strengthened. The process is iterative. Several rounds of discussion and several drafts may be involved, as was the case with the report of the Panel. While a final consensus on all points is not essential from the viewpoint of effectiveness, general agreement on the principal findings is usually desirable.

This Panel ultimately agreed on 19 findings. Without reproducing the supporting arguments, it may be of interest to list them.

1. For both blacks and whites the quality and convenience of housing and neighborhood services take precedence over racial prejudice in housing decisions.

2. To be successful, a marketing strategy should emphasize the positive racial attitudes that do exist and should take into account the variations in these attitudes. At the same time, the marketing strategy should recognize that there are no clearly identifiable groups holding distinctive racial attitudes with respect to housing.

3. Attitude changes are affected where the physical and social conditions encourage and support behavioral changes.

4. There is no ratio of blacks to whites that is known to ensure success in racial mixing. The ratios or proportions must be adapted to the particular populations involved.

5. Any fragmentation of the housing market constitutes a basis for segregation. Existence of multiple autonomous governments and private institutional barriers contribute to fragmentation.

6. Even in the absence of multiple autonomous governments, the lack of adequate mechanisms for the distribution of housing information among realtors and home seekers tends to fragment a housing market.

7. Experience demonstrates that success in racial mixing in rental properties is influenced in considerable degree by the attitudes, skill, and wisdom of property managers.

8. New, large-scale developments of residential properties for sale have been more amenable to racial mixing than have been older housing units widely scattered in established neighborhoods. Factors of importance in this respect appear to be (a) the central control of sales policy, (b) the strong market orientation of the home building industry, and (c) the absence of precedent in the newly created developments.

9. Mortgage financing institutions have had separate lending policies for blacks and for whites. They have been timid in developing policies for realizing mixed residential areas.

10. Despite the Supreme Court decision concerning the nonenforceability of restrictive covenants, there is reason to believe that such covenants continue to have some effect in preventing the development of interracial neighborhoods.

11. It is unlikely that a policy of racial mixing can be consistently applied in metropolitan areas where there are two or more autonomous governments. For any one locality to serve in the total social interest, it must put itself in a position to be beggared by others who do not accept similar responsibility voluntarily.

12. While the low-income status of blacks is a factor in their segregation, race prejudice exerts a strong independent influence on the separation of the races.

13. In general, socioeconomic status rises with distance from the center of the metropolitan area. However, there are many contextual variations. The stratification process and the pattern that results are not as yet well understood. Thus, the effect of efforts to alter the process is uncertain.

14. At present, the desirability of intervention to foster socioeconomic mixing in residential areas is uncertain. In question are not only the possible benefits, but untested assumptions concerning the amount and kind of present interaction across socioeconomic lines.

15. There is no evidence from field studies that socioeconomic mixing is feasible. The trend in the movements of urban population is toward increasing separation of socioeconomic categories—a tendency manifested among blacks as well as among whites.

16. A more adequate knowledge base is needed in order to determine the feasibility of socioeconomic residential mixing. More information is needed about why people live where they do—specifically, (a) housing preferences and attitudes; (b) "real costs" for different socioeconomic groups; (c) public sector costs and benefits, both perceived and actual; (d) alternative approaches to correcting public sector costs and changing individual "real costs"; and (e) the "human costs" of socioeconomic stratification.

17. Stratification by socioeconomic characteristics, as with segregation by race, tends to raise the employment opportunity costs of workers least able to bear costs. Such costs are being lowered, however, by the suburbanization of blue-collar workers.

18. Local government autonomy in metropolitan areas results in an uneven distribution of public sector costs; some government units are forced to assume the costs of decisions and policies adopted by other units.

19. Experiments in socioeconomic mixing at a number of different scales could help to provide a better basis for policy formulation. The same procedure would be valuable with respect to racial mixing.

Attitudes on Race and Housing: A Social-Psychological View

THOMAS F. PETTIGREW

ABSTRACT: White attitudes toward open housing have become increasingly more favorable over the past generation. However, the trend appears to be the result of factors largely outside the housing realm. Black attitudes favoring open housing have remained stable, perhaps even strengthening in recent years. The attitudes of both whites and blacks are more derivative than causal in the total process of how access to housing is distributed in the United States. Behavioral change typically precedes, rather than follows, attitude change, Pettigrew concludes. Support for the view that interracial living will itself effectively erode opposition to open housing to the degree that it satisfies Gordon Allport's four situational criteria is found in the research literature. These criteria are equal status of the groups in the situation, common goals, group interdependence, and social sanction. Achievement of open housing requires that undue emphasis not be placed on hostile white opinions, that there be effective enforcement procedures for existing laws, and that government act in a consistent fashion on a broad front with a view to achieving the necessary institutional changes. Finally, an instructive simulation model is discussed, which could provide a very useful tool for practical planning in the future.

Thomas F. Pettigrew is Professor of Social Psychology, Harvard University.

21

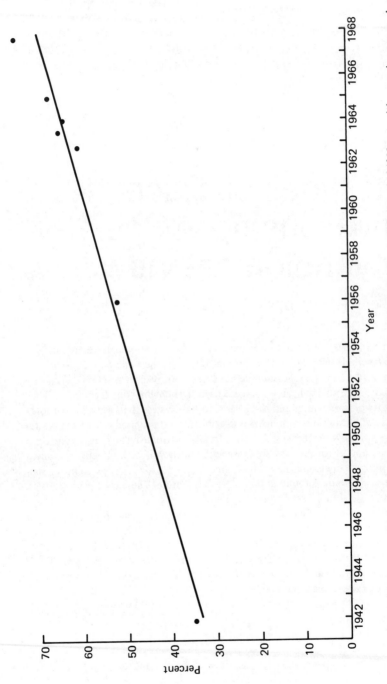

FIGURE 1 Least squares trend line in percent total white respondents who would not mind if Negro with same income and education moved on same block, 1942–1965. Adapted from Schwartz (1967, p. 55).

Over the past generation, the attitudes of white Americans toward interracial neighborhoods have become markedly more favorable and the ability of black Americans to move to interracial neighborhoods has increased; yet, the nation's housing since 1940 has become *more,* not less, segregated by race. The contradiction between these facts is actually more apparent than real. It is the purpose of this paper to explore these recent trends and the complex and subtle relations between them.

Together with a general reduction in antiblack sentiments in numerous realms, the attitudes of white Americans toward interracial housing have definitely become more positive over the past three decades. Figure 1, adapted from Schwartz (1967, p. 55), shows the trend in white responses to the standard race and housing query of the National Opinion Research Center (NORC): "If a Negro, with just as much income and education as you have, moved into your block, would it make a difference to you?"[1] The trend from 1942 to 1968 is quite clear; the percentage of white respondents who report that they would not mind black neighbors at all more than doubles from 35 to 76 percent. As we shall see in the next section, a variety of other survey questions asked at different times by other agencies lead to the same conclusion.

Similarly, there can be little question that the ability of black Americans to afford housing in predominantly white areas has greatly increased in recent years. After remaining at just over half that for whites—around $3,000—for some years, the median family income of Negroes rose in the late 1960's to roughly 60 percent that of whites and thus over $5,300 (United States Departments of Labor and Commerce, 1970, p. 15). These figures, however, are sharply reduced by southern data as evidenced by comparable data in 1968 for the Midwest (75 percent and $6,900) and for the West (80 percent and $7,500). Using the crude rule of thumb that a family can afford to purchase a home costing about 2½ times their gross annual income, one interprets this to mean that the median black family in 1968 in the Midwest could have considered purchasing a $17,000–$18,000 home or an $18,000–$19,000 home in the West.

The other black factor needed to reduce racial segregation by residence—the willingness to move to interracial areas—is less clear, and we shall explore this topic at some length later.

---

[1] The simplified wording in the 1944 NORC survey read: "Would it make any difference to you if a Negro family moved in next door to you?"

The trend toward greater housing segregation by race has been challenged by some observers;[2] but there is no debate over the fact that residential patterns within central cities have become considerably more segregated by race since 1940 (Taeuber & Taeuber, 1965). A significant rise in black penetration of the suburbs did not occur until the close of the 1960's. And Taeuber and Taeuber (1966, p. 133–134, 136) have shown for metropolitan Chicago how most of the scant Negro suburban population is itself concentrated in either overwhelmingly black suburbs or in black pockets within suburbs.

To unravel this apparent contradiction between the potential for more interracial living and the harsh facts of growing racial separation, we need, first, to carefully examine the available trend data for attitudes on race and housing; second, we must place these attitude data in their social context. Finally, we shall attempt to draw some policy implications from our discussion.

Trends in Attitudes on Race and Housing

WHITE ATTITUDES

As Figure 1 has already shown, the attitudes of white Americans on race and housing have changed fundamentally over the past three decades. This clear trend emerges regardless of the type of question asked or the survey agency conducting the study (Table 1). Coupled with survey data concerning discrimination in other realms, these results indicate that a basic shift toward favoring black rights evolved between World War II and the mid-1950's. This shift was fueled in all probability by economic prosperity over these years together with the resounding decision of the U.S. Supreme Court in 1954 against *de jure* segregation of public schools. In any event, the race and housing opinions of white Americans appear to have remained rela-

---

[2]See, for example, Bradburn et al. (1970, p. 207): "While our data on the number of integrated neighborhoods do not in and of themselves tell us whether there have been similar trends in behavior, the general non-systematic evidence suggests that the country is making some progress toward increasing residential integration." The discrepancy between this statement and the position taken in this paper *may* involve only a difference between an absolute and a relative judgment. There is good reason to agree with Bradburn and his colleagues that the absolute number of interracial neighborhoods is on the increase, while also maintaining that the relative percentage of black Americans residing in such neighborhoods is not increasing.

TABLE 1   White American Attitudes toward Race and Housing[a]

a. If a Negro, with just as much income and education as you have, moved into your block, would it make any difference to you?
   Survey Agency: NORC

Date	White Sample	Percentage of Agreement
		Yes, make a difference
June 1942	National	62
June 1956	National	46
May 1963	National	39
Dec 1963	National	35
May 1964	National	36
June 1965	National	32
Apr 1968	National	21

b. If colored people came to live next door, would you move?
   Survey Agency: AIPO, Gallup

Date	White Sample	Percentage of Agreement
		Yes, definitely, or might move
Oct 1958	National	46
June 1963	National	45
May 1965	National	35
July 1966	National	34
Aug 1967	National	35

c. Would you move if colored people came to live in great numbers in your neighborhood?
   Survey Agency: AIPO, Gallup

Date	White Sample	Percentage of Agreement
		Yes, definitely, or might move
Sept 1958	National	77
May 1963	National	78
May 1965	National	69
July 1966	National	70
Aug 1967	National	71

d. ... tell me if you personally would or would not object to: Having a Negro family as your next door neighbor.
   Survey Agency: Harris

Date	White Sample	Percentage of Agreement
		Would object
Aug 1963	National	55
Oct 1963	National	51
Oct 1965	National	37
Aug 1966	National	51

e. Do you think [that] (i) there should be laws compelling Negroes to live in certain districts; or (ii) there should be an unwritten understanding, backed up by social pressure, to keep Negroes out of the neighborhood where white people live; or (iii) Negroes should

TABLE 1 (continued)

be allowed to live wherever they want to live, and there should be no laws or social pressure to keep them from it?
Survey Agency: Roper

Date	White Sample	Percentage of Agreement		
		Alternatives		
		(i)	(ii)	(iii)
1939	National	41	42	13

f. White people have a right to keep Negroes out of their neighborhoods if they want to, and Negroes should respect that right.
   Survey Agency: NORC

Date	White Sample	Percentage of Agreement
		Agree that whites have right to exclude
Dec 1963	National	56
Apr 1968	National	54
Apr 1970	National	43

g. Which of these statements would you agree with: (i) white people have a right to keep Negroes out of their neighborhoods if they want to; (ii) Negroes have a right to live wherever they can afford to, just like white people.
   Survey Agency: Survey Research Center

Date	White Sample	Percentage of Agreement	
		Alternatives	
Sept–Oct 1964	National[b]	(i)	(ii)
		Strongly	*Strongly*
		24	28
		Not strongly	*Not strongly*
		6	22
		Alternative	
Jan–March 1968	15 key central cities[c]	(i)	(ii)
		30	62

h. Negroes are not ready to live in better neighborhoods.
   Survey Agency: Harris

Date	White Sample	Percentage of Agreement
		Agree
July 1963	National	61

i. Would you favor a Federal law forbidding discrimination in housing against Negroes?
   Survey Agency: Harris

Date	White Sample	Percentage of Agreement
		Oppose law
Oct 1963	National	56
Aug 1966	National	52
Oct 1966	National	51
June 1967	National	63

TABLE 1 (continued)

j. Do you favor or oppose laws to prevent discrimination against Negroes in . . .
Survey Agency: Survey Research Center

Date	White Sample	Percentage of Agreement		
		Favor	*Oppose*	*Don't know*
Jan–March 1968	15 key central cities[c]			
job hiring and promotion		67	23	10
buying or renting houses and				
apartments		40	51	9

k. In your own words, what is "open housing"–what does this term mean? [If answers
correctly] Would you like to see Congress pass an "open housing" bill or reject it?
Survey Agency: AIPO, Gallup

Date	White Sample	Percentage of Agreement		
		Answers correctly		
Apr 1967	National	59		
		Pass	*Reject*	*No opinion*
		35	54	11

l. Would you be willing to live in the same general neighborhood with members of the
other race?
Survey Agency: Gaffin

Date	White Sample	Percentage of Agreement		
		Yes	*No*	*No opinion*
May 1958	National[d]	52	44	4

m. Would it make any difference to you if a Negro family moved in next door to you?
Survey Agency: NORC

Date	White Sample	Percentage of Agreement		
				Qualified or
		Yes	*No*	*no opinion*
May 1944	National	69	22	9

n. Would you be willing to live next door to members of the other race?
Survey Agency: Gaffin

Date	White Sample	Percentage of Agreement		
		Yes	*No*	*No opinion*
May 1958	National[d]	41	53	6

o. Suppose a Negro family moved next door to you. What would you do?
Survey Agency: AIPO, Gallup

Date	White Sample	Percentage of Agreement	
		Would dislike, move, or	*Depends on*
		wouldn't socialize	*family*
June 1965	National	24	9

TABLE 1 (continued)

p. As far as your own personal feelings go, would you be personally concerned or not if a Negro neighbor moved in next door?
    Survey Agency: Harris

Date	White Sample	Percentage of Agreement
		Concerned
Oct 1966	National	56

q. Now I want to give you a list of groups and institutions. Do you think [real estate companies] have tended to help Negroes or have tended more to keep Negroes down?
    Survey Agency: Harris

Date	White Sample	Percentage of Agreement		
		Helping	*Keeping down*	*Not sure*
Aug 1963	National	22	44	34
Aug 1966	National	30	34	36

r. Now on each of the following I'd like to ask you, if you were in the same position as Negroes, would you think it justified or not to protest against discrimination in:
    Survey Agency: Harris

Date	White Sample	Percentage of Agreement		
		Justified	*Not justified*	*Not sure*
Aug 1966	National			
jobs		59	30	11
education		60	30	10
housing		49	36	15

s. Do you think that in [central city] many, some, or only a few Negroes miss out on good housing because white owners won't rent or sell to them?
    Survey Agency: Survey Research Center

Date	White Sample	Percentage of Agreement		
		Many	*Some*	*Few or none*
Jan–March 1968	15 key central cities[c]	38	30	26

t. On the average, Negroes in [central city] have worse jobs, education, and housing than white people. Do you think this is due mainly to Negroes having been discriminated against, or mainly due to something about Negroes themselves?
    Survey Agency: Survey Research Center

Date	White Sample	Percentage of Agreement		
		Discrimination	*Themselves*	*Both*
Jan–March 1968	15 key central cities[c]	19	56	19

u. If a Negro family with about the same income and education as you moved next door to you, would you mind it a lot, a little, or not at all?
    Survey Agency: Survey Research Center

TABLE 1 (continued)

Date	White Sample	Percentage of Agreement		
		Mind		
		A lot	*A little*	*Not at all*
Jan–March 1968	15 key central cities[c]	19	25	49

v. Suppose there are 100 white families in a neighborhood. One white family moves out and a Negro family moves in. Do you think it would be a good idea to have some limit on the number of Negro families that move there, or to let as many move there as want to?

   Survey Agency: Survey Research Center

Date	White Sample	Percentage of Agreement		
		Some limit	*No limit*	*Don't know*
Jan–March 1968	15 key central cities[c]	48	40	12

[a]Sources: Schwartz (1967), Erskine (1967, p. 482–498), Brink & Harris (1967), Sheatsley (1966, p. 303–324), Campbell & Schuman (1968, p. 1–67).
[b]Data adjusted slightly from those published by Survey Research Center to correct for inclusion of nonwhites in sample.
[c]The fifteen cities sampled include, with few exceptions (e.g., Los Angeles and Dayton, Ohio), all of the larger cities outside of the South with significant black populations: Baltimore, Boston, Chicago, Cincinnati, Cleveland, Detroit, Gary, Milwaukee, Newark, New York City (Brooklyn only), Philadelphia, Pittsburgh, San Francisco, St. Louis, and Washington, D.C.
[d]Gaffin provided data by regions only; thus, the national data shown represent an extrapolation based on the fact that southern respondents represent roughly one fourth of the nation's white adults.

tively stable into the sixties, only to become more pro-desegregation between 1963 and 1965 (see items b, c, d, n, o of Table 1). This was the fateful period of the assassination of President John Kennedy followed by the passage of the sweeping Civil Rights Act of 1964.[3]

The much publicized "white backlash" of the mid- and late-1960's did not, in fact, materialize in survey data in any manner similar to its lurid descriptions in the mass media of the period (Pettigrew, 1971b). Neither is it to be noted in the data shown in Table 1, except possibly for the 1966 results of item d; rather, these and other opinion findings covering this period indicate that possibly some polarization occurred with whites of many different persuasions adopting stronger positions in the direction they already leaned, but

[3]Other survey data analyzed by the author and his associates demonstrate clearly that it was indeed the murder of Kennedy that motivated the shift, and that this shift was in turn furthered by the *fait accompli* effects of the resulting passage of the Civil Rights Act of 1964. However, this Act was not so sweeping as to include measures against residential discrimination, for these would have to wait four more years before becoming law (Pettigrew, Riley, & Ross, in preparation).

that the overall effect led to little change in racial views similar to the
1958–1963 period. Indeed, the most recent results on items a and f
suggest the possible resumption of the trend since 1968, the year of
the murder of Dr. King and the issuance of the Kerner Commission
Report.

Within these broad trends, Table 1 enables us to obtain a sense of
the order of magnitude of present white opposition to open housing.
About a fourth of the nation's white adults object to a Negro family
of the same social class as themselves moving into their block (item a),
and this proportion rises to over two fifths if the Negro family were
to move into a house immediately next door (items d, o, p, u). Indeed, one third claim that if Negroes of unspecified class background
moved next door, they would move (item b). And the fear of "great
numbers" of black families coming to the neighborhood causes seven
in ten to report that they would move, a percentage that has declined
only slightly in recent years (item c, 77 percent in 1958 and 71 percent in 1967). In key central cities of the North and West, this fear
leads half of the white respondents to favor limits being placed on
the number of Negro families who could come to a single, previously
white neighborhood (item v).

Most white Americans are well aware that racial discrimination in
housing exists. Two thirds of the urban northern respondents realize
that at least "some Negroes miss out on good housing" because of
discrimination (item s). And in a list of 14 white institutions, ranging
from "Congress" and "local government" to "retail stores" and "labor unions," "real estate companies" comprise the *only* institution
rated by whites in 1966 as "keeping Negroes down" more than
"helping Negroes" (item q). Moreover, half the whites believe black
protest against housing discrimination to be "justified," though this
proportion is 10 percent below that thinking protests against job and
education are justified (item r). Yet only a minority of whites favored
laws against housing discrimination prior to the passage of such federal legislation in 1968 (items i, j, k). Note in the urban northern results (item j), too, that while only 40 percent favored antidiscrimination legislation for housing, two thirds did so for employment. This
huge difference would seem to point to a joint function of how employment and housing differ in racial opinions (as also in item r) as
well as the *fait accompli* effect we shall discuss shortly, In 1968, at
the time of this 15 city survey, federal legislation against job discrimination was 4 years old and gaining increasing acceptance, but
such legislation for housing was under debate at that point with

prestigious national figures opposing it with such seemingly legitimate and nonracial arguments as its constitutionality.[4]

A conflict in two widely held beliefs undergird these white attitudes on race and housing. On the one hand, many whites feel
strongly that they should have the right to restrict Negroes from
their areas (items e, f, g). On the other hand, a rapidly growing
number of whites believe that Negroes as American citizens have
a right to live where they wish and can afford (items e, g). What is
more, many of the same white Americans hold *both* of these beliefs. One study in a New Jersey suburb set out to confront directly
its middle-class survey respondents with this conflict, and found
both the conflict and similar means of handling it to be widespread
(Friedrichs, 1959). Often white Americans assume that their values
are different from those of Negroes. We shall return to this critical
phenomenon later. But at this point note how it operates to ease
the belief in consistency of many white respondents: 61 percent
in 1963 thought "Negroes are not ready to live in better neighborhoods" (item h), and 75 percent of urban Northerners in 1968 believed that Negroes have "worse jobs, education, and housing than
white people" at least in part because of "something about Negroes
themselves" (item t).[5]

Interestingly, a similar dilemma between the urge to discriminate
and a basic sense of fairness emerged in a recent survey in Great
Britain (Rose, 1969, p. 576–579; Bagley, 1970, p. 15–18). Respondents in five English boroughs with above-average percentages of
colored immigrants were asked if they thought " . . . the authorities
should let or refuse to let a Council house [or flat] " to an immigrant family. About 44 percent said, "No." But then these resisters
were asked if the authorities should " . . . still refuse if the family
had been on the waiting list the right length of time." Faced with
this clear contradiction of "fair play," only 20 percent of the full
sample still maintained that the immigrants should be refused.

The millennium, then, has not arrived. Despite steady erosion of

---

[4]Intensive analyses of survey data of the 1960's suggest that such periods of civil rights
legislative debates coincided with increased anti-integration sentiment among whites
(Pettigrew, Riley, & Ross, in preparation). Consistent with this view are the results for
item i in Table 1. Observe the large 12 percent jump in white opposition to an act in
this area following its *defeat* in 1966 (51 percent in 1966 and 63 percent in 1967).

[5]In a follow-up item, however, only 6 percent thought that "Negroes are born that way,"
compared to 66 percent who believed "changes are possible" (Campbell & Schuman,
1968).

TABLE 2 Percentages of Whites with Experience on Interracial Blocks, 1965[a]

Negro Family Lived on Same Block	Region and Education (%)					
	South			North		
	Grade School	High School	College	Grade School	High School	College
Yes, live there now	6	3	5	15	10	15
Yes, used to	21	27	14	24	25	22
No, never	73	70	81	61	65	63

[a]Adapted from Schwartz (1967, p. 61).

white attitudinal resistance to interracial residential patterns over the past generation, there remains an enormous degree of fear, reluctance, and downright opposition. Part of this resistance stems from not having experienced interracial living, for we shall later see that attitudes often follow behavior rather than precede it.[6] Table 2 reveals how few white respondents in 1965 report ever having lived on a block together with a Negro family. Observe that while there is a regional difference there is little or no difference by education.[7]

A closer look at white attitudes on interracial housing can be achieved by seeing how they range across geographic and demographic categories. Two of the most important controls are region and education. Whites in the South are consistently more opposed to housing desegregation than other whites. This fact, of course, is consistent both with other racial attitudes of southern whites and with the greater degree of residential segregation in the urban South.[8] More surprising, however, is the relationship with education. As Figure 2 illustrates, there was little or no association between education and housing opinions in 1956, especially in the

[6]Bradburn et al. (1970, p. 248) have shown how previous integrated experience, as a child and as an adult, are related to selection of an integrated neighborhood in which to live. Thus, 44 percent with both experiences chose integrated neighborhoods, compared to about 32 percent with one; only 18 percent of those who had not had previous interracial experience as either a child or as an adult chose an integrated neighborhood.

[7]Opportunities to reside in a racially mixed neighborhood also vary widely across cities in the North and West: They are relatively available in San Francisco and Boston and unavailable in Chicago and Cleveland (Schuman & Gruenberg, 1970).

[8]This is particularly true of the newer cities in the South, such as Atlanta and Miami. There still lingers a trace of the old master–slave quarters pattern in such older southern cities as Macon, New Orleans, and Charleston, South Carolina, giving them slightly lower indices of residential segregation by race.

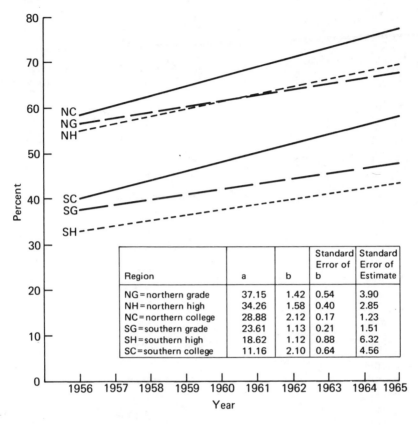

FIGURE 2   Least squares trend lines by region and education in percent who would not mind if Negro with same education and income moved on same block, 1956–1965. Adapted from Schwartz (1967, p. 56).

North. But the shift in attitudes by 1965 had created significant differences between the college-educated in both regions and other whites, though high-school-trained Southerners remained the most opposed to accepting equal status Negroes on their block. In short, while Figure 2 shows that all six regional and educational groups participated in the increasing favorable white attitudes toward inter-racial living from 1956 to 1965, the college-educated throughout the country disproportionately contributed to the shift.

Campbell and Schuman (1968, p. 35) unravel this phenomenon in their 1968 study of 15 northern cities by relating both age and

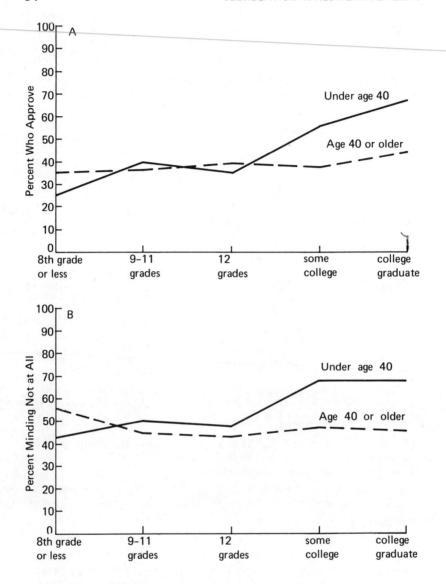

FIGURE 3 Relation of racial housing attitudes to educational levels among
white men. A: "How about laws to prevent discrimination against Negroes in
buying or renting houses and apartments? Do you favor such laws?" B: "If a
Negro family with about the same income and education as you moved in next
door to you, would you mind a lot, a little, or not at all?" From Campbell &
Schuman (1968, p. 35).

education to two measures of white racial attitudes concerning housing. Figure 3 supplies the Taeubers' results for white males. Witness the virtually flat education percentage line for those 40 years or older on both graphs. By contrast, see the remarkably more favorable opinions on both graphs of those under 40 who had attended at least a few years of college. Figure 3 deserves perusal, for its findings bear important and interesting implications. They suggest, as Campbell and Schuman point out, that schools at all levels through World War II accepted the prevailing culture in race relations and possessed little or no potential for changing the racial opinions of their products. Indeed, this situation holds generally for the nation's elementary and secondary schools even after 1945. But the colleges appear to have changed as noted by Campbell and Schuman (1968, p. 35):

Since World War II those white students who have gone on to college have evidently been exposed to influences which have moved their attitudes away from the traditional pattern in the directions we have observed. We cannot say whether this resulted from specific instruction regarding questions of race or from a general atmosphere of opinion in the college community but it is clear that a sizable proportion of these postwar generation college students were affected.

In other words, age seems to be critical only for the college-educated as a predictor of racial housing attitudes. Even sex is not a critical predictor. In general, white women are only slightly less in favor of neighborhood integration than white men. Similarly, Bradburn and his colleagues could find *no* consistent relation between the belief that whites have the right to keep Negroes out of their neighborhood (item f of Table 1) and such variables as central city versus suburbs, size of metropolitan area, and ownership (Bradburn *et al.*, 1970). There was some evidence to suggest that renters and those living in "open neighborhoods," with two or more Negro families but less than 1 percent Negro, were more likely to disagree with the right of whites to exclude Negroes (Bradburn *et al.*, 1970).

Somewhat more interesting predictors are the particular city and ethnicity. Schuman and Gruenberg (1970) have demonstrated with ingenious analyses that the city variable itself in the Campbell–Schuman 15 city study constitutes an interesting predictor for particular racial variables. It relates to the belief of whites that there is much housing discrimination in their city, but less so than to whether the respondent had ever moved to get away from Negroes.

Robin Williams (1964, p. 34, 67) found wide differences in racial attitudes between his samples from four widely scattered small cities. His most deviant pattern was found in tradition-bound Savannah, Georgia. Here in the early 1950's, 26 percent of the white respondents lived within one or two blocks of Negroes, but only 16 percent said they did not "mind the idea of Negroes living in my neighborhood"; only 4 percent would not find it "distasteful" to have a Negro family living next door, and only 3 percent approved of racially mixed neighborhoods.

Two more recent studies point to differences between white ethnicities in reactions to residential integration in the urban North. Harris in his 1966 *Newsweek* survey found Polish-Catholic respondents particularly "upset" by the thought of Negroes moving into their neighborhoods, followed by Italian-Catholics and Irish-Catholics (see Table 3) (Brink & Harris, 1967, p. 108–110). This rank order was confirmed by Crawford and Rosenberg in an intensive study of church-going Roman Catholics in Chicago; 40 percent of their Polish-American respondents favored residential integration by race, compared to 54 percent of Italian-Americans, 58 percent of Irish-Americans, and 59 percent of German-Americans (Crawford & Rosenberg, 1970, p. 6). One is tempted to speculate that the underlying variable here is the degree to which each ethnic group maintains its own relatively homogeneous neighborhoods; the more this is true, it seems to follow that the greater the opposition is to all "outsiders" moving in. It is known that Polish-Americans are one of the most residentially segregated of all white ethnic groups, while Irish-Americans are one of the least (Lieberson, 1963). Moreover, Polish-Americans have had a relatively small college-educated sector until recently.

TABLE 3   Ethnicity and Attitudes toward Neighborhood Integration[a]

Would it upset you . . . if Negroes moved into this neighborhood?	Ethnicity			Total for National Sample (%)
	Polish-Catholic (%)	Italian-Catholic (%)	Irish-Catholic (%)	
A lot	40	24	36	24
Some	15	24	21	16
Only a little	24	14	2	12
Not at all	21	38	41	48

[a]Adapted from Brink and Harris (1967, p. 109, 209).

In sum, significant shifts in white American opinions on racial residential mixing have come about over the past generation. Despite the growing percentage of those who favor open desegregated housing, however, there remains a large and critical minority who oppose it. A number of related phenomena seem to underlie this pattern. First, the shift in opinion, while reflected in all regional and educational groups, is particularly strong among those who have received their college training since World War II. Second, this leaves particularly intense opposition to interracial neighborhoods among many white Southerners, relatively homogeneous groups of ethnic Northerners, the old, and the poorly educated. Third, opposition to black neighbors is often just one part of a conflict with national and religious values of fair play and equal opportunity for all. On the abstract level of what is "right," an overwhelming number of white Americans believe a black family should be able to live where it wishes and can afford. But, in the face of their own block and the house next door, many of these same whites shift ground and believe whites have the right to exclude blacks. It is more than a simple fear of lowered property values that motivates this threatened response on the concrete level. Many white Americans assume "blacks aren't ready yet," that they are typically of a different and lower social class. We shall return to this phenomenon later; but recall at this point that few whites have ever experienced interracial neighborhoods in their past, and this adds to their unease and fear.

One further point of caution requires mention. A stable pattern over the years in white racial thought involves the intimacy of black–white contact: that is, the more intimate the contact, the more white opposition to it. At the extremes, interracial dating and marriage are still opposed by a large majority of white adults, but casual interracial contact in such formal situations as hotels and restaurants is now overwhelmingly approved. Table 4 shows this pattern for white Texans before and after the assassination of Dr. Martin Luther King in April 1968. Note that housing integration is perceived as relatively intimate and is well down the list in approval. Note also that the dramatic increase in the acceptance of interracial contact following King's murder was confined largely to the realms of formal and informal contact perceived as less intimate than residential contact. In other words, King's death seems to have created positive changes in the racial attitudes of white Texans socially, but had relatively little effect on attitudes toward interracial neighborhoods. In short, the

TABLE 4 Racial Attitudes of White Texans before and after King Murder[a]

Area of Desegregation	Nov 1967	Feb 1968	May 1968	Aug 1968	(May + Aug) − (Nov + Feb) / 2 Raw Change
Formal contact					
Same buses	62.9	64.5	74.3	69.7	+8.3
Same jobs	66.8	69.1	76.1	76.4	+8.2
Same restaurants	57.9	59.9	66.8	66.4	+7.7
Same hotels	53.0	53.8	60.2	59.6	+6.5
Informal contact					
Same schools	53.7	57.6	61.4	61.7	+5.8
Same churches	57.4	60.0	62.5	65.4	+5.2
Teach your child	49.4	51.2	54.3	55.6	+4.7
Intimate contact					
Same social gatherings	39.3	38.9	41.8	44.2	+3.9
Live next door	*29.5*	*32.1*	*32.0*	*36.6*	*+3.5*
Same swimming pools	30.9	27.1	29.5	34.6	+3.1
Same house party	26.2	26.2	26.5	29.0	+1.5
College roommate of your child	17.4	17.8	17.1	18.0	0.0

[a]Adapted from Pettigrew (1971b, p. 309).

shift served to accentuate the degree of intimacy pattern.[9]

The taboo against intimate racial contact, as perceived by many white Americans, acts as a formidable barrier to rapid change in racial attitudes on housing. This is not a surprise, even if one assumes that the trends of Figures 1 and 2 will continue unabated. It would not be until the start of the twenty-first century that 90 percent or

[9]There is, however, an interesting upturn in the acceptance of a Negro neighbor in Table 4 between May and August 1968. We have named this a "ripple effect," since change appears to have come for the nonintimate realms first and then "rippled" or percolated down to the less-accepted intimate realms. In any event, the effect is a small one compared to the dominant pattern under discussion (Pettigrew, 1970, p. 59–81). National survey data bear out these Texas findings concerning the manner in which most whites perceive housing integration as relatively intimate contact. In the 1963 and 1965 surveys, Harris asked white respondents if they "would object to" interracial intimacy ranging in degree from "working next to a Negro on a job" to "having your daughter dating a Negro." "Having a Negro family as next door neighbors" was one of the most objected to, surpassed only by two sexually related items involving marriage and dating (item d of Table 1) (Schwartz, 1967).

more of noncollege white Southerners would not object to Negroes of comparable class living on their block (Schwartz, 1967, p. 117).[10]

HOW ACCURATE ARE SURVEY DATA?

Before we turn to reviewing black American attitudes on the subject, we should first consider a standard reaction to the survey data presented so far. Some observers, unfamiliar with competent survey research, doubt whether the poll interview can fathom the full depth of racial prejudice. What has really changed over recent decades, they argue, is not prejudice or unwillingness to have a black neighbor, but the respectability of prejudice and segregationist attitudes. Even if only this standard of respectability had changed, that would itself be noteworthy. For what is "real" prejudice? A change in verbal behavior is certainly "real" in a most important sense.

In any case, need we be so limiting? No doubt the open espousal of antiblack attitudes became markedly less respectable during the past generation. But this change would seem to be only one among many symptoms of a deeper, more meaningful lessening of prejudice. Indeed, there are a number of reasons for accepting the major shifts reported by the opinion polls as genuine, at least in large part.

First, rapport in the survey situation is generally far greater than those unfamiliar with the technique realize. A pleasant, attentive stranger who has gone to some trouble to record your opinion on vital issues, and who does not provide any cues of disagreement, is often a much safer and more rewarding confidant than acquaintances.

Second, the remarkable consistency of the trends in attitudes toward minority groups extends to a wide variety of questions, asked by different polling agencies. Presumably, the questions vary considerably in "respectability bias" (or, to use the parlance of modern testing theory, in "social desirability"); thus, if the results were largely a reflection of "respectability bias," we would not expect the consistency noted previously in Table 1.

Third, certain questions tapping prejudice and attitudes toward discrimination, which appear to involve a built-in "respectability

---

[10]For question c of Table 1 concerning not moving if large numbers of Negroes moved into the neighborhoods, the 90 percent figure would not be reached for grade-school Southerners until 2102; high-school-educated Northerners, 2067; and college-educated Southerners and Northerners, 1997.

bias" as great as those of Table 1, have *not* changed over the past few decades. For example, the National Opinion Research Center has repeatedly asked representative nationwide samples if they "think most Negroes in the United States are being treated fairly or unfairly." The responses have remained stable for a decade; in both 1946 and 1956, 63 percent answered, "fairly" (Erskine, 1962, p. 139).

Fourth, the typical way for survey interviewees to avoid a difficult or threatening question is merely to say that he has no opinion on it or "does not know." In fact, many questions in survey results provoke large percentages of these "don't know" responses—usually a sign that the question has little salience for the respondents or is in some manner threatening. Race questions of all types, however, typically provoke far *fewer* "don't know" responses than the average survey question. The issue is salient for the vast majority of American respondents; as a result, there seems to be little tendency to "leave the field" by answering, "don't know."

Finally, election results have borne out the evidence from surveys on intergroup attitudes. Ithiel de Sola Pool and his associates (1964) attempted to simulate the 1960 Presidential election using only data from polls gathered before 1959. To predict the crucial anti-Catholic vote against John F. Kennedy, Pool used the simple and straightforward question, "Would you be willing to vote for a qualified Catholic for President?"—surely as frontal a measure of prejudice as any employed to explore attitudes toward race and housing. Yet, for all its obviousness, the question produced a response that proved remarkably accurate and useful in simulating the actual 1960 election. As the authors state in their intriguing volume (de Sola Pool *et al.*, 1964, p. 115):

Millions of Protestants and other non-Catholics who would otherwise have voted Democratic could not bring themselves to vote for a Catholic. In total—so our model says—roughly one out of five Protestant Democrats or Protestant Independents who would otherwise have voted Democratic bolted because of the religious issue. The actual number of bolters varied with the voter-type and was determined in the model by the proportion of that voter-type who had replied on surveys that they would not want to vote for a Catholic for President. What our model tends to show is that the poll question was a good one. The model suggests that the number of people who overcame the social inhibitions to admitting prejudice to a polltaker was about the same as the number who overcame the political inhibitions to bolting their party for reasons of bias.

Furthermore, attitudes concerning housing integration directly have proved effective predictors of voting in elections with racial significance. For example, a survey of 250 white voters in Gary, Indiana, conducted in October 1968, just prior to the Presidential election, found those who supported residential segregation were much more likely than other respondents to be planning to vote for Governor George Wallace for President (Pettigrew, 1971b, p. 244). Thirty-seven percent of those who agreed that "whites have a right to keep Negroes out of their neighborhood" supported Wallace, while only 19 percent of those who disagreed supported Wallace. Also, 46 percent of those who "would mind a lot if a Negro family with the same income and education moved next door" supported Wallace in contrast to 27 percent of those who would "mind a little" and only 21 percent of those who would "not mind at all."[11]

Figure 4 presents additional prediction examples. In 1965, 317 of Boston's white voters were twice interviewed concerning their voting intentions for or against Mrs. Louise Day Hicks, a local politician who has gained a national reputation for strong resistance to racial change not unlike that of Governor Wallace (Pettigrew, 1971b, Ch. 9). Within each of the three educational categories shown in Figure 4, white Bostonians who supported Mrs. Hicks for both the school committee and for mayor are in all cases more opposed to housing integration than those who supported her for just the school committee, who in turn, are in all cases more against housing integration than those who opposed her for both offices. Indeed, of all the attitude variables measured by this Boston survey, those items tapping attitudes toward interracial neighborhoods proved the best predictors of the "Hicks phenomenon." Such a finding prompts the speculation that the often-heard theme of Mrs. Hicks for "neighborhood schools" represents less a fear of interracial education than it does interracial living; the adjective "neighborhood" is more critical than the noun "schools." This possibly is consistent, too, with the ordering of racial attitudes in Table 4, indicating that housing integration is more resisted than school integration.

---

[11]It could be argued that verbally indicating your voting preference is merely an attitude, too, so that these relationships are attitude-to-attitude associations rather than attitude-to-nonverbal-behavior associations. This is true; but the same study, sampled by precinct, found that the projections for the vote by precinct based on the respondents' reports were extremely close to the actual votes cast.

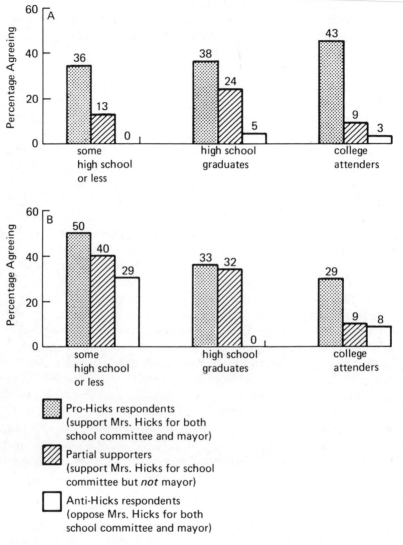

FIGURE 4   Attitudes toward interracial housing and support for Mrs. Hicks among white voters in Boston. A: "White people have a right to keep Negroes out of their neighborhoods if they want to." B: "Negroes certainly have their rights, but it is best to keep them in their own districts and schools and to prevent too much contact with whites." Adapted from Pettigrew (1971b, p. 224–225).

A final example derives from a late 1970 survey of 296 white voters in Gary, Indiana (Pettigrew, 1971a). Each respondent was asked about his voting intentions in that city's 1971 mayoralty race as well as an array of other questions, including the standard query— "Would you mind if a Negro family with about the same income and education as you moved next door?" The results are clear-cut. Among those white respondents who supported incumbent Richard Hatcher, Gary's famous black mayor, none would mind "a lot," only 12 percent would mind "a little," and 88 percent would not mind at all.

Among those who could consider voting for Hatcher but who are not now among his followers, 17 percent would mind "a lot"; 39 percent, "a little"; and 44 percent, "not at all." Among the intensely anti-Hatcher white respondents, 23 percent would mind "a lot"; 28 percent, "a little"; and 50 percent, "not at all."

To return to the basic query of this paper, why, then, have white attitudes toward residential mixing been improving over recent decades, while housing segregation grows more severe? Our discussion so far eliminates in large part two possible answers. First, the attitude trend itself could be questioned; yet, as we have seen, this trend is reflected in the results of many different questions posed by a variety of survey agencies. To be sure, a critical mass of resistance and ambivalence remains, but the trend toward greater acceptance is strong and definite. Second, attitude results themselves can be derogated. But, we have just reviewed a number of reasons why survey data need to be taken seriously as relatively accurate reflections of the nation's racial attitudes. Now we turn to inspect survey data relevant to a third possibility: White Americans have become increasingly more willing to live on interracial blocks, but black Americans have become less willing to do so; thus, the ever mounting segregation by residence goes largely unchallenged by blacks.

BLACK ATTITUDES

Table 5 summarizes a variety of survey findings concerned with black attitudes. When presented with a meaningful choice between an all-black neighborhood and a mixed neighborhood (items a, e, g, h, k), black respondents overwhelmingly favored the latter. This trend is clearest for respondents outside of the South; yet, in 1969, 63 percent of even low-income black Southerners favored desegregated residential areas. Those who favored mixed areas made it clear that

TABLE 5   Black American Attitudes toward Race and Housing[a]

a. In living in a neighborhood, if you could find the housing you want and like, would you
    rather live in a neighborhood with Negro families, or in a neighborhood that had both
    whites and Negroes?
    Survey Agency: Newsweek

Date	Black Sample	Percentage of Agreement		
		Negro	*Both Negro and white*	*Not sure*
Aug 1963	National	20	64	16
Aug 1966	National	17	68	15
May 1969	National	16	74	10
	By Category			
1963	South	27	55	18
1966		26	57	17
1969		21	67	11
1963	Non-South	11	75	14
1966		8	79	13
1969		11	80	9
	South			
1969	Low income	24	63	14
1969	Low middle	20	69	11
1963	Middle income	6	69	25
1966		17	70	13
1969		23	69	8
	Non-South			
1963	Low income	19	75	6
1966		10	79	11
1969		10	76	14
1963	Low middle	11	75	14
1966		7	78	15
1969		9	84	7
1963	Middle income	12	69	19
1966		6	80	14
1969		11	81	8
1966	Under 35 yr	12	75	13
1969		18	71	7
1966	35–49 yr	17	67	16
1969		15	73	11
1966	50+ yr	21	63	16
1969		16	75	10

b. [Of those who answered item a "both whites and Negroes"] Why do you feel this way?
    Survey Agency: Harris

Date	Black Sample	Percentage of Agreement		
		Races should mix	*Quieter, cleaner, etc.*	*Other*
Aug 1963	National	49	26	25

TABLE 5 (continued)

c. [Of those who answered item a "Negro families"] Why do you feel this way?
   Survey Agency: Harris

Date	Black Sample	Percentage of Agreement		
		Get along better	*Less tension, conflict*	*Can't get used to rival groups*
Aug 1963	National	52	14	24

d. If both neighborhoods were equally well kept up, would you rather live in a neighborhood that was mostly Negro or mostly white?
   Survey Agency: Marx

Date	Black Sample	Percentage of Agreement		
		Mostly Negro	*Mixed or no difference*	*Mostly white*
Fall 1964	Non-southern metro-			
	politan areas[b]	55	38	4
	New York	52	35	9
	Chicago	68	25	5
	Atlanta	74	18	5
	Birmingham, Ala.	69	27	1
	Total	62	31	4

e. Would you personally prefer to live in a neighborhood with all Negroes, mostly Negroes, mostly whites, or a neighborhood that is mixed half and half?
   Survey Agency: Survey Research Center

Date	Black Sample	Percentage of Agreement				
		All Negro	*Mostly Negro*	*Mostly white*	*Mixed half and half*	*No difference*
Jan–March 1968	15 key central cities[c]	8	5	1	48	37

f. [Of those who answered item e "mixed half and half"] Why do you feel that way?
   Survey Agency: Survey Research Center

Date	Black Sample	Percentage of Agreement			
		Learn to get along together	*Less crime, quieter, etc.*	*Better services*	*Other*
Jan–March 1968	15 key central cities[c]	44	24	10	22

g. Would you be willing to live next door to members of the other race?
   Survey Agency: Gaffin

Date	Black Sample	Percentage of Agreement		
		Yes (whites)	*No (whites)*	*No opinion (whites)*
May 1958	National[d]			
	Total	87	5	8
		(41)	(53)	(6)

TABLE 5 (continued)

Date	Black Sample	Yes (whites)	No (whites)	No opinion (whites)
		Yes (whites)	*No* (whites)	*No opinion* (whites)
	South only	79	8	13
		(19)	(78)	(3)
	Non-South only	97	1	2
		(48)	(45)	(7)

h. Would you be willing to live in the same general neighborhood with members of the other race?
　　Survey Agency: Gaffin

Date	Black Sample	Yes (whites)	No (whites)	No opinion (whites)
		Yes (whites)	*No* (whites)	*No opinion* (whites)
May 1958	National			
	Total	91	4	5
		(52)	(44)	(4)
	South only	86	6	8
		(32)	(65)	(3)
	Non-South only	98	1	1
		(59)	(37)	(4)

i. Do you think that most Negroes want to live in white neighborhoods, or in Negro neighborhoods, or that it doesn't matter to them?
　　Survey Agency: Gaffin

Date	Black Sample	Negro neighborhoods (whites)	White neighborhoods (whites)	Doesn't matter (whites)
		Negro neighborhoods (whites)	*White neighborhoods* (whites)	*Doesn't matter* (whites)
May 1958	National			
	Total	17	8	68
		(52)	(18)	(23)
	South only	24	3	65
		(74)	(12)	(10)
	Non-South only	9	13	73
		(44)	(20)	(26)

j. Would you prefer to live on a block with people of the same race or of every race?
　　Survey Agency: Center for Urban Education

Date	Black Sample	Every race
		Every race
Summer 1968	Bedford-Stuyvesant (Brooklyn, N.Y.)	80

k. Would you rather live in a neighborhood with only Negro families or in a neighborhood that had both Negro and white families?
　　Survey Agency: Meyer

TABLE 5 (continued)

Date	Black Sample	Percentage of Agreement		
		Only Negro	*Both Negro and white*	*Don't know*
Aug 1967	Detroit	17	61	22
Sept 1968	Detroit	13	75	12

l. Which do you think is more important now—to get more and better housing in and around where Negroes already live, or to open housing for Negroes in other parts of the city and suburbs?
    Survey Agency: Meyer

Date	Black Sample	Percentage of Agreement			
		More and better housing	*Open up interracial housing*	*Both equally vital*	*Don't know*
Sept 1968	Detroit	44	41	14	1

m. An owner of property should not have to sell to Negroes if he doesn't want to.
    Survey Agency: Marx

Date	Black Sample	Percentage of Agreement		
		Agree	*Disagree*	*Don't know*
Fall 1964	Non-southern metro-politan areas[b]	50	47	3
	New York	33	64	3
	Chicago	58	37	5
	Atlanta	50	47	3
	Birmingham, Ala.	53	43	4

n. An owner of property should not have to sell to Negroes if he doesn't want to.
    Survey Agency: Meyer

Date	Black Sample	Percentage of Agreement		
		Agree	*Disagree*	*Don't know*
Sept 1968	Detroit	38	54	8

o. On the whole, would you say you are satisfied or dissatisfied with your housing situation?
    Survey Agency: Gallup

Date	Black Sample	Percentage of Agreement		
		Satisfied (whites)	*Dissatisfied* (whites)	*No opinion* (whites)
1949	National	59	32	9
		(67)	(28)	(5)
Oct 1963	National	43	54	3
		(76)	(21)	(3)
Sept 1965	National	29	66	5
		(77)	(20)	(3)
Nov 1966	National	51	44	5
		(77)	(19)	(4)

TABLE 5 (continued)

Date	Black Sample	Percentage of Agreement		
		Satisfied (whites)	*Dissatisfied* (whites)	*No opinion* (whites)
May 1969	National	50 (80)	48 (18)	2 (2)

p. Let me read you some situations you might find yourself in. Suppose in each situation you had to see a white person. Tell me . . . if you think you would be likely to be given a hard time by the white person or not.
    Survey Agency: Harris

Date	Black Sample	Percentage of Agreement		
		Hard time	*Not a hard time*	*Not sure*
Feb–March 1970 National				
Looking for new housing		66	25	9
Applying for a job in a big company		59	26	15
Applying for a loan in a bank		48	38	14
Enrolling child (self) in integrated				
school		33	49	18

q. In general, if you were to get a house or apartment (flat) the same as a white person, do you feel you would pay more rent or the same as the white person would pay?
    Survey Agency: Harris

Date	Black Sample	Percentage of Agreement		
		More rent	*Same rent*	*Not sure*
Aug 1963	National	53	30	17

r. Believe "many" or "some" Negroes in this city miss out on good housing because of racial discrimination.
    Survey Agency: Survey Research Center

Date	Black Sample	Percentage of Agreement
Jan–March 1968	15 key central cities[c]	76

s. Believe there are "many" places in this city where they could not rent or buy a house because of discrimination.
    Survey Agency: Survey Research Center

Date	Black Sample	Percentage of Agreement
Jan–March 1968	15 key central cities[c]	43

t. Believe that racial discrimination in housing is increasing or not changing.
    Survey Agency: Survey Research Center

Date	Black Sample	Percentage of Agreement
Jan–March 1968	15 key central cities[c]	54

TABLE 5 (continued)

aa. People have different ideas about what causes riots like the one in Detroit last summer. Let me read you a list of possible riot causes . . . . Please tell me whether it might have a great deal to do with causing a riot, something to do with causing a riot, or nothing at all to do with causing a riot.
    Survey Agency: Meyer

Date	Black Sample	Percentage of Agreement	
		A great deal to do with causing a riot	
Aug 1967	Detroit		
Sept 1968	Detroit	1967	1968
Police brutality		57	71
Poor housing		54	61
Poverty		44	60
Lack of jobs		45	57
Overcrowded living conditions		55	55
Dirty neighborhoods		44	43

bb. Which of the following do you think is a "big problem" for Negroes here?
    Survey Agency: Meyer

Date	Black Sample	Percentage of Agreement	
		Big Problem	
Feb–March 1968	Miami		
May–July 1968	Miami	Winter 1968	Summer 1968
Too many school dropouts		80	82
Rents too high		63	78
Poor housing		57	75
Overcrowded living conditions		58	75
Too much crime		71	74
Dirty neighborhoods		67	73
Poverty		41	73

[a]Sources: Erskine (1967), Brink & Harris (1967), Campbell & Schuman (1968), Marx (1969), Goldman (1970), Gallup (1969, p. 11), Harris (1970), Meyer (1967, 1968, 1969).
[b]The "non-southern metropolitan area" sample of blacks was drawn by the National Opinion Research Center apart from the special probability samples of blacks drawn for the four cities studied in detail and listed separately.
[c]The fifteen cities sampled include, with few exceptions (e.g., Los Angeles and Dayton, Ohio), all of the larger cities outside of the South with significant black populations: Baltimore, Boston, Chicago, Cincinnati, Cleveland, Detroit, Gary, Milwaukee, Newark, New York City (Brooklyn only), Philadelphia, Pittsburgh, San Francisco, St. Louis, and Washington, D.C.
[d]Gaffin provided data by regions only; thus, the national data shown represents an extrapolation based on the fact that southern respondents represent roughly one fourth of the nation's white adults.

they did so for positive reasons of racial harmony even more than for the obvious advantages of good neighborhoods (items b and f). Similarly, those who preferred all-black areas made it equally clear that their reasons center around a desire to avoid interracial tension and strife (item c).

Where, then, is the turn to black separatism heralded by the mass media as the chief black shift of the late 1960's? These housing data are actually consistent with a host of other survey data that demonstrate the media have grossly exaggerated this trend. Campbell and Schuman (1968), for example, show that the basic black ideological shift stresses cultural emphasis far more than racial separatism. They show that what little attention is given to separatism is concentrated among young Northerners, though even for them integration was the overwhelming choice. This trend is evident in the present results in an age and region interaction (Goldman, 1970). In the 1969 survey, young respondents in the North were the strongest segment in their desire for all-black neighborhoods—though this still came to only 17 percent compared to 77 percent desiring *mixed* neighborhoods.

Important for our discussion is that these black attitudes favoring interracial housing do not appear in the aggregate to be declining. Indeed, the results for item a in Table 5 suggest that, if any trend is occurring, it is toward greater willingness to live in mixed areas. It is also clear, however, that there is no widespread desire among black Americans to live in "mostly" or overwhelmingly white areas. Marx (1969) asked his question d of Table 5 by giving only the two alternatives, "mostly Negro" and "mostly white." Although this inadequate wording greatly enhances the percentages selecting "mostly Negro," two remarkable findings emerge from his results. First, relatively large percentages of his black respondents said "mixed" or "it does not matter," even though these alternatives were not even offered by the question. Second, the percentages favoring "mostly Negro" for the four cities are almost linearly related to the Taeubers' 1960 indices of racial segregation by block for these central cities. New York, of the four sampled, has, by far, the lowest index (79.3) and the lowest percentage wanting "mostly Negro" areas, while Chicago (92.6) and Birmingham, Alabama (92.8), are relatively intermediate and Atlanta is the most segregated (93.6) (Taeuber & Taeuber, 1966, p. 39–41). This suggests that there is a "reality" factor involved: Separatist attitudes are often formed *after* the harsh facts of racial discrimination and segregation in housing.

Such a conclusion is supported by a special survey of black opinion conducted in 1968 in Bedford-Stuyvesant in New York City (Center for Urban Education, 1968). As item j in Table 5 shows, four fifths of the respondents in this relatively dense ghetto

area would still prefer to live on a multiracial, rather than a uni-
racial, block. Significantly, however, the most favorable group to
heterogeneous living in the entire sample were the black residents
of a still-desegregated public housing development, 88 percent of
whom favored multiracial blocks. We shall return to this important
point in the next section.

Naturally, a desire for better housing undergirds these data. This
becomes apparent as soon as we compare the findings of items a, j,
and k with l in Table 5. When the choice is simply between all-black
or genuinely mixed areas, roughly four-to-one majorities preferred
the latter. But when the hard policy choice is presented between
improving ghetto housing and opening up housing for blacks outside
of the ghetto, a clear split in the Detroit sample (item l) occurs with
a seventh of the respondents who realistically argued for both even
though the question did not list this response alternative. The findings of item i in Table 5 bear this out further. Whites in both the
North and South tended to comfort themselves with the idea that
"most Negroes want to live in . . . Negro neighborhoods," but the
overwhelming majority of blacks in both regions believed that it
"does not matter."

Conservative notions about property rights are not limited to
white Americans. As the data for items m and n reveal in Table 5,
close majorities of urban blacks, save for New York City and Detroit,
believed in the 1960's that "an owner of property should not have to
sell to Negroes." This finding is made all the more remarkable when
we inspect the results for item o in Table 5. About half of the nation's
blacks remained dissatisfied with their housing throughout the 1960's.
This situation contrasts sharply with white dissatisfaction with housing, which has steadily declined from 28 percent in 1949 to only 18
percent in 1969. Note, too, that black dissatisfaction with housing
increased sharply between 1949 and 1963—from 32 percent to 54 percent—even though we know from considerable census data that black
housing significantly improved in the aggregate throughout the 1950's.
This interesting situation affords yet another example of the phenomenon of rising aspirations and *relative* deprivation as a source of growing dissatisfaction; beyond survival levels, the difference between
aspiration and achievement is socially and psychologically more critical
than *absolute* deprivation itself (Pettigrew, 1964, Ch. 8, 1968; Geschwender, 1964; Runciman, 1966; Hyman & Singer, 1968).

One might naively ask at this point why blacks do not seek better
housing in presently white areas now that many of them have rising

incomes. One answer, of course, is that blacks are keenly aware of the
the discrimination and possible abuse they face in such efforts. Item
p in Table 5 shows that blacks throughout the nation anticipated "a
hard time" from whites more in "looking for new housing" than in
any of twelve situations offered by the Harris survey question. Only
"applying for a job in a big company" and ". . . for a loan in a bank"
rival the search for new housing, and looking for a suitable mortgage
from a bank is itself likely to be involved in seeking to purchase new
housing. By contrast, only one third of the black respondents anticipated "a hard time" over seeking integrated schooling, conflict-
ridden as that process has been, compared to the two thirds who
anticipated it in the house-hunting process.

Additional data round out this view of black perceptions of housing discrimination. A definite majority were correctly aware in 1963
of the "race tax" they must pay in higher rents compared to those
paid by whites (item q in Table 5).[12] In their 15-city study for the
Kerner Commission (items r, s, and t), Campbell and Schuman (1968)
found in 1968 that three in four blacks believed that numbers of
blacks "miss out on good housing" because of racial discrimination;
and three in seven believed that many parts of their cities were closed

to them because of discrimination—a proportion that might have well
been higher had "suburbs" been included in the item wording.
Roughly half believed that the pervasive pattern of racial discrimination in housing is not eroding (items t and u)—a belief that, apart from
its validity, probably acts to discourage black attempts to grapple with
white officials and real estate dealers for housing outside of the ghetto.
A policy implication of this possibility immediately emerges: *Successful efforts at decreasing racial discrimination in housing must, among
other things, be made widely known among black Americans.* It
should be observed, too, in the results for item u in Table 5, that it
is the young and northern blacks who are the most skeptical—the very
segments who otherwise are the most likely to take advantage of new
interracial housing opportunities.

Black estimations of how they are personally faring in the housing
market did not change in the aggregate much over the 1960's (item v
of Table 5). When these data are disaggregated, however, we find diverse trends by region, which, again, suggest the operation of the rela-

---

[12]One rigorous study of race and housing conducted in 1956 in Chicago concluded that
for roughly equivalent housing, nonwhites had to pay about $15 more a month than
whites (Duncan & Hauser, 1960).

tive deprivation process. Black Southerners consistently perceived more progress in their housing conditions than black Northerners, whose percentage reporting "better off" declined 6 percent over the 7 years from 1963 to 1970. Furthermore, in 1970, rural and small city blacks reported far greater housing improvements than big city blacks, and both the poorest and richest blacks reported more progress than the middle-income ($3,000–9,999). Finer analyses than shown in Table 5 unravel these findings. The poor blacks who saw advances in their personal accommodations are found largely on the farm and in smaller communities in the South—a phenomenon that is a comment on the incredibly bad living conditions for these Americans in the past rather than a comment on the status of their present living conditions. The well-off blacks who saw advances in their personal accommodations are found largely in the larger cities of both regions, a phenomenon that largely reflects their ability to rent and purchase housing in the central city vacated by suburban-bound whites.

Housing, together with schools, was rated by a national sample of blacks as one of the "biggest problems facing Negro people that . . . something should be done about" (item w in Table 5). Yet, 60 percent listed "jobs and pay," compared to only one third listing housing. This difference probably reflects the pressing immediacy of economic problems for many blacks as well as the prior need for greater income in order to seek better accommodations.

Two questions on interracial contact (item x in Table 5) provide suggestive results. Only 29 percent of a 1970 national sample of blacks reported family contact with a white neighbor. But 81 percent of those with such contacts reported them to be "pleasant and easy"—the second highest percentage of twelve types of contact presented by Harris and surpassed only by that for "a friend socially." At the other end of the scale, 22 percent reported family contact with a white landlord or rent collector, and only 67 percent of these contacts were described as "pleasant and easy"—a percentage reflecting tension surpassed only by contact with an "employer or supervisor at work" or "a policeman in the neighborhood." These findings, though hardly surprising, bear reflection, too, by those who are concerned about generating greater racial harmony in our torn society. Interracial contact on a neighborly basis is reported by blacks themselves as typically achieving the type of interaction (to be discussed in the next section) necessary for reducing intergroup prejudice. The contact with landlords and collectors is understandably often unpleasant and likely to generate greater intergroup intolerance and conflict. Obviously, we must have effective housing policies that expand the former type of contact while they shrink the latter type.

The next two items of Table 5 (y and z) narrow this point further. By 1969, two out of every three blacks with an opinion on the subject think real estate companies were more harmful than helpful "to Negro rights." If Rose Helper's research (1969) on the real estate industry can be generalized nationally, this dominant black view is correct. Indeed, of the twelve white groups and institutions employed in the *Newsweek* surveys, real estate companies were rivaled only by "the local police" for a negative black view. Again, this negative view is held strongest by those segments of black population most likely otherwise to seek housing in interracial areas: i.e., Northerners, those under 30 years of age, and those with higher incomes (Goldman, 1970, p. 255–256).

Item z in Table 5 illustrates with 1967 and 1968 survey data from Detroit how real estate dealers in the neighborhood were viewed relative to five other types of business. Local grocery stores drew particular fire as "unfair" both years. While there is some improvement as more time passes after the 1967 Detroit race riot, four types of businesses—related, in part, to housing—all continued to be rated as "unfair" by sizable minorities of black respondents: real estate brokers, home improvement companies, furniture stores, and loan offices.

The six leading causes of race riots cited by Detroit blacks from a list of 25 are shown under item aa in Table 5 (Meyer, 1968). "Police brutality," as might be expected, leads the list in both surveys. But three of the six perceived chief causes of race riots relate directly to housing: "poor housing," "overcrowded living conditions," and "dirty neighborhoods." Clearly, in the minds of Detroit's blacks, housing needs have a high priority in assessing the conditions underlying the type of racial riot they witnessed.

The final item of Table 5 (bb) attempts to show changes among Miami's blacks over the brief and tragic spring of 1968 that saw Dr. Martin Luther King assassinated, a new rash of race riots, and the issuance of the forthright report of the National Advisory Commission on Civil Disorders (the Kerner Commission Report) (Meyer, 1969). Interestingly, some of the biggest shifts in rating the issues that are "a big problem" involve housing. "Rents too high" rose from 63 percent to 78 percent over the spring of 1968; "poor housing," from 57 percent to 75 percent; "overcrowded living conditions," from 58 percent to 75 percent; and "dirty neighborhoods," from 67 percent to 73 percent. By the summer of 1968, then, four of the seven issues considered by Miami blacks as "big problems" for them involved housing—yet another indication of the special importance granted this realm by black Americans.

In summary, black Americans rate better housing as one of their most pressing needs. They would be more than willing to obtain it in racially mixed neighborhoods if they could, though typically, they do not wish to reside in an overwhelmingly white area. In fact, their willingness to move to genuinely interracial neighborhoods appears motivated by a desire to live in racial harmony as well as to achieve better housing and services. As it is, blacks are far more dissatisfied with their present housing situation than whites; and only a minority feel "better off" personally from recent improvements in the housing stock of blacks. Yet they are reluctant to seek housing in presently white areas, in part, because of the discrimination and abuse they anticipate they would suffer. Furthermore, it is precisely those blacks—the young, well-off, and living in the North—who otherwise are most likely to seek interracial housing, who most often harbor these fears as well as the belief that residential discrimination is not receding.

In conclusion, one important dimension must be added. Although we are concentrating in this paper on the factor of *race* for both whites and blacks, race is only one of many factors involved in residential choice—one that is often not critical to either whites or blacks. Thus, we should not let our focus on race cause us to overlook the many other factors that people do actively take into account in housing selection. This point is underlined by data from Bradburn and his University of Chicago colleagues (1970, p. 242–244, 261–263). They sought information on what families thought were the chief advantages causing them to move to their present home. When they compared these factors for whites and blacks who had moved into either integrated or segregated neighborhoods, extremely similar patterns emerged for both groups. Of these, four dominant advantages emerged: convenience to work; the dwelling unit was of appropriate size; specific features of the dwelling other than size (e.g., presence of a garage, fencing, or a particular architectural style); and financial advantages. Mention of these essentially nonracial, but often decisive, factors impresses on us the need to place the attitude data just reviewed in their socially meaningful context.

The Social Context of Attitudes on Race and Housing

Other papers commissioned by the Academy deal directly and in detail with the many critical social and economic factors that govern the racial patterns in housing in the United States. Consequently, this section will focus on only a few of these factors selected for their importance to understanding the role of racial attitudes in the larger process. This section will also introduce a number of social–psychological concepts and theories that enable us to relate the attitude level of analysis to the larger societal level.

The dilemma posed at the start of this paper between the rising approval of interracial living by whites over the past generation and the increased degree of housing segregation over these same years is, of course, more apparent than real. The trends in white attitudes toward favoring open housing are real enough. Surveys have proven their ability to measure with predictive accuracy racial beliefs and attitudes, and black attitudes favoring open housing have remained stable, perhaps even strengthened. But, the dilemma dissolves as soon as we accept that attitudes, as such, are not *primarily* causal but rather *largely* derivative of basic market considerations in housing. There is, to be sure, an interface between the two levels of analysis that is in some ways causal in both directions; and we shall probe this interface in this section. It is, however, the contention of this paper, to repeat, that *the attitudes of both whites and blacks are more derivative than causal in the total process of how shelter, as a resource, is distributed by race in the United States.*

The survey results just reviewed provided evidence for this contention. Recall that whites are far more likely to move into an interracial neighborhood if they have experienced integration previously as a child or as an adult—particularly, if both. Recall, too, that blacks across four cities preferred all-black neighborhoods in direct relation to the degree of residential segregation by race within these cities and that the most pro-desegregation blacks in the Bedford-Stuyvesant study were those who resided in one of the few remaining interracial developments in the area. These findings coincide with those of a 1966 survey study of the urban North and West designed by the U.S.

Commission on Civil Rights (1967, Vol. I, 108–113; Vol. II, 221–241) to test this phenomenon explicitly. It found that white adults who had attended interracial schools as children expressed more willingness to reside in an interracial neighborhood, as well as other more positive attitudes towards blacks, and were, in fact, more likely to be living in interracial neighborhoods and to have close black friends than comparable whites. Also, it found that black adults who had attended interracial schools as children were more trusting of whites than comparable blacks, more eager for their children to attend desegregated schools, and more willing to live in an interracial neighborhood, even if they would have to "pioneer" to do so. What is more, the biracially educated blacks were more likely to be living in mostly white neighborhoods, to be sending their children to desegregated schools, and to have close white friends. Thus, interracial experience is a cumulative process for both races and even spans generations.

According to this model, then, behavior change typically precedes, rather than follows from, attitude change. There is considerable social psychological evidence to support this principle (Pettigrew, 1971b), although it is almost precisely the opposite process from that popularly assumed to be true. One practical corollary of this thesis is that *an effective way to alter opposition, white and black, to interracial housing is to have them live successfully in such housing.* Extensive research in social psychology supports this contention (Pettigrew, 1971b), and at once raises two problems. First, how can we ensure that the interracial living will in fact be "successful," rather than a reenactment of the painful American drama of racial confrontation and conflict? Second, how can we overcome the hostile attitudes in order to achieve the interracial housing in the first place? Let us consider each of these questions in turn.

Many well-meaning Americans have expressed the opinion that if only blacks and whites could experience more contact with each other, the nation's racial difficulties would solve themselves. Unfortunately, the case is not so simple. Black and white Americans have more contact in the South than in any other region of the nation; yet, the region is not conspicuous for its interracial harmony. It appears almost as if contact between the two peoples exacerbates, rather than relieves, intergroup hostility; but this conclusion would be just as hasty and fallacious as the naive assumption that contact invariably lessens prejudice.

Increasing interaction, whether it be of groups or individuals, intensifies and magnifies the processes already under way. Hence, more interracial contact can lead either to greater prejudice and rejection or to greater respect and acceptance, depending on the situation in which it occurs. The basic issue, then, concerns the types of situations in which contact leads to distrust and those in which it leads to trust.

Gordon Allport, in his review of the relevant research (1954), concludes that four characteristics of the contact situation are of utmost importance. Prejudice is lessened when the two groups (1) possess equal status, (2) seek common goals, (3) are cooperatively dependent on each other, and (4) interact with the positive support of authorities, laws, or custom.

If groups are of widely different social status, contact between them may do little more than reinforce old and hostile stereotypes. In the typical southern situation of interracial contact, most blacks encountered by white Southerners are servants and other low-status service workers. Many whites eventually conclude that these are the types of jobs best suited for blacks, that somehow this is the black's "proper place." To be sure, there are black professionals in the South, but, as noted above, segregation has forced them to stay deep within the black ghetto where whites rarely meet them. The segregationist who boasts that he "really knows blacks" is usually referring to his casual encounters with blacks of lower status. This is a principal reason that the plentiful black–white patterns of contact in the South have not led to better interracial understanding.

Many whites are convinced that blacks do not share their interests and values, a belief that compounds racial prejudice with assumed value conflict. *Equal status* contact attacks this problem in two ways. First, people of equal status are more likely than others to possess congruent outlooks and beliefs simply by virtue of their common positions in society. Second, equal status situations provide the optimal setting in which this congruence can be mutually perceived.

When groups work together toward *common goals,* further opportunities are presented for developing and discovering similarities of interests and values. The reduction of prejudice through general contact requires an active, focused effort, not simply intermingling for its own sake. Athletic teams furnish a pertinent example. In striving to win, interracial teams not only create an equal status contact situation, but one in which black and white team members cannot achieve their common goal of winning without the assistance of each other. Under such conditions, race loses importance.

Not only must groups seek common goals, but the attainment of these goals must be a *mutually dependent* effort involving no competition along strictly racial lines. For instance, if the San Francisco Giants were an all-white baseball team and the Los Angeles Dodgers were all black, they could probably play indefinitely and not become more racially tolerant. Though equal status and common goal conditions would prevail, the lines of competition would make race important. The contact situations that lead to interracial harmony must involve cooperative interdependence.

The final factor concerns the auspices of the contact. If the situation has *explicit social sanction,* interracial contact is more readily accepted and leads to more positive effects. Though the situation may be a bit awkward at first, the support of authorities helps make it seem "right." Failure of local authorities, law, and custom to bolster even minimal desegregation in much of the South is a chief reason for the failure of many white Southerners to respect federal court orders.

Research literature abounds with examples of these contact principles in operation. One study found that white merchant marines tended to hold racial attitudes in direct relation to how many voyages they had taken with equal status Negro seamen—the more desegregated voyages, the more positive their attitudes (Brophy, 1945–1946).[13] Another investigation noted that white Philadelphia policemen who had personally worked with Negro colleagues were far more favorable toward the desegregation of their force than other white policemen (Kephart, 1957, p. 188–189). A third study of white government workers, veterans, and students found that those who had known Negro professionals were far less prejudiced toward Negroes than those who had known only unskilled Negroes (MacKenzie, 1948).

Evidence appears even in times of crisis. While Negro and white mobs raged during the Detroit race riot of 1943, co-workers, university students, and neighbors from integrated sectors peacefully carried on their lives side by side (Lee & Humphrey, 1943, p. 97, 130, 140). Mention of neighborhood integration introduces the most solid research evidence available. Repeated studies have found that

---

[13]One possible explanation for the results of this study and others cited below is that the people who were the least prejudiced to begin with sought out interracial contact. Most of these studies, however, rule out the operation of this self-selection factor.

integrated living in public housing developments, which met all four of Allport's contact criteria, sharply reduces the racial prejudice among both black and white neighbors. These same studies demonstrate that living in segregated, but otherwise identical, housing developments, if anything, enhances racial bitterness.

One major study by Deutsch and Collins (1951) took advantage of a made-to-order social experiment in the late 1940's. In accordance with state law, two public housing projects in New York City were desegregated; in all cases, apartment assignments were made regardless of race or personal preference. In two other comparable projects in Newark, New Jersey, the two races were assigned to separate buildings. Striking differences were noted between the attitudes toward blacks of randomly selected white housewives in the desegregated and the segregated developments. The desegregated women held their black neighbors in higher esteem and were considerably more in favor of interracial housing (75 percent to 25 percent). They had more direct contact with blacks in situations meeting Allport's four criteria—e.g., contact as neighbors in the same building, outside on benches, and at laundry and grocery facilities. When asked to name the chief faults of blacks, they mentioned such personal problems as feelings of inferiority and oversensitivity; by contrast, the segregated women listed such group stereotypes as troublemaking, rowdy, and dangerous (Deutsch & Collins, 1951).

Basically, these differences in attitude center upon the fact that the desegregated housewives viewed blacks as individuals more often, as people like themselves. Witness these sample quotations from Deutsch and Collins (1951):

Living with them my ideas have changed altogether. They're just people . . . they're not any different.

I started to cry when my husband told me we were coming to live here. I cried for three weeks. . . . Well, all that's changed. I've really come to like it. I see they're just as human as we are.

I was prejudiced when I moved in here but not any more. . . . I find there is no such thing as "my kind.". . . I know the people. I have been in their homes . . . been to church with them. . . . I know they're not dirty.

Wilner, Walkley, and Cook (1955; see also Jahoda & West, 1951) conducted a later investigation of four other public housing projects, replicating the Deutsch and Collins findings and extending them.

They found physical proximity to blacks to be even more important than whether the individual building was officially desegregated or not. This was true because intimacy of contact and consequent behavior change was directly dependent on proximity. Thus, favorable attitudes toward blacks, in general, developed among only one third of the white tenants who did not interact with their black neighbors beyond casual greetings, compared to almost half of those who had extended street conversations with blacks and three fourths of those who behaved like neighbors with blacks in numerous ways. In short, those who acted like neighbors, felt like neighbors. Herein lies the fundamental reason why optimal contact can lessen prejudice; it generally leads first to changed *behavior* that, in turn, results in attitude change. In these housing projects, this changed behavior most often had its most dramatic effects on the attitudes of those initially most bigoted.[14]

Both of these public housing researches also established the importance of the intricate relationship between a person's attitudes and his perception of what other people expect of him. Underlining once again the need for social sanction, Deutsch and Collins noted that the white housewives in the desegregated projects anticipated approval from their neighbors for their friendly interaction with blacks, while housewives in the segregated projects feared social ostracism for such behavior. The racial policy of the housing development thus fixed a social climate that influenced the expectations, behavior, and attitude change of the occupants. Wilner and his associates concluded (1955, p. 106): "Contact and perceived social climate tend to reinforce each other when their influence operates in the same direction, and to cancel each other out when their influence works in the opposite direction."

The vital role played in race relations by social climate is difficult to overemphasize. At this point, it is interesting to observe its power in the Republic of South Africa. Patterned after the public-housing studies in the United States, research on a racially mixed neighborhood in Durban uncovered subtle differences (Russell, 1961). One half of the neighborhood consisted of whites (largely working class), 20 percent of coloureds (working class and white collar), and 30 percent of Indians (white collar and professional)—a rare South African example of close contact between lower-status whites and relatively upper-status nonwhites. Even in South Africa, this situation led the

[14]For a theoretical and methodological critique of this finding, see Brehm and Cohen (1962, p. 274–277).

whites to develop positive attitudes toward their coloured and Indian neighbors; but, unlike the public-housing results in the northern United States, these favorable attitudes did not extend beyond the immediate neighborhood to nonwhites in general. Indeed, the South African whites in this unusual situation were defensive about their interracial contacts, some of them even attempting to avoid contact as much as possible. Moreover, the contact that did take place was not truly equal and reciprocal. Whites received neighborly aid from nonwhites and entered nonwhite homes far more frequently than the other way around. In fact, the whites rationalized their interracial contact in terms of the mildly exploitative aspects of the relationship. Both the whites and nonwhites were fully aware that the social climate of South Africa does not support, in fact punishes, equal status contact between races, an atmosphere that poisons true neighborliness at the core.

While housing research has concentrated on the attitudes of whites toward blacks, one investigator focused on the attitudes of blacks toward whites. Do the same principles of contact and change apply in reverse? Works (1961, p. 47–52) demonstrated that they do. He noted that increased equal status interaction with whites in a public-housing project was related both to more positive feelings and to attitudes toward whites. Furthermore, this result held for husbands as well as wives, though the wives experienced more interracial contact in the project. Ninety-nine percent of the black wives in the desegregated part of the development, for example, had favorable feelings toward whites, compared to only 44 percent of those in the segregated part. Sample statements by desegregated husbands provide the flavor of the changed attitudes (Works, 1961, p. 50–51):

I thought they were going to be a lot worse than they are.

When I first came in . . . I thought they were going to be like some other people I have had dealings with. They have not been like that at all.

They're nice. Can tell by the way they come over and talk with my wife.

One important qualification attends attitude change through interracial contact: At least in the early stages, the change is often limited to the specific situation involved. Consider the apparent inconsistencies of a neighborhood group of white steel workers in the Chicago area (Reitzes, 1953). These men were all members of the same thoroughly desegregated union and all worked in desegregated plants. In fact, blacks held elected positions, such as shop stewards, executive board members, and vice president of the union, and shared with whites the same locker rooms, lunch rooms, showers, and toilets in both the union hall and the plants. Of the 151 whites studied, only 12 percent evidenced "low acceptance" of blacks in the work situation; and the deeper their involvement in union activities, the greater their acceptance of blacks as co-workers. Neighborhood acceptance, however, was a vastly different matter to these men. Bolstered by a neighborhood organization that opposed desegregation, 86 percent of the white workers rejected the idea of allowing blacks to live near them; those men most involved in the collective existence of the neighborhood tended to reject the idea most adamantly. The effects of optimal interracial contact at work did not extend to housing. No relationship existed between acceptance of blacks as fellow workers and acceptance of them as neighbors.

The important key to understanding this process is the operation of the organizations in each of these situations. Most of the steel workers, like members of mass society in general, conformed to what was expected of them, even when these expectations countered one another. Thus, the inconsistency is more apparent than real; it appears conflicting to the observer, but to the person involved their behavior is perfectly reasonable. In both situations, they are living by the norms of the groups to which they refer their behavior—their *reference groups*. It is these group norms that may act to restrict the generalization of contact-induced attitude change.

To sum up, interracial living itself will effectively erode racial opposition to open housing to the degree that it is characterized by Allport's four key criteria: equal status of the groups in the situation, common goals, group interdependence, and social sanction. The rapidly changing neighborhood, with whites selling low in panic, is a classic urban housing situation that grossly violates all of Allport's factors and generates intense hostility on both sides of the color line. Stable interracial neighborhoods—which are far less publicized, but were found by Bradburn and his associates (1970) to be more numerous than many thought—illustrate the positive operation of Allport's factors and are, in fact, characterized by greater interracial acceptance and tolerance. Desegregation in other realms, even when successful, does not necessarily generalize to housing, however, as shown in the study of white steel workers.

An understanding of this social psychological process helps to explain a number of otherwise puzzling phenomena in the area of race and housing. For example, Bahr and Gibbs (1967) have shown that residential segregation is not an accurate indicator of other urban racial phenomena. Analyzing 1960 data from 33 randomly selected Standard Metropolitan Statistical Areas (SMSA's) throughout the nation, they note no relationship between residential segregation and racial discrepancies in education, occupation, and income. This contrasts to the consistently positive correlations across cities between educational, occupational, and income differences of blacks and whites. Indeed, for their subsample of 13 southern cities, Bahr and Gibbs discovered that residential segregation is actually slightly *negatively* correlated with racial educational (–.32), occupational (–.12), and income (–.14) differences. Consistent with this southern finding, Schnore and Evenson (1966) noted that the age of southern cities is negatively associated with residential segregation.[16] They believe that this is a twentieth century carry-over of old urban slavery patterns, where lower-status blacks live near upper-status whites in a type of "backyard desegregation." Of course, these same legacies of slavery also make for wide discrepancies between blacks and whites on such indices as education, occupation, and income.[17]

The Bahr–Gibbs aggregate phenomenon, when looked at from the individual level, is easily accounted for by the social psychological model of contact proposed here. The South's older cities probably have more actual contact between the two races than the region's newer cities. Yet this contact between blacks and whites of sharply different social status is likely to violate Allport's key criteria and vitiate any positive, prejudice-reducing effects. More likely, this unequal status contact serves largely to reinforce hostile stereotypes on both sides. This process, combined with the stronger influence of traditional racial norms, allows us to understand readily how greater residential desegregation can be directly related to greater racial disparities in the South's older cities.

The attitude-contact model as presented, however, remains obviously incomplete. If, as it has been indicated, pro-desegregation attitudes in housing are generated easiest by actual experience in

[16]Thus, of the Taeubers' Gini-type index (1965, p. 40–41) of 1960 residential segregation, old cities, such as Charleston, South Carolina (79.5), Macon, Georgia (83.7), and New Orleans (86.3), tend to boast lower indices than modern cities, such as Atlanta (93.6), Dallas (94.6), and Miami, Florida (97.9).

[17]In addition, Winer (1964) has shown that the newer and more prosperous southern cities were the first to initiate and enlarge the process of racial desegregation of their public schools.

interracial neighborhoods as characterized by Allport's four conditions, how is it that these attitudes have been improving steadily for whites (Table 1) while residential segregation was increasing? This is the reverse order of our original question, and the answer is similar. Housing is not a closed system. Attitudes toward interracial housing have been subject to considerable influence and change by other factors. To be sure, as the steelworker investigation indicated, these other factors are likely to possess less potential for changing white opinions about interracial housing than has optimal neighborhood experience. Cumulated over an entire generation as part of wider racial attitudes, race and housing attitudes have slowly altered. Recall the results presented earlier on the delayed shift in the interracial housing opinions of white Texans following Dr. King's murder. Presumably, the dramatic racial events of recent years have repeatedly served this function together with the optimal interracial contact that has been increasing in employment and higher education.

Supportive of this interpretation is the fact that white attitudes toward interracial housing, in general, have not improved as fast as they have in those realms where optimal contact has been becoming more widespread. Remember from Table 1 that large numbers of white Americans are still resistant to neighborhood mixing. Two additional reasons for this resistance are also apparent. The first one we have already discussed. Housing contact is perceived as far more intimate than many other areas of contact, as illustrated in the Texas data. Critical sexual and status fears underlying American race relations make perceived intimacy an important barrier to change.

The other reason for resistance involves what is known in social psychology as acquaintance and similarity theory. Newcomb (1965) states the fundamental tenet as follows:

> Insofar as persons have similar attitudes toward things of importance to both or all of them, and discover that this is so, they have shared attitudes; under most conditions the experience of sharing such attitudes is rewarding, and thus provides a basis for mutual attraction.

Rokeach (Rokeach & Mezer, 1966; Rokeach et al., 1960) has applied these notions to American race relations with some surprising results. He maintains that white American rejection of black Americans is motivated less by racism than by assumed belief and value differences. In other words, whites generally perceive blacks as holding contrasting beliefs, and it is this perception, and not race per se, that leads to rejection. Indeed, a variety of subjects (Smith *et al.*, 1967; Stein, 1966; Stein *et al.*, 1965; Hendrick *et al.*, 1971) have supported Rokeach's ideas by typically accepting in a social situation a black with similar beliefs to their own over a white with different beliefs.

Additional work specifies the phenomenon more precisely. Triandis and Davis (1965) have shown that the relative importance of belief and race factors in attraction is a joint function of the interpersonal realm in question and personality. Belief similarity is most critical in more formal matters of general personal evaluation and social acceptance, where racial norms are ambiguously defined. Race is most critical in intimate matters of marriage and neighborhood, where racial norms are explicitly defined. For interpersonal realms of intermediate intimacy, such as friendship, both belief and race considerations appear important. Moreover, there are wide individual differences in the application of belief similarity and race, especially in contact realms of intermediate intimacy.

Seen in the light of this work, racial isolation has two negative effects. First, isolation prevents each group from learning of the common beliefs and values they do in fact share. Consequently, blacks and whites kept apart come to view each other as so different that belief dissimilarity typically combines with racial considerations to cause each race to reject contact with the other. Second, isolation leads in time to the evolution of genuine differences in beliefs and values, again making interracial contact in the future less likely.

Thus, one investigation found that racially isolated, white ninth-graders in California assumed an *undescribed* black teen-ager to be similar to a black teen-ager who is described as being quite *different* from themselves; but they assumed an *undescribed* white teen-ager to be similar to a white teen-ager who is described as being quite similar to themselves (Stein *et al.*, 1965). A number of other replications of this phenomenon have been completed; one such study indicates that it operates strongly only for racially prejudiced subjects (Hendrik *et al.*, 1971). If this finding can be extrapolated for white Americans in general, it provides another important link in our argument. Thus, a new white neighbor who moves onto a white block may typically be assumed to be *similar* in values and outlook until he proves otherwise. But a new black who moves onto a previously white block may typically be assumed to be *different* in values and outlook until he proves otherwise. Riots and media coverage of Black

Panthers and other militant blacks probably add to this *"assumed*
dissimilarity" factor.

The paucity of optimal interracial contact at the neighborhood
level, the perceived intimacy of housing, and the assumption of dissimilarity erode the more abstract beliefs in equality held by most
white Americans when the issue of race and housing is made directly
relevant to the individual white. Once combined with fears of declining house values, these factors help account for the voting data
on the subject to date. Despite the attitude trends and data shown
in Table 1, civil rights referenda on housing in Akron, Detroit,
Seattle, and California during the 1960's lost by roughly two-to-one
margins. The most interesting and important of these votes was that
cast in 1964 for California's Proposition 14, an initiative constitutional amendment that precluded state and local fair-housing legislation. It carried by a handsome 65.4 to 34.6 percent margin of
2,130,000 votes (Eley & Casstevens, 1968, p. 237–284).[18] At the
same election, the Democratic Party's ticket of Johnson and Humphrey swept the Goldwater–Miller ticket by 59 to 41 percent, indicating that a minimum of one in every four Californian voters
in 1964 cast his ballot against fair housing *and* the conservative Republican candidates at the same time. Nevertheless, surveys demonstrated that white support for Proposition 14 was strongest among
Protestants, Republicans, men, homeowners, and the middle class,
weakest among Jews and renters. Age, interestingly, did not predict opinion on the issue. Social class variables provided complex
results: In general, the more prosperous whites backed Proposition
14, but it was the moderately educated (i.e., high school graduates
plus those with one or two years of college) who backed it (Eley &
Casstevens, 1968, p. 275–281). There is, then, the suggestion that
those whose status was marginal and inconsistent—high income,
but modestly educated middle-class homeowners—were particularly
enthusiastic over the discriminatory measure.

Voting, of course, is an imperfect guide to attitudes, since it is
also importantly determined by the political structure and situation
in which it occurs. Indeed, referenda of all types with racial significance often go in the conservative direction by the same two-to-one
majorities. The Civilian Review Board of New York City's police
force, which was resoundingly defeated at the polls in 1966, is a

[18]This volume offers the best available overview of this issue below the federal level.

dramatic case in point (Abbott *et al.*, 1969).[19] In this New York referendum, fear of crime more than anti-black sentiment was the key; in the housing referenda, fear of lowered property values and the traditional American view of the rights of private individuals to own and control their property more than anti-black sentiment were the key. The real estate industry aids this process vociferously in the fair-housing campaigns. Indeed, virtually all of the industry's efforts can be seen as attempts to heighten these fears and the traditional view that the authority of the state ceases at the doorstep of the home, while deemphasizing the equally traditional principle of fair play for all Americans.

Small wonder, then, that laws whose avowed purpose is the elimination of racial prejudice in private housing have triggered long and bitter conflict across the nation. Once again the gains in this realm underscore the importance placed by this paper on the *fait accompli* effects upon attitudes of structural alterations. In spite of the fierce opposition, between December 30, 1957, when New York City's historic ordinance was passed, and July 1, 1967, some 40 cities, 22 states, the District of Columbia, Puerto Rico, the Virgin Islands, and a metropolitan county adopted and often later strengthened fair-housing laws covering at least part of the private housing market (Eley & Casstevens, 1968). Admittedly, as other papers document, these laws have not as yet been typically administered in an effective manner. Nonetheless, they set the national political scene that enabled the nation's first act on this issue to be passed in 1968. Their momentum has accumulated over time into increasingly broader and more effective legislation. For example, the fair-housing ordinance of Oberlin, Ohio, once sanctioned by the state supreme court, led directly and quickly to a similar 1965 law at the state level after attempts at such a statute had failed in 1961 and 1963 (Hale, 1968, p. 149–185).[20] Similarly, Ann Arbor, Michigan, another college town, witnessed a bitter struggle for many years over a fair-housing ordinance; but, once it finally was adopted in 1963, it gained wide-

[19]Interestingly, the survey pattern of social correlates for this vote in Brooklyn resembles that of Proposition 14. Catholics, the moderately educated, those with middle-range incomes, and males were most opposed to civilian review, college-educated Jews most in favor, and age again does not predict opinion.
[20]Significantly, the Republican Governor, James Rhodes, joined Democratic legislators in influencing Republicans to accept a modest bill and in dissuading realtors from mounting another massive referendum campaign to defeat the enactment.

spread acceptance in the community and led to gains in other areas of civil rights (Eley, 1968, p. 285–351).

The most striking example of this cumulative legislative process and its influence on white attitudes comes from Flint, Michigan. Governmental responses to the rising pressure for fair-housing policies, according to Walker (1968, p. 353–382), had to bypass the clogged legislative process. These end-runs included an abortive attempt at administrative regulation and a sweeping interpretation of the civil rights provision in the new state constitution. In the late 1960's, fair-housing laws were enacted in Detroit, Muskegon, Lansing, Flint, and other cities in the state. Most significant as an indication of altered white views, however, is the fact that the Flint law was approved in a public referendum in February 1968. This marked the first time in the nation that a fair-housing statute was approved at the polls, a feat made all the more remarkable by the fact that Flint was a northern stronghold for George Wallace in his presidential race months later.

THE ACHIEVEMENT OF INTERRACIAL HOUSING

Mention of the cumulative nature of legislative support for open housing introduces this second problem posed by the model advanced here. If attitudes on race and housing are more derivative than causal, *the clear policy implication is to achieve more interracial housing without placing undue emphasis on hostile white opinions. How* is the question.

Our discussion to this point has touched on a number of factors relevant to this problem. Thus, we have noted that black and white attitudes concerning open housing are not in a vacuum; they are subject to alteration by dramatic events as well as the national tide in public opinion about civil rights in general. Indeed, the openness of these attitudes to influence by nonhousing events accounts in large part for the definite, if slow, trend in white opinion toward favoring fair housing (Table 1). In turn, this trend has aided the process of increasingly rigorous legislative attempts to open private housing racially just reviewed—a process that feeds back to furthering the favorable trend itself. Obviously, then, *the achievement of interracial housing requires additional gains on these legislative and judicial fronts.*

These additional gains would be most strategically effective if they came more in terms of more effective enforcement procedures rather than in terms of simply more statutes modeled after our present, largely unsuccessful laws. Mayhew (1968) provides a critical example of such a shift.[21] He demonstrates with both employment and housing data on discrimination in Massachusetts how class, rather than individual action, is essential. In general, local and state fair-housing statutes apply a case-by-case approach, relying on individual complaints; yet complaint cases are largely nonstrategic. The problem has such deep structural roots—ranging from zoning ordinances to land use planning—that only direct confrontation of these fundamental issues and the housing industry as a whole promises truly effective enforcement. That is, racial discrimination in housing is institutionally patterned; consequently, only patterned enforcement offers hope for success.

One of the basic problems at the attitude level is that the thorough separation by residence of the races has conditioned both whites and blacks to think largely in terms of two separate housing markets. Many in both races come to expect it as "the way things are done," as the "right" as well as the normal pattern of housing. Status considerations have naturally developed around this idea that the real estate industry blatantly advertises as the desirability of *exclusive* areas. Once such a process has been given force for decades, even by leading agencies of the federal government, it is not surprising that it is difficult to reverse.

Hidden in this sad national history, especially since the building boom of suburbia following World War II, is a key principle: Federal government policy, even more than the regressive policies of the real estate industry, is itself largely responsible for the extreme situation of dual housing markets in which we find ourselves today.[22] It would seem that a pattern established largely by federal policy could be disestablished if altered federal policy led the way. What the law giveth, the law can taketh away!

Moreover, it is not an exaggeration to say that inspiration for the shape these new federal policies could take can be gleaned directly from simply reversing 180 degrees some of the policies of former years. Consider, for instance, the consistent policies of the Federal

[21]For documentation of blatant discrimination even in a small city (Schenectady, New York), which has a tiny black population and operates under a relatively well-administered state antidiscrimination statute, see Mercer (1962).

[22]For evidence for this point, see Abrams (1966, p. 512–524) and Grier (1966, p. 525–554).

Housing Authority (FHA) in the late 1940's and 1950's, which
not only biased its mortgage programs in favor of whites but also
in favor of new housing in the rapidly growing suburbs rather than
old housing in the central city. This policy, like many of the FHA's
discriminatory policies of the period, furthered racial segregation
and established the present pattern of "white nooses" around the
increasingly black central cities. Why not reverse the incentive?
Why not bias federal mortgages, including those granted by the Veterans' Administration, in favor of whites seeking to rehabilitate older
housing in the central city and blacks seeking to purchase new homes
in the suburbs? Other papers in this volume develop more comprehen-
sively such policy and structural changes necessary to alter today's
racially dual markets in housing. Until such policy changes are
adopted and rigorously applied, however, concern over the attitudes
of Americans about race and housing is misplaced and fruitless.

THE INTERFACE OF ATTITUDES AND SOCIETAL FACTORS

Attitudes, although more derivative than causal in the housing segregation process, are not completely derivative. It remains, then, to
discuss the two-way causal interface of attitudes on the individual
level with the powerful market factors on the societal level. Here,
we can greatly benefit from an ingenious and valuable computer
simulation of the varieties of residential segregation by Freeman and
Sunshine (1970).

These investigators begin by viewing the residential segregation
process as the output of the confluence of (a) market income factors, (b) economic interest factors, (c) ethnic proximity-proportion
factors, and (d) racial prejudice. These four classes, argue Freeman
and Sunshine, control the degree of residential segregation both
by preventing blacks from buying houses in white areas and by encouraging whites to move out of, or not to move into, areas containing blacks. This organization of the problem coincides closely
with the best social science research available on the subject at
present, and it provides the framework for the simulation of the
process.

In more detail, the researchers reduce the issue to five steps of a
cycle: Can blacks compete economically for houses in good quality
white neighborhoods? Are brokers willing to bring homes in white
neighborhoods to the attention of black clients? Are white homeowners willing to sell to prospective black buyers? Can a black who

has successfully bought a home in a white area actually live peacefully in his house? Finally, how likely is it that whites will move
out of, or refuse to buy a home in, a racially heterogeneous neighborhood? Freeman and Sunshine maintain that the prejudiced attitudes of whites enter into each of the answers to these questions.
Their simulation employs all four classes of factors in order to shed
light on the interface of prejudiced attitudes with other factors for
each of these five queries.

To simulate the first step in the cycle, Freeman and Sunshine
distinguish in their model between two kinds of economic difficulties for blacks: their inferior position in the economy and racial
discrimination in lending. This distinction is important, for the
Taeubers (1965) have shown that the reduced economic resources
of blacks account for only a small portion of racial separation by
residence compared to the enormous effects of direct discrimination
in all its forms.

For the second step in the cycle, Freeman and Sunshine introduce the fact that the probability of a black being shown a house
by real estate brokers is a function of the proportion of houses on
the market in the neighborhood and of the mean level of white
prejudice in the neighborhood. Five specific axioms are applied
that attempt to provide reasonable approaches to the complex
relations between these factors. Thus, in the limiting case of virtually no prejudice in the neighborhood, the two researchers assume
that the other two factors are inoperative. Also, when there is considerable prejudice, the model assumes that a large proportion of
vacant houses will "open up" the neighborhood to black families
and sets the occasion for panic selling and a quick racial turnover.
More interesting is the difficult situation in which there are no blacks
in the neighborhood and only moderate levels of prejudice. As the
proportion of houses on the market increases to the assumed tipping
point of 33 percent, the broker will feel pressure to sell. However, the
white prejudice of the area is likely to direct hostile reactions to the
broker for his activities on behalf of black clients. The broker is thus
placed in a conflict between his short- and long-range interests, and
the model predicts that he will more often show homes to black applicants as vacancy rates rise and prejudice levels decline.

The third step concerning white willingness to sell to blacks presents a similar problem to that of broker reactions. The two extremes
here involve a bigoted builder selling new suburban homes in his development, on the negative end of the continuum, and, on the posi-

tive end, an unprejudiced owner of a home in an interracial neighborhood who wants to obtain the best sale price and who is relatively oblivious to his neighbors. In an attempt to capture these situations in their model, Freeman and Sunshine set white willingness to sell to blacks as a function of four factors: prejudice of the owner, the number of cycles the house has been on the market, the acquisitiveness level of the owner, and the proportion of black households in the neighborhood. Five axioms are established similar to those for broker reactions.

The probability that a black "pioneer family" will be "pushed out" of a white neighborhood—the fourth step relevant to the cycle—is considered a function of three factors: the neighborhood's mean prejudice level, the *number* of other black households in the neighborhood, and the number of previous attempts made to push this black family out ("fatigue factor"). The first of these heightens the probability; the others reduce it in the model.

The final step in the cycle involves the likelihood that whites will move out of, or refuse to move into, a mixed neighborhood. By an ingenious formula, Freeman and Sunshine (1970) derive a reasonable, though necessarily arbitrary, measure that taps both proximity to, and proportion of, black neighbors for each house of a neighborhood. Thus, a next door neighbor is assumed in the model to have a saliency of 25, while that of a house in the next block is assumed to have a saliency of only four. For simplicity of their trial model, they omit from their model such variables as sentimental ties to the neighborhood, perceptual awareness of the density and proximity of blacks, and the realistic alternatives that are available. Consequently, they establish probabilities of whites leaving or refusing to buy into an interracial neighborhood as functions of personal prejudice levels and their proximity and density measure.

We have described this simulation by Freeman and Sunshine of the residential segregation process in some detail so that their results can be appreciated and evaluated. Despite obvious simplification of a complex social process into 20 variables, this early effort at a serious simulation of this realm is able to generate in a series of 150-cycle "experiments" many of the phenomena noted in the research literature as well as new possibilities. Hence, a color-blind neighborhood, where prejudice is nonexistent and both races have the same purchasing power, naturally responds like a one-race neighborhood, except that the ratio of blacks to whites grows as the experiment continues until it reaches the black proportion of these seeking housing.

"The social class ghetto" results when there is no prejudice, but the black purchasing power mean is realistically set at only 72 percent of the white mean. Fewer blacks are able to enter this neighborhood and higher vacancy rates obtain, but those who can are not segregated within the neighborhood.

The model can also simulate the more common case of "invasion," panic, and racial succession (Duncan & Duncan, 1957; Wolf, 1957).[23] This occurs when white prejudice is set at moderately high levels and black buying power is set at 72 percent that of whites. At the onset of this experiment, blacks have a difficult time entering the neighborhood; blacks do not become established until the twenty-sixth cycle. As indicated earlier, it is the combination of individual and neighborhood-wide prejudice that causes this delayed entry; the social class ghetto experiment is identical to this, save for no prejudice existing and has blacks entering from the beginning.

Once the black penetration of the neighborhood is achieved, however, it becomes rapidly easier for blacks to enter. Freeman and Sunshine write (1970, p. 64–65):

Whites begin to leave, those with the highest prejudice levels and living closest to Negroes leaving first. And, although some whites continue to enter the community, prejudice exercises inhibitory effects so that demand cannot be maintained by new white purchasers. The upshot is that the vacancy rate builds up and prices turn downward.

The process is cumulative and irreversible. The fall in prices brings the houses within the range of the Negro purchasing power distribution. Simultaneously, the fall in price increasingly inhibits whites from entering through the price-to-low-bid constraint. Then, as the proportion of Negroes builds up to rather large values, even relatively unprejudiced whites are unwilling to enter. The final result at Cycle 150 shows a neighborhood with 197 non-whites, 4 whites and 39 vacancies. This clearly is a case of invasion and succession. Furthermore, as one might expect, the segregation index achieves rather large values. Thus, segregation is maintained both within the neighborhood and in the larger community by the device of "turning this neighborhood over" to the Negroes. If equality in purchasing power had been allowed, the situation would be altered only in minor detail. . . .

The fact that this critical succession pattern is not influenced more by purchasing power differentials is an interesting output of the

---

[23]In the practical case of succession, black demand is so pent up that it more than substitutes for white demand. Prices thus rise if white panic does not ensue (Laurenti, 1959).

model that is consistent with our discussion earlier of belief similarity: In prejudiced communities, whites prefer whites as neighbors, even though this results in considerable "social-class desegregation." Or put in our earlier terms, the strongly prejudiced choose race over belief similarity, especially for the relatively intimate area of housing.

When white prejudice is set at extremely high levels with differential buying power, "a South African neighborhood type" is generated by the model. In 150 cycles, *no* blacks secure a home under these conditions. Prices and vacancies are determined wholly by white demand and blacks are shut out of the market. Interestingly, home values find a range somewhat lower than in the color-blind neighborhood. "This is a consequence," write Freeman and Sunshine (1970, p. 67), "of the restricted demand that results from excluding Negroes from competing for homes. As a matter of fact, prejudice *always* reduces demand—either by excluding Negroes or through the refusal of whites to enter a mixed neighborhood—so there is always an economic cost to prejudice."

What about the possibility of a stable interracial neighborhood? Freeman and Sunshine produce one of several possibilities for this goal by assuming moderately low prejudice, high white demand, and moderate black demand combined with the black buying power again set at 72 percent that of whites. In this experiment, blacks enter the neighborhood from the beginning. Some are pushed out, but most remain. Those whites with the highest prejudice levels leave and prices drop somewhat. Unprejudiced whites still buy into the neighborhood, internal segregation does not develop, prices recover much of their lost ground, and the black proportion stabilizes around cycle 100. Bradburn and his colleagues (1970) apparently uncovered a number of interracial neighborhoods throughout the nation that resemble this experiment.

This work by Freeman and Sunshine marks an important beginning of the application of sophisticated computer simulation methods to the realm of residential segregation, demonstrating the complex interface of prejudiced attitudes with social and market factors. Moreover, some of the policy implications of the model are interesting and not necessarily obvious (Freeman & Sunshine, 1970, p. 77–78):

First, we note that equality of purchasing power alone does not prevent a condition of intra-neighborhood segregation; in the face of local prejudice such equality merely speeds up the process of population turnover. If there is no residential prejudice, and ethnic inequality in purchasing power exists, there will still be seg-

regation, this time by the systematic exclusion of Negroes from "better" neighborhoods. It follows, then, that equal access to decent neighborhood and housing conditions requires equality across the board. . . .

Second, the model indicates density and spatial distribution factors should be
related in an ameliorative policy. Specifically, if prejudice obtains and the nonwhite population is segregated in a certain area of a neighborhood, houses on the
perimeter of the non-white area are offered for sale. Since these will be filled by
newly entering whites only with difficulty, they are likely to be sold to Negroes.
This wave process culminates in a more or less complete turnover of the population. On the other hand, if the same initial number of non-whites could be dispersed, the turnover process would be slowed. This has not been demonstrated
experimentally so far, but it appears to be a reasonable conclusion.

Third, there is a class of "administrative" solutions implied by the model.
Negro demand could be cut off at a certain point, and in conjunction with this,
white demand could be maintained—if need be—by subsidies. Perhaps, it would
be possible to arrange the addresses of incoming white applicants judiciously so
that the distance of a prejudiced white from the closest Negro is proportional
to his prejudice level.

Naturally, it is hard to see how these principles could be invoked without
weakening the doctrine of consumer sovereignty. There is some reason to suspect, however, that if Negro demand can be kept fairly low and white demand
high, that unprejudiced whites would tend to form a "buffer zone" between
Negroes and prejudiced whites. This might well result from a "natural" process,
and require only the manipulation of demand through the control of alternatives. . . .

There are a number of ways this and comparable models can be
made more realistic in addition to more research facts needed to fill
in gaps in our present empirical knowledge. Thus, future models
could simultaneously treat three or more contrasting neighborhoods
to include competing alternatives for buyers as part of the experiments. New models could also attempt to deal with contagion processes that collectively encourage panic and flight, harsh resistance,
or adaptation. Most important from the viewpoint of this paper,
however, is that future models must treat prejudiced attitudes as
derivative as well as causal. The Freeman–Sunshine simulation treats
prejudice as a static variable; hypothetical individuals in their study
are assigned a prejudice score that does not change at all over the
150 cycles of the experiment. This feature of their model is unrealistic. Furthermore, it seems likely that inclusion of prejudice as a
dynamic property that becomes significantly better or worse under
a wide range of interracial housing patterns would serve to increase

greatly the span of conditions that could produce stable and successful biracial neighborhoods as well as those that could produce
rapid racial succession. In other words, the cumulative quality of
the effects of optimal and far-from-optimal intergroup contact
would serve as a catalyst in speeding up whatever neighborhood
process is under way.

Summary and Policy Implications

The chief points of this paper can be briefly summarized and their
policy implications indicated by the following assertions:

1. White American attitudes toward open housing have become
increasingly more favorable over the past generation. This definite
trend appears to result largely from factors outside of the housing
realm, e.g., dramatic racial events, the general trend in racial attitudes apart from housing, and increasing racial desegregation in
other realms. The rapid growth of fair-housing legislation over the
last decade and a half appears to have had an especially important
influence on this trend; but the most direct technique for improving
white attitudes on this subject—actual neighborhood contact between the races under optimal conditions—has not been widespread
enough to account for the attitude trend.

2. Black American attitudes favoring open housing have remained
stable, perhaps even strengthening in recent years. Now that the black
middle class is making significant economic gains, it appears that fear
of a hostile white reception together with binding ties with, and "a
stake and status" in, the black community is primarily responsible
for black reluctance to move into previously all-white areas (Watts
et al., 1964).

3. The attitudes of both whites and blacks are more derivative
than causal in the total process of how shelter as a resource is distributed by race in the United States. Desegregation is a cumulative
process for both races: The more optimal intergroup contact you
have had, the more you favor and seek it in the future. Behavior
change, then, typically precedes rather than follows attitude change.
The practical implication of this principle is that an effective way to
alter opposition, white and black, to interracial housing is to have
them live successfully in such housing. But, what constitutes "suc-

cessful"? How does one achieve such housing before the attitudes are altered?

4. Interracial living will itself effectively erode racial opposition to open housing to the degree that it is characterized by Gordon Allport's four situational criteria: equal status of the groups in the situation, common goals, group interdependence, and social sanction. This principle has considerable research support for both blacks and whites, with many of the best studies having been conducted in public-housing developments. The policy imperative for the housing planner is clear: We need not only more interracial living, but efforts to achieve more mixed neighborhoods must also strive to ensure the operation of Allport's four optimal conditions in these neighborhoods.

5. The actual achievement of interracial housing requires: (a) that undue emphasis not be placed upon hostile white opinions, that affirmative efforts not be inhibited by initial opposition or wait until "educational" programs for attitude change can be mounted; (b) additional gains on the legislative and judicial fronts, gains less in terms of simply more statutes and rulings and more in terms of more effective enforcement procedures (e.g., patterned class actions rather than nonstrategic, case-by-case complaints); and (c) vigorous federal action that sharply contrasts with federal housing practices of the past (e.g., mortgage incentives for whites to buy in the central city and blacks to buy in the suburbs). Other necessary structural alterations are discussed in detail by others in this volume.

6. Finally, the interface of prejudiced white attitudes and racial residential patterns are explored through an ingenious, 20-variable simulation model constructed by Freeman and Sunshine. White prejudice enters into every step of a housing cycle, according to this model, from the ability and willingness of blacks to seek good housing in white neighborhoods to whites who move out of, or refuse to buy into, an interracial neighborhood. Realistic facsimilies of "the color-blind neighborhood," "the social class ghetto," the classic pattern of invasion and rapid succession, "the South African neighborhood" of total black exclusion, and the stable "racially mixed neighborhood" are simulated. The model leads to a number of not-so-obvious policy implications. This model, with extensions such as the addition of the property of attitudes to shift with various types of intergroup contact, offers great promise as a needed tool both for theory on the subject as well as for practical planning for the future.

References

Abbott, D. W., Gold, L., & Rogowsky, E. T. *Police, politics and race: The New York City referendum on civilian review.* Cambridge, Mass.: Harvard University Press, 1969.

Abrams, C. The housing problem and the Negro. In T. Parsons & K. Clark (Eds.), *The Negro-American.* Boston: Houghton Mifflin, 1966.

Allport, G. W. *The nature of prejudice.* Cambridge, Mass.: Addison-Wesley, 1954. Chapter 16.

Bagley, C. *Social structure and prejudice in five English boroughs.* London: The Institute for Race Relations, 1970.

Bahr, H. M., & Gibbs, J. P. Racial differentiation in American metropolitan areas. *Social Forces,* 1967, 45, 521–532.

Bradburn, N. M., Sudman, S., & Gockel, G. L. *Racial integration in American neighborhoods.* Chicago: National Opinion Research Center, 1970.

Brehm, J. W., & Cohen, A. R. *Explorations in cognitive dissonance.* New York: Wiley, 1962.

Brink, W., & Harris, L. *Black and white.* New York: Simon & Schuster, 1967.

Brophy, I. N. The luxury of anti-Negro prejudice. *Public Opinion Quarterly,* Winter 1945–46, 9, 456–466.

Campbell, A., & Schuman, H. Racial attitudes in fifteen American cities. In *Supplemental Studies for National Advisory Commission on Civil Disorders.* U.S. Government Printing Office, 1968.

Casstevens, T. W. California's Rumford Act and Proposition 14. In L. W. Eley & T. W. Casstevens [Eds.], *The politics of fair-housing legislation: State and local case studies.* San Francisco: Chandler, 1968.

Center for Urban Education. Survey of the residents of Bedford-Stuyvesant. Unpublished paper of the Center for Urban Education, New York City, 1968.

Crawford, T. J., & Rosenberg, M. J. Results of analyses of Chicago Catholics and racial prejudice data. Unpublished paper, Department of Psychology, University of Chicago, 1970.

de Sola Pool, I., Abelson, R. P., & Popkin, S. L. *Candidates, issues, and strategies: A computer simulation of the 1960 presidential election.* Cambridge, Mass.: MIT Press, 1964.

Deutsch, M., & Collins, M. *Interracial housing: A psychological evaluation of a social experiment.* Minneapolis: University of Minnesota Press, 1951.

Duncan, O. D., & Duncan, B. *The Negro population of Chicago: A study of residential segregation.* Chicago: University of Chicago Press, 1957.

Duncan, B., & Hauser, P. M. *Housing a metropolis—Chicago.* New York: Free Press, 1960.

Eley, L. W. The Ann Arbor Fair-Housing Ordinance. In L. W. Eley & T. W. Casstevens [Eds.], *The politics of fair-housing legislation: State and local case studies.* San Francisco: Chandler, 1968. Pp. 285–351.

Eley, L. W., & Casstevens, T. W. [Eds.], *The politics of fair-housing legislation: State and local case studies.* San Francisco: Chandler, 1968.

Erskine, H. G. The polls: Race relations. *Public Opinion Quarterly,* 1962, 26, 139.

Erskine, H. G. The polls: Negro housing. *Public Opinion Quarterly*, 1967, 31, 482–498.

Freeman, L. C., & Sunshine, M. H. *Patterns of residential segregation.* Cambridge, Mass.: Schenkman, 1970.

Friedrichs, R. W. Christians and residential exclusion. An empirical study of a northern dilemma. *Journal of Social Issues*, October 1959, 15, 14–23.

Gallup International, Inc. *Gallup opinion index.* Report No. 47. Princeton, N.J., May 1969.

Geschwender, J. A. Social structure and the Negro revolt: An examination of some hypotheses. *Social Forces*, 1964, 43, 248–256.

Goldman, P. *Report from black America.* New York: Simon & Schuster, 1970.

Grier, E. & Grier, C. Equality and beyond: Housing segregation in the great society. In T. Parsons & K. Clark [Eds.], *The Negro American.* Boston: Houghton Mifflin, 1966. Pp. 525–554.

Hale, M. Q. The Ohio Fair-Housing Law. In Lynn W. Eley & T. W. Casstevens [Eds.], *The Politics of fair-housing legislation: State and local case studies.* San Francisco: Chandler, 1968. Pp. 149–185.

Harris, L. Harris overlay on *Time* black poll. Unpublished paper of study No. 2014, March 1970.

Helper, R. *Racial policies and practices of real estate brokers.* Minneapolis: University of Minnesota Press, 1969.

Hendrick, C., Bixenstine, V. E., & Hawkind, G. Race versus belief similarity as determinants of attraction: A search for a fair test. *Journal of Personality and Social Psychology*, 1971, 17, 250–258.

Hyman, H. H., & Singer, E. [Eds.] *Readings in reference group theory and research.* New York: Free Press, 1968.

Jahoda, M. & West, P. Race relations in public housing. *Journal of Social Issues*, 1951, 7, 132–139.

Kephart, W. M. *Racial factors and urban law enforcement.* Philadelphia: University of Pennsylvania Press, 1957.

Laurenti, L. *Property values and race: Studies in seven cities.* Berkeley and Los Angeles: University of California Press, 1959.

Lee, A. M., & Humphrey, N. D. *Race riot.* New York: Dryden Press, 1943.

Lieberson, S. *Ethnic patterns in American cities.* New York: Free Press, 1963.

MacKenzie, B. The importance of contact in determining attitudes toward Negroes. *Journal of Abnormal and Social Psychology*, 1948, 43, 417–441.

Marx, G. T. *Protest and prejudice.* (Rev. ed.) New York: Harper & Row, 1969.

Mayhew, L. *Law and equal opportunity: A study of the Massachusetts Commission against Discrimination.* Cambridge, Mass.: Harvard University Press, 1968.

Mercer, N. A. Discrimination in rental housing: A study of resistance of landlords to non-white tenants. *Phylon*, 1962, 23, 47–54.

Meyer, P. *The people beyond 12th street: A survey of attitudes of Detroit Negroes after the riot of 1967.* Detroit: Detroit Urban League and Detroit Free Press, 1967.

Meyer, P. *Return to 12th street: A follow-up survey of attitudes of Detroit Negroes, October 1968.* Detroit: Detroit Free Press, 1968.

Meyer, P. Aftermath of martyrdom: Negro militancy and Martin Luther King. *Public Opinion Quarterly*, Summer 1969, 33(2), 160–173.

Newcomb, T. M., Turner, R. H., & Converse, P. E. *Social psychology: The study of human interaction.* New York: Holt, Rinehart & Winston, 1965.

Pettigrew, T. F. *A profile of the Negro American.* Princeton: Van Nostrand, 1964.

Pettigrew, T. F. Social evaluation theory: Convergences and applications. In D. Levine [Ed.], *Nebraska symposium on motivation, 1967.* University of Nebraska Press, 1968.

Pettigrew, T. F. A study of school integration. Unpublished U.S. Office of Education Final Report of Cooperative Research Project No. 6-1774, August 1970.

Pettigrew, T. F. Initial findings on the Gary mayoralty election, 1971. Unpublished paper, Department of Social Relations, Harvard University, February 19, 1971a.

Pettigrew, T. F. *Racially separate or together?* New York: McGraw-Hill, 1971b.

Pettigrew, T. F., Riley, R. T., & Ross, J. M. *The nature of racial change: Research in American race relations.* Cambridge, Mass.: Harvard University Press, 1972.

Reitzes, D. C. The role of organizational structures: Union versus neighborhood in a tension situation. *Journal of Social Issues,* 1953, 9(1), 37–44.

Rokeach, M., & Mezei, L. Race and shared beliefs as factors in social choice. *Science,* 1966, 151, 167–172.

Rokeach, M., Smith, P., & Evans, R. Two kinds of prejudice or one? In M. Rokeach [Ed.], *The open and closed mind.* New York: Basic Books, 1960.

Rose, E. J. B. *Colour and citizenship.* London: Oxford University Press, 1969.

Russell, M. A study of a South African interracial neighborhood. Unpublished master's thesis, University of Natal, Durban, South Africa, 1961. Cited by P. L. van den Berghe, Some trends in unpublished social science research in South Africa. *International Social Science Journal,* 1962, 14, 723–732.

Runciman, W. G. *Relative deprivation and social justice.* London: Routledge & Kegan Paul, 1966.

Schnore, L. F., & Evenson, P. C. Segregation in southern cities. *American Journal of Sociology,* 1966, 72, 58–67.

Schuman, H. & Gruenberg, B. The impact of city on racial attitudes. *American Journal of Sociology,* 1970, 76, 213–261.

Schwartz, M. A. *Trends in white attitudes toward Negroes.* Chicago: National Opinion Research Center, 1967.

Sheatsley, P. B. White attitudes toward the Negro. In T. Parsons & K. Clark [Eds.], *The Negro American.* Boston: Houghton Mifflin, 1966. Pp. 303–324.

Smith, C. R., Williams, L., & Willis, R. H. Race, sex and belief as determinants of friendship acceptance. *Journal of Personality and Social Psychology,* 1967, 5, 127–137.

Stein, D. D. The influence of belief systems on interpersonal preference. *Psychological Monographs,* 1966, 80 (Whole No. 616).

Stein, D. D., Hardyck, J. A., & Smith, M. B. Race and belief: An open and shut case. *Journal of Personality and Social Psychology,* 1965, 1, 281–290.

Taeuber, K. E., & Taeuber, A. F. *Negroes in cities.* Chicago: Aldine, 1965.

Taeuber, K. E., & Taeuber, A. F. The Negro population in the United States. In J. P. Davis [Ed.], *The American Negro reference book.* Englewood Cliffs, N.J.: Prentice-Hall, 1966. Pp. 133–134, 136.

Triandis, H. C., & Davis, E. E. Race and belief as determinants of behavioral intentions. *Journal of Personality and Social Psychology,* 1965, 2, 715–725.

U.S. Commission on Civil Rights. *Racial isolation in the public schools.* Washington, D.C.: U.S. Government Printing Office, 1967. 2 vols.

U.S. Departments of Labor and Commerce. *The social and economic status of Negroes in the United States, 1969.* Washington, D.C.: U.S. Government Printing Office, 1970.

van den Berghe, P. L. Some trends in unpublished social science research in South Africa. *International Social Science Journal,* 1962, 14, 723–732.

Walker, J. L. Fair housing in Michigan. In L. W. Eley & T. W. Casstevens [Eds.], *The politics of fair-housing legislation: State and local case studies.* San Francisco: Chandler, 1968. Pp. 353–382.

Watts, L. G., Freeman, H. E., Hughes, H. M , Morris, R., & Pettigrew, T. F. *The middle-income Negro family faces urban renewal.* Waltham, Mass.: Heller Graduate School for Advanced Studies in Social Welfare, Brandeis University, 1964.

Williams, R. W., Jr. *Strangers next door.* Englewood Cliffs, N.J.: Prentice-Hall, 1964.

Wilner, D. M., Walkley, R., & Cook, S. W. *Human relations in interracial housing: A study of the contact hypothesis.* Minneapolis: University of Minnesota Press, 1955.

Winer, M. L. *White resistance and Negro insistence: An ecological analysis of urban desegregation.* Unpublished honors thesis, Department of Social Relations, Harvard University, 1964.

Wolf, E. P. The invasion-succession sequence of a self-fulfilling prophecy. *Journal of Social Issues,* 1957, 13, 7–20.

Works, E. The prejudice-interaction hypothesis from the point of view of the Negro minority group. *American Journal of Sociology,* 1961, 67, 47–52.

Institutional and Contextual Factors Affecting the Housing Choices of Minority Residents

DONALD L. FOLEY

ABSTRACT: Institutional barriers to freedom of choice in the housing market may be grouped into three main classes: (a) private institutional practices in the rental, sale, and financing of housing; (b) public institutional practices in urban planning and land use controls for urban renewal and the financing, development, and managing of housing; (c) the array of activities that form the community context for housing choice. Within this last class are the distribution of employment, welfare policies, the school system, transportation, and such intangibles as community leadership.

This paper focuses on opening up housing choice for minorities and the prospects of this choice being extended by "dispersal" beyond the main inner-city communities. Institutional practices that serve to limit or block housing opportunities are impersonel and bureaucratic in character. Any single representative of some part of the organization can blame others and does not have to accept direct responsibility for blocking opportunities. In other words, there exists a web of institutional discrimination in which virtually no one is obliged to accept direct responsibility for hindering access to housing.

Comprehensive, up-to-date research on institutions that provide or block

Donald L. Foley is Professor of City and Regional Planning, University of California at Berkeley.

access to housing is difficult to locate. Typically, scholarly research is neither
sustained over time nor fully representative of the changing situations in urban
America. Reports of governmental commissions and advocate organizations are
more current and comprehensive, but of varying reliability. Change is rapid,
but the question remains: What has changed and what remains the same,
nationally as well as in particular areas?

It has long been common knowledge that blacks and other disadvantaged minorities are denied free choice of housing. Typically,
they have been segregated in black or ethnic communities, usually
in the inner city. Although segregation has been exercised *de facto,*
schools and other local services have functioned as though *de jure*
segregation exists. The result has been a low level of service to minorities and a high level of indifference by unaffected majority-
whites. Rapid metropolitan growth and the migration of large
numbers of blacks, Puerto Ricans, Mexican-Americans, and
American Indians to inner districts have brought about a significant change in the dimensions or residential segregation—from small
ethnic enclaves to vast ghettos that constitute a substantial part of
the inner city in many metropolitan areas. In contrast, most of the
outer districts in these metropolitan areas have remained overwhelmingly white. The result is an inner city–suburban difference that
threatens to perpetuate itself and to create two societies within
each metropolis.

   We focus on the opening up of housing choice as the antidote to
housing discrimination and on the prospects that this housing choice
can be extended beyond the main black or minority inner-city communities. We might term this extension "dispersal," since it suggests
opportunities to find housing in sections other than the ghetto or its
immediately surrounding gray areas. This might also be termed
"macrointegration," as contrasted to microintegration within a
social block or a small neighborhood. We believe it is more important to focus on macro- than microintegration.

   First, research evidence suggests that although most minority residents support the principle of integration, they seem to interpret it
as "the right to live in integrated situations" rather than as an end in
itself. Indeed, minority households (like majority households) look
for features that constitute good housing and a good neighborhood
with an associated high level of services. The desire for high-quality
schools, for example, is consistently emphasized (Watts *et al.,*

1964; Schermer & Levin, 1968; Billingsley, 1968; Mack, 1968).
Second, housing market decisions are so decentralized that microintegration is beyond the control of individual governmental or private managements. Integration is a particular situation in which an
open market is at work and in which minority households have
moved into a district and majority-white households have refrained
from moving out. (Theoretically, this could be reversed—i.e., there
could be an ethnic or racial majority in the district and an influx of
majority-whites). In general, it would appear that majority-white
residents control the integration process. They can prevent or discourage minorities from entering, or they can flee if they feel that
the district is being overrun. Only in specific instances, such as
within apartment buildings or other rental projects or in large tract-
housing developments, however, can a single owner "manage" integration by means of benign quotas or some other method.

   Third, some minority households, perhaps at certain points in
their life and mobility-cycles, may choose housing that in "micro"
terms is not integrated, such as a racial or ethnic enclave in a suburban area. There is evidence that many minority households are
not prepared to move from an inner-city segregated neighborhood
to a suburban integrated neighborhood in one jump. The household
is more likely to move in stages; in this manner, no single move simultaneously combines all of the various possible changes. Thus, a household may move from the inner city to an intermediate situation—
possibly into the older, more urban suburbs or into a black or ethnic
enclave. This may then provide a staging point for a subsequent move
into an integrated or a preponderantly majority-white residential
district. Similarly, a minority household may move from inner-city
to suburban rental housing (if it can be obtained) and only later to
a suburban-owned home (Bullough, 1969; Watts *et al.*, 1964;
Grodzins, 1958).

   This by no means denies the significance of successful microintegration of specific housing projects or subdivisions. Above all, it can
provide a successful experience in integrated living; and success may
beget further success as direct contact among different ethnic groups
breaks down stereotypes and prejudices. Unless integration at a micro-
level of social environment is successful, continuing efforts to change
attitudes are unlikely to succeed. However, this paper focuses on
those larger-scale aspects of housing choice and residential integration that are affected by institutional practices.

Household Characteristics Bearing on Open-Housing Choice by Minorities

We restrict our discussion to three considerations: income, employment, and welfare; the interrelations of income, class, and race; and household composition and stage in the family cycle. These are all related to our subsequent main focus on institutional practices as they affect housing choice.

INCOME, EMPLOYMENT, AND WELFARE

It has been demonstrated that minority families are less well-off than majority families. For example, much larger percentages of black families than of majority-white families have low incomes or are below the poverty level. Furthermore, minority income may be irregular, and the meager assets of many minority families do not provide reserve funds. A national survey in 1962 (Lansing *et al.,* 1969, p. 49) showed that the average net worth of Negro families was less than one fifth of that of white families; this was true at all age levels. A large and growing number of households are headed by females, and a large number are composed of older persons. Such households are likely to have income problems (Downs, 1970; U.S. Bureau of the Census, 1970b; Bernstein, 1970).

The employment situation is directly related to minority choice of housing. As a result of deficient education, lack of professional or technical skills, and a tradition of occupational discrimination, minority workers typically receive lower earnings, both in absolute terms and in relation to their educational and experience levels, than do majority-white workers. Although low wages, by and large, are a greater contributor to poverty than is unemployment, unemployment remains distressingly high for minorities in ghetto areas (Gwartney, 1970; Riessman, 1969; U.S. Bureau of the Census, 1970a; Grebler *et al.,* 1970).

The system of welfare assistance is also related to housing choice. Forceful arguments have been made to establish a base minimum income level (Tobin, 1968; Downs, 1970; Haggstrom, 1968; Miller & Roby, 1970). In the words of a recent Presidental Task Force (U.S. President's Task Force on Urban Renewal, 1970, p. 8):

Increased incomes would give lower income families the means for better satisfying their individual needs, in particular for acquiring better housing on the private market. The Task Force therefore urges the enactment of income maintenance and job training programs to increase the incomes of lower income families.

To which a dissent by Messrs. Muth and Tolley from the same report (p. 11) adds:

... We would emphasize more strongly than does the Report [of the Task Force] the need for measures directly attacking poverty. . . . Income maintenance strikes directly at the heart of the poverty problem rather than nibbling at its edges as many other programs have attempted to do.

Another recent report (Birch, 1970, p. 38) suggests, "it should be clear that any program that raises the incomes of the poor will accelerate the out-migration of the present city population and thereby facilitate the growth of the new [i.e., the suburbs]."

THE RELATION OF INCOME, SOCIAL CLASS, AND RACIAL OR ETHNIC STATUS

The great American dream is that, over time, households will raise both their income level and their social-class position. Expectation of upward mobility also extends to educational attainment, to occupational niche, and to life style. But social climbing meets both overt and covert resistance by those who have already arrived. Distinctions based on racial or, less sharply perhaps, on ethnic or nationality lines may provide bases for blocking upward mobility. Insofar as the racial distinctions approach castelike differentiation, the ensuing systematic discrimination, however impersonal or institutional, severely impedes upward social mobility by a minority member. Different households may be limited by different factors. A household may simultaneously lack money and social-class position, as well as be of minority-group status. In such a case, it faces several serious barriers to mobility. Or it may have the money without the social position. Or it may have the money and the social-class position, but still be limited by its minority-group status.

As minority households continue to share in rising incomes, improved education, and better occupations, they also may be expected to increase their social-class position. Such households will overcome the income and social-class barriers and will be in a significantly improved position to consider housing in suburban or other residential districts previously closed. For such households, however, racial or ethnic prejudice persists as a final hurdle. It seems reasonable to believe that minority households confronted with only one major barrier—race or ethnic status—are in a relatively better position than those minority households faced by resistance on the grounds of race, social class, and lack of money (Simpson & Yinger, 1965; Drake, 1965; Billingsley, 1968).

Movement to a new residential district can take on great social significance, to both the household moving and those households already residing there (Rossi, 1955, p. 184).

Residential mobility is often the spatial expression of vertical social mobility. As families rise in social class positions, they often change their residence to accord with their class destination. Inferential data on this aspect of mobility were shown in this study; more direct research is necessary to show the extent of this type of movement and its significance for the American social structure.

It follows that middle- or upper-middle-class residents, once established in a district, will be concerned about any "potential deterioration of class image" (Werthman et al., 1965, p. 114).

HOUSEHOLD COMPOSITION AND STAGE IN THE FAMILY CYCLE

Minority households, like majority-white households, differ in composition. There are, for example, single-person households, especially young persons and elderly persons; young married couples without children; households with children, including (particularly among lower-income households) a considerable number with very large families. We have already alluded to the importance of female-head families with children among black households. These households vary in their interest in considering housing in districts other than those already heavily settled by fellow minority members. Some of these households (e.g., elderly persons and young people, or couples without children) may find that residential location in the central city offers the greatest advantages on balance, even though they might find other advantages to moving out of ghetto areas. Other households, particularly those with young children, may seek the advantages of good schools and other improved services and the physical amenities of housing at much lower density than those in the inner city. Each household has its own preferences and judgments as to desirable residential location.

General sociological and housing literature suggests that a combination of several factors would be necessary before a household would consider a move to the suburbs: The household would need to have the money; it would need to be at a stage of its family cycle

that made it inviting to find different housing; it would need to hold
attitudes favoring integration or, at a minimum, not to remain firmly
attached to its present neighborhood; and, presumably, it would need
to have become sufficiently middle class to be drawn to the features
offered by a suburban-like district. We lack an adequate research
literature about such families. As Watts *et al.* (1964, p. 110) have
put it:

... there is but limited information about the middle-class Negro family in
Boston, or for that matter, in the whole United States. Since the classic work
of Frazier on material now two decades old, there has been little systematic
examination of the stake and status of the middle-income or middle-class
Negro family. Many of those we studied are of a different type and generation of Negroes. They grew up during and after World War II, and their experiences in the armed forces, their education, inspired and prolonged by
veterans' legislation, the changed climate of opinion, and the new definitions
of appropriate community responsibility toward minorities makes of them a
group in transition....

More recently, Billingsley (1968) has suggested a current typology
of black families that helps to fill this knowledge void.

Minority Attitudes toward Housing

From Rossi's study of why families move, we can draw inferences
about how any family—majority or minority—approaches moving.
Families may have reactions to their present housing and their present neighborhood that "push" them to seek other housing; they
develop certain specifications that narrow their search and apply
criteria as bases for their choice of new housing—the "pull" factors.
Rossi (1955), however, deliberately avoided the complexities confronting minority households, and no Negro families were interviewed.

Presumably, there is a great range of outlook and consideration
among minority households. One extreme is a middle-class outlook
comparable to that of other middle-class Americans (Mack, 1968).
In Billingsley's words (1968, p. 181–182):

Ask almost any Negro family head what he (or she) wishes most for his family,
and the response would be "a decent house in a decent neighborhood." Ask
that same parent what he wishes most for his children and the response would
be "a decent and effective education."...

A 1968 national poll of blacks resulted in this identification of needs (Beardwood, 1968, p. 41):

More education for my children	97%
More desegration in schools, neighborhoods, jobs	93
A better job	87
Some kind of special training	77
Better police protection	69
More education for myself	62
Making neighborhood a better place to live	60
More money to spend	53
Moving out of the neighborhood	20

Blacks and other minorities may not wish to leave their present district. This has been explained in terms of the social ties and the familiar patterns and contacts for coping with life that are available in their neighborhood (Hartman, 1963; Fried & Levin, 1968). A perceptive study made in the Boston area resulted in the observation (Watts *et al.,* 1964, p. 11):

... we wish again to emphasize that the middle-income Negro family sees itself as having a personal stake in Washington Park [from which urban renewal was about to displace a number of families]. It must be borne in mind that *non-discrimination is not the same thing as integration.* ... The family willing to support the Negro rights organizations in striving for wider choice in housing may perhaps be personally committed to life in Washington Park, at the same time regarding it as a social responsibility to fight for the opportunity not to live there. One must recognize that the individual Negro family will decide for itself the right and the wrong and the appropriateness or unsuitability of moving out, the same decision as other ethnic groups in the city must make.

Outlying residential areas, particularly those in the suburbs, may seem uncongenial and remote. Some minority families, like some majority families, may just not care much for suburban living. Some may like some of its physical features, but be wary about moving into an overwhelmingly white area (Schermer & Levin, 1968, p. 20):

A few market surveys conducted among middle- and moderate-income Negro households indicate a strong preference for detached houses, individual lots, and other features that are more characteristic of suburbia than central city. However, there appears to be considerable resistance to outlying suburbs. Many Negroes would like suburban-style living, but they do not trust the suburbs. They feel unwelcome and unwanted. They are likely to continue feeling that way until there are affirmative programs to help them feel otherwise.

Some researchers have reported that only a small proportion of minority households are willing to make a persistent search for housing in neighborhoods completely separated from concentrated minority areas. Determination and self-confidence are needed to carry a household into unfriendly territory and likely rebuffs. In the case of Washington Park in the Boston area, "less than five percent of the families in a ten-month period actually inspected a dwelling outside of Roxbury and the families used public and voluntary bodies very little to assist them in hunting outside. . ." (Watts *et al.,* 1964, p. 10). In a recent Los Angeles study, most Negroes still living in concentrated Negro areas had made no attempt to look for housing outside these areas. Some "characteristically told of a single experience in which they looked and were rebuffed or decided they really preferred the central city" (Bullough, 1969, p. 61). Of those who finally succeeded in moving into white areas in the San Fernando Valley, many reported negative experiences along the way (Bullough, 1969, p. 61):

... most of the discrimination encountered was not overt. Only occasionally were people met with open refusals. More often they were faced with a long series of evasions and deceit, including realty salesmen who were "out" or ran to hide from them in the other room, managers who had no authority to rent apartments, owners who could not be located, forms that could not be processed, returned deposits, and so on. The persistence shown by some of the families in the sample in the face of one disappointment after another is worthy of note.

Some generalizations about what types of family are most likely to move into white neighborhoods have been made. The Negro "pioneers" tend to be relatively young, of above average economic and occupational status, well educated, and of lighter skin color. Most have had previous experiences with integration (Northwood & Barth, 1965; Bullough, 1966; Weinstein & Giesel, 1962). They are less alienated and more committed to the idea of integration than those remaining in minority areas. And, as Bullough in particular (1969, p. 103) has emphasized, there is an inevitable circularity between experience and attitudes.

Past segregation is related to present alienation, and present alienation is related to segregated housing patterns. . . . [Those Negroes who succeeded in moving to a suburban location] were able to escape the ghetto because they were not as alienated. They tended to reflect less of the powerlessness and feelings of separation and despair. . . . The integrated subjects in this study had not necessarily grown up with more socioeconomic advantages than ghetto subjects, but they did report more past experience with integration.

Residential desegregation was anything but a sudden or isolated incident in the lives of the people studied. It was a part of a total overall pattern which had developed over a long period of time. . . .

To consider moving from the concentrated minority area is to risk not only discriminatory responses from majority persons, but complications in relations with fellow minority persons and ambivalence of psychological identification. Clark's observations (1965, p. 194–195) provide an articulate summary:

The Negro who dares to move outside of the ghetto, either physically or psychologically, runs the risk of retaliatory hostility, at worst, or of misunderstanding, at best. To do so requires strength and individualism. It may reflect, in addition a desire to escape a negative racial identification and an urgent, anguished, realistic desire to affirm himself as an individual without regard to the white or the Negro world, without regard to the tendency of whites to shackle or imprison his spirit, or the tendency of Negroes, in a different but just as effective way, to do the same. Yet escape, whatever the motive, can never be complete as long as racial oppression exists. The Negro, no matter how successful his flight may appear, still remains in conflict, a conflict stemming from his awareness of the ambivalence of other Negroes toward him and from his awarenesss that the larger white society never accepts him fully. He is in conflict within himself, with whites, and with Negroes, confronted by a sense of guilt, alienation, resentment, and random bitterness directed as much against Negroes as against whites.

Integration—A Two-Way Street

It is often presumed that integration occurs when minority families move into the residential territory of the majority. Efforts to facilitate integration have concentrated on making it possible for minority or moderate-income families to move to the suburbs. But integration may also be brought about by the move of majority families into minority areas or be preserved by their determination to remain in mixed areas in spite of a rising proportion of minority residents. Thus, Watts and colleagues (1964, p. 11) wrote:

. . . an implication of our study is that the cause of integration in housing may best be served by private and public organizations, actively encouraging the moving of white families into Washington Park, in addition to striving to bring Negroes freer access to housing.

Selectively, some majority-white households seek inner-city residence locations for a variety of reasons. Urban renewal has often sought to reintroduce higher-income housing into districts that had been deteriorating. But the overwhelming trend is for majority households, particularly at certain points in their family cycles, to consider outward moves, sometimes in stages, toward suburbia.

Sudman and colleagues (1969) reported a higher proportion of American households living in integrated situations than is commonly believed. This suggests that there are other, more haphazard, methods of achieving integration than the more dramatic focus on "pioneering" minority families implies. Other researchers have claimed that the Sudman study uses measures that overstate the amount of stable residential integration by including neighborhoods that are in the path of imminent black residential invasion and succession (Pascal, 1970).

We need research relative to the significance of assured high level of services and amenity in maintaining stable integrated residential districts. Friedman (1968) has, for example, suggested: "Mixed income neighborhoods would be stable if they were highly desirable neighborhoods."

Institutional Barriers to Free Choice in the Housing Market

Although barriers to integration have been lowered in "realms of relatively formal contact," they have remained high in "realms of intimate contact—desegration of social gatherings, housing, swimming pools, house parties and college dormitories" (Pettigrew, 1969, p. 54). Housing remains a sensitive sphere, reflecting various mutually reinforcing socioeconomic considerations.

In the United States, there is widespread acceptance of the idea that one's residence is an indicator of social status as well as physical housing (Warner et al., 1949). Consistent with a concern about status and prestige, residents may resist encroachment by lower-status households. This is based mainly on social class considerations; it may also include broader presumptions by majority-whites that minority members are, *ipso facto,* of lower social status. Or the argument may run that the acceptance of middle-class minority households will inevitably lead to further "invasion" by minority members of lesser social status.

Resistance to minority households may also be couched in economic terms. Home owners, in particular, may view their house as an
investment from which they fully expect to make a capital gain. They
may therefore be frightened by any suggestion, valid or not, that the
economic value of this investment is threatened by an influx of households with lesser income or minority status (Werthman *et al,* 1965;
McEntire, 1960; Simpson & Yinger, 1965).

Individual prejudice toward minority members, while significant,
may be mainly covert. Majority-whites may simply avoid personal
contact with minority persons, unless the contacts are an integral
part of everyday work or service. This is conveniently reinforced by
a spatial pattern of residential segregation. Even the verbal liberal,
for all his professed open-mindedness, may live and operate in essentially majority-white social circles as a result of *de facto* segregation
(Daniels & Kitano, 1970).

Majority-whites also rely on certain gatekeeper mechanisms to
"guard their turf." These mechanisms include the various institu-
tionalized arrangements for maintaining law and order (the police),
dealing with matters of poverty and family problems (the social
welfare system), channeling students into expected occupational
niches (the school system), etc. Gatekeeper mechanisms have also
been used to maintain the housing market—or, more accurately, to
maintain appropriate submarkets for minority families or low-income
families. Most such families are kept from full and open access to the
main market, which is presumably reserved for majority families with
the economic, social, and ethnic status to take full advantage of it
(Daniels & Kitano, 1970).

The institutional web that blocks the minority family from the
main housing market comprises a great many interlocking components, among which are the outlook and social behavior of residents
(and, often, homeowners); the services of realtors, mortgage lenders,
appraisers, and developers; the laws, government regulations, and
administrative and political behavior of government officials; and
the relevant patterns and practices related to employment, schools,
transportation, and community services. As a young Negro scholar
expressed it (Hastie, 1970) in an unpublished appraisal:

... The foundations of exclusion [of the large majority of blacks from the open
housing market] are found in institutional practices like restrictive zoning, realtor practices, governmental inadequacies, and other subtle, conscious and un-
conscious actions. Standing alone any one of these procedures might be short-

lived, but co-existing they become mutually supportive creating what Harold Baron has called the "web of urban racism."

We now discuss private institutional practices and governmental practices, respectively, in the next two main sections. This is a division merely for convenience in our presentation, for the interlocking of private institutional, governmental, and personal behaviors is an essential characteristic of the phenomenon we are seeking to identify.

Private Institutional Practices in the Rental, Sale, and Financing of Housing for Minority Families

A recent significant report on real estate practices in the San Francisco Bay Area concludes that a hierarchy of discrimination in the housing market exists. It is most difficult for minorities to rent housing, less difficult to buy older houses, and least difficult to buy new housing in tracts (Denton, 1970).

RENTAL HOUSING

Various studies support the conclusion by Denton that Negroes and other minorities have the greatest difficulty in obtaining rental housing outside established minority areas (Watts et al., 1964; NCDH, 1970; Meyer et al., 1965). A 1965 mail questionnaire, to which 164 members of the Greater Pittsburgh Board of Realtors responded, found that 72 percent of these realtors had never shown housing to, and 79 percent had never completed rental arrangements with, black prospects in predominantly white areas (Biochel et al., 1969).

In part, this reflects the selectivity of landlords, apartment managers, and real estate agents, whether or not in nonminority residential areas. For example, a 1960 survey in Schenectady, New York, reported the following objections stated by 200 landlords of vacant apartments: 65 percent objected to renting to Negroes (compared with 75 percent, 1951 survey of same city), of which 36 percent would "under no circumstances" rent to Negroes and 29 percent would prefer not to rent to Negroes; 55 percent objected to renting to families with children; 53 percent objected to renting to families with pets; and 6 percent objected to renting to non-Christians (Mercer, 1962, p. 49). Landlords, either apartment owners or managers, may be gatekeepers to their apartment building and the immediate neighborhood for various reasons: They may live there themselves and wish to screen their own prospective neighbors; they may seek to protect what they take to be the interests of present or prospective majority-white tenants; they may be unfavorably influenced by stereotypes about housing maintenance by minority tenants; and they may believe that minority households, once admitted, will stimulate pressures for further minority tenancy.

A great increase in construction of new apartments has taken place in the suburbs since the late 1950's. This has meant that new rental housing has become readily available in the suburbs; such housing has often been attractively designed and located, sometimes in well-landscaped settings. Better housing and more services for the rental dollar were offered than were available in the central city. Generally, however, such apartments, located in predominantly or all majority-white residential areas, are even more likely to discriminate against prospective minority tenants than older apartment buildings in or closer to the inner city (Neutze, 1968).

Unfortunately most research on housing discrimination does not make a clear distinction between rental and owner housing. The most illuminating recent research we could uncover that deals separately with the practices of apartment owners and managers is that by John Denton, cited above. We do not know if his findings apply to other geographic regions. We need further work that sharply differentiates between various parts of the housing market. Denton, in his conclusion—quoted at length because of its significance (1970, p. Jb23–Jb24)—implies that one important service of the real estate broker is his ability to cope with minority prospects.

Our conclusion from our research is that the vast majority [of apartment owners] discriminate, and almost all believe that their white tenants will leave if they rent any of their apartments to minority families. Their usual tactics for avoiding integration are delay and red tape, i.e., the minority prospect gets delay and red tape and the white prospect gets the apartment. Where housing is as tight as it is in the Bay Area, discrimination becomes very difficult to prove and easy to practice. If a minority prospect can be held off for as little as four hours, it is usually time to get a bona fide white tenant signed up in time. . . .

Time is bought in all kinds of ways by setting requirements almost no one can meet: by forms; by demanding references; by myriad uncertainties, even by failing to call back when an initial phone inquiry suggests that the prospect may be of a minority ethnic group. . . . Actually, most minority prospects are easily turned away. They are too proud to force the issue, and also very worried about the amount of time it takes to follow through a complaint.

Some of the data suggests that because of their determination to discriminate, more mamma–poppa operations are using agents than was formerly the case. The obvious reason is that [real estate] brokers have developed skills to fend off minority prospects and can do this more clearly than an owner. Moreover, where all else fails, it can turn out that "the owner had already rented the apartment and forgotten to tell the broker.". . .

As will be further discussed below, the broker has become more sophisticated in the performance of this "service" in the face of fair-housing laws and other anti-discrimination legislation (NCDH, 1970; Denton, 1970).

It is essential for minority households that the rental market be opened up. Because of severe housing shortages, fierce competition for rental housing, and the restrictions imposed by discriminatory practice, minority households are victims of an unusually tight market or submarket. It has long been understood that minority households get less housing for the money than do majority households, and this discrepancy may be widening (Abrams, 1965; Kerner Commission, 1968; Douglas Commission, 1969; Kaiser Committee, 1968; U.S. Commission on Civil Rights, 1967; New York City Rand Institute, 1970; Grebler *et al.,* 1970, Ch. 11). No matter how advantageous and desirable home ownership may be in the long run, rental housing remains the immediate prospect for most minority families. Available rental housing in the suburbs could facilitate the staging of moves, so that the family could face up to the spatial move before taking the next step of a tenure change. Moreover, a rental base in an outer locality would provide an advantageous base for the search for a house to buy.

SALE OF OLDER HOUSING

Most slum clearance and relocation transactions are handled through real estate brokers. The broker paired with an owner may provide a formidable gatekeeping arrangement. The seller may feel a sense of responsibility on behalf of his majority-white neighbors and may determine, almost as a matter of course, to instruct the realtor not to consider "undesirable" prospects. The real estate broker, in addition to a loyalty to the seller, may have an eye to future business and may interpret such a dictum as his "professional" responsibility to maintain the stability of the neighborhood. While the National Association of Real Estate Boards (NAREB) has openly stated that all realtors are expected to conform to the fair-housing laws, there is

evidence that the brokers have continued their screening responsibilities, but with greater care in order not to be caught openly in viola-
tion of the new legislation.

In the San Francisco Bay Area study, Denton (1970, p. Jb5)
concluded:

. . . by and large, the vast majority of realtors still believe in residential segregation and believe that to maintain their control of the market for used homes
they must find ways to prevent minority prospects from finding housing in all-
white neighborhoods.

Of the sample of Pittsburgh realtors studied in 1965, 53 percent
had never shown housing for sale and 79 percent had never completed housing sales to black prospects in predominantly white areas
(Biochel *et al.*, 1969). In the Washington, D.C., area, realtors had
at one time been instructed not to sell (or rent) to "colored people."
Later this instruction was modified, but the realtors still tend to
urge sellers to specify terms of the sale as to whom they would not
want to sell or would not sell (Simpson & Yinger, 1965, p. 332).

In understanding discriminatory practices in the sale of houses,
it is essential to distinguish between specific mechanisms and the
underlying spirit and outlook that pervade the setting in which
transactions are carried through. Regarding these transactions,
Denton (1970, p. Jb6–Jb7) reports:

Our conclusion about how discrimination takes place is that every routine
act, every bit of ritual in the sale or rental of a dwelling unit can be performed
in a way calculated to make it either difficult or impossible to consummate a
deal. Everyone in real estate recognizes how easily deals are killed by poor
salesmanship, ignorance and ineptitude on the part of the intermediaries,
failure to show property to good advantage, and other non-purposive errors.
Yet no one has made an analysis of how these devices are intentionally used
to destroy the interest of minority people in looking for housing in all-white
neighborhoods. Perhaps this is because most of these devices can not be
reached by law. . . .
Since brokers almost invariably act as agents for landlords and homesellers,
the general rule of law is that they are under no obligation to renters or buyers
to offer them service. Theoretically, California solved this problem with the
Unruh Act, passed in 1959, which requires all business . . . to provide every
prospective customer with the same services. However, in recent years, there
has been so little attempt to enforce this act, that we discovered that many
salesmen and brokers make frank verbal avowals of their unwillingness to serve
minority prospects. It should be noted that we found no evidence of outright
refusals, but we think this is a specious difference. . . .

Denton goes on to show that since negotiated bargaining is so crucial to the typical real estate transaction, it is difficult for a minority client (or for someone seeking to police fair-housing laws) to know whether the broker has at critical points failed to represent the client's interest with integrity. It is safe to speculate that minority buyers are more likely to settle for the full asking price rather than jeopardize the purchase by bargaining.

Majority-white persons are able to spend a long period searching for housing and can expect the cooperation of a real estate broker; they are not screened until financial negotiations begin. Minority prospects, however, may be screened at the very start before a broker even expresses willingness to be of direct assistance. Various discouraging or delaying tactics may be employed by the broker; if delaying tactics fail, the broker may delay the submission of a client's order or find technical difficulties (Denton, 1970; NCDH, 1970; McEntire, 1960; Helper, 1969).

Real estate brokers are also in a position to foster "panic" selling, although this may be more characteristic of the central city than the suburbs (Leacock *et al.*, 1965, p. 32).

When it becomes apparent that a particular neighborhood is undergoing change, [real estate agents] are in a position either to speed up or slow down the process. It has been the pattern throughout the country for real estate interests to play an extremely destructive role in relation to interracial communities. They spread mis-information about declining values in changing neighborhoods, using it to manipulate desegregation and "re-segregation" by causing a rapid turnover once Negro families have started to move in. In some cases they simply do not show houses in one section to prospective Negro buyers, nor houses in another section to whites; at times they use genuine scare tactics to speed up turnover to their own advantage.

THE SALE OF NEW HOUSING

In earlier periods, the sale of new housing, particularly tract housing built by large developers, was also subject to prevalent discriminatory practices. The cases of exclusion of minorities from the Levitt's large suburban developments are generally known; once forced, the New Jersey Levittown was smoothly integrated (Gans, 1967; [U.S.] HHFA, 1964). Large firms of homebuilders, in particular have been changing their practices. The Denton survey in the Bay Area (1970, p. Jb20)

... tends to show that minority prospects get much better treatment from tract builders with their own sales forces than from realtors. To some extent this is due to the differences in marketing factors, i.e.,

1) the prospect transports himself to the site and needs very little service from the sales agent on the premises.
2) the price and terms are usually fixed and widely advertised, so that there is very little room for bargaining.

In addition, there seems to be no organized resistance from the homebuilding industry, as there obviously is within the fields dominated by N A R E B. In our judgment, the different attitudes of white realtors and white homebuilders is at least partially a reflection of the fact that the National Association of Home-builders has a more favorable attitude toward residential integration than does N A R E B. . . . [We] made trips to new subdivisions and were pleasantly surprised to find that most of those in modest price brackets had at least a few minority homeowners. . . .

New homes for sale are increasingly provided in large scale tracts and, as we have just indicated, there is evidence that practices have shifted considerably during the past few years. But most of the general research literature is based on earlier studies and may provide outdated conclusions. Ten years ago the McEntire study (1960, p. 176–177) could report:

The combination of large-scale building methods with racial discrimination has given rise to the phenomenon of the totally white community. . . . [The] developer has the power and generally uses it, to exclude unwanted minority groups completely.

But just as the large developers had the monolithic power to exclude, so, too, have they the power to institute changes in policy. We judge this to be a needed area of research; it is important to monitor the practices and experiences of the tract builders. Indeed, it would be valuable to know about their initial sales to minority households and to follow through the impact of the pattern thus created on attitudes and practices with respect to resales in subsequent years. McEntire reported (1960, p. 177), ". . . as several experiences have demonstrated, a pattern of total minority exclusion, once established, is extremely difficult to change." We could hypothesize, alternatively, that a pattern of racial mixture, once established, would make it more likely that integration within the development would continue.

We need to research the role and effectiveness of black builders and contractors. This should include information on types and location of housing built, marketing and financing arrangements, and the characteristics for the buyers. Does this lead to black enclaves? Does it promote dispersal to suburban areas?

One additional research approach deserves particular note. In this approach, a sample survey of the sale of new homes is coupled with an analysis of the chain of moves into the housing successively left vacant. This approach was suggested in earlier work by Kristof (1965) and used in a significant national study by Lansing and his associates (1969). The Lansing study concluded that only six tenths of the number of Negroes that one would predict on the basis of income actually occupied new dwellings. In the national sample, of all the Negro families moving into new homes, only one third moved into owned homes, whereas of all white families moving into new homes, over one half moved into owned homes. This lower fraction for Negro families appears to reflect both a relative dearth of assets among Negro families and the impact of discrimination. Applying the filter theory of housing, the Lansing study concluded that the building of new housing is of less indirect help to Negro families than to white families in opening up other vacancies along chain-of-moves paths and that it is of even less assistance to poor families (of either race).

Real estate boards cut across real estate brokers' involvement in the rental of housing and in the sale of both old and new homes. They have typically resisted taking in minority persons as brokers. In the San Francisco Bay Area, real estate board membership has gradually opened to minorities in the core cities (only after law suits, however, still pending as recently as 1966), but memberships have not been generally available "to nonresident minority brokers in all-white suburban real estate boards" (Denton, 1970).

Sale of housing to minorities is also affected by the multiple-listing practices of real estate boards. In the San Francisco Bay Area, at least, a broker is on the distribution list for listings produced by his own real estate board, but he only has access to the listings produced by other boards if he can establish his own reciprocity with brokers in these other boards or if he can take out a nonresident membership in these areas. A minority broker who is a member of a core-city real estate board thus may find it difficult or impossible to have access to listings of suburban real estate boards. He therefore has great difficulty in providing the full range of listings in suburban areas to a minority client, and the client is at the mercy of majority-white brokers in these suburbs. In Denton's words (1970, p. Ja31),

The conclusion we have drawn from our survey of listing practices is that they effectively bar minority people looking for housing from having access to indispensible information about what is offered. Moreover, so long as multiple listing is voluntary in most Bay Area cities there is no way it can be made into area wide "exchange" of homes for sale. . . .

RESTRICTIVE COVENANT OR DEED RESTRICTION

Probably no institutional device has been more insidiously woven into the web of practices bearing on the rental and sale of real estate than the restrictive covenant or deed restriction. Weaver (1948), for example, was able to show that in the period just before and after World War II these covenants carried much, and probably the brunt of, discriminatory restrictions. A very large number of urban and suburban residential properties were at that time covered by covenants. Real estate boards and property owners' associations had vigorously campaigned to get signatures or resignatures on the covenants. That very year, the Supreme Court in *Shelley v. Kraemer* withdrew any role for courts in enforcing restrictive covenants, although it did not outlaw the covenants as such. We lack full up-to-date evidence about how these millions upon millions of covenants, still part of deeds, are interpreted by prospective sellers and buyers and by the real estate brokers and others involved in the complex process of transferring property. Some participants may act as though the covenants had no force. Some participants who believe in fair-housing and integration may avoid the purchase of such properties or take pains when selling to see that an open market is maintained. But it is quite possible that a large number of persons use the covenants to maintain discrimination. Drawing upon a report issued in 1962 by the U.S. Commission on Civil Rights, Simpson and Yinger (1965, p. 331) argued that covenants were still being effectively used:

In the Washington D.C. area, builders in at least 13 communities utilize [restrictive covenants]. Their effectiveness is seen in the racial composition of the census tracts covering these communities. It is not clear why they continue to be effective despite the fact that they are no longer enforceable in the courts, but one possibility is that some homeowners are not aware of the 1948 Supreme Court decision. Also, it has been suggested that those who have entered into these agreements feel under moral pressure to keep them. The

U.S. Commission on Civil Rights thinks that the best explanation for the effectiveness of these covenants in the District of Columbia and environs is that simple exclusion is used to enforce the policy they declare.

Perhaps beyond the purview of social scientific research—for it involves judicial and political considerations—is the question of whether it is reasonable that restrictive covenants be permitted to persist. Although *Shelley v. Kraemer* implied that such covenants based on race, creed, or color were legal, critical differences in views remain. One observer has said, "Most commentators today are of the opinion that such a covenant is illegal and should be so regarded, rather than accepting the incongruous fiction that it is legal but unenforceable" (Robinson, 1964, p. 36). We believe research should be done on covenants—their prevalence, their use in new housing, and their meaning to the various persons concerned with the sale and rental of housing and the sale and development of residential land.

MORTGAGE FINANCING

In 1960, McEntire reported (p. 218–219):

Mortgage credit is the key to acquisition of good housing via home ownership. . . . Whites and nonwhites of comparable economic status and owning similar properties seem to receive, on the whole, similar treatment from most lending agencies, with the crucial exception: institutional lenders traditionally have required properties for nonwhite occupancy to be located in recognized minority residence areas, and many lenders continue to enforce this special requirement. By making mortgage credit available to minorities in certain areas and withholding it in others, lending agencies help to maintain segregation.

Simpson and Yinger (1965, p. 332), drawing upon evidence submitted to the U.S. Commission on Civil Rights (1962 report) suggested that this practice was continuing:

A spokesman for the Mortgage Bankers Association of Metropolitan Washington wrote [to the Commission] : "Applications from minority groups are not generally considered in areas that are not recognized as being racially mixed, on the premise that such an investment would not be attractive to institutional lenders."

Denton, in his recent San Francisco Bay area study, said (1970, p. Jb32):

Based on our discussions with black brokers and fair housing brokers we believe it is fair to say that minority people trying to move out of the ghetto have *even* more trouble than formerly in obtaining mortgage loans. Earmarking "minority mortgage money" for loans on so-called ghetto property means that minority applicants are more likely than ever to find it hard to get loans for purchase in suburban areas.

He stresses that, just as there are no minority suburban real estate firms, there are no Bay area minority-group mortgage bankers. He doubts that there are any in the entire United States, but he is careful to state he lacks conclusive evidence.

We are advised that Fred Case (Graduate School of Business, University of California, Los Angeles) has been engaged in a large study of mortgage lending practices as they bear on minority housing choices; this study has apparently not yet been published.

REAL ESTATE APPRAISERS

It is reported that in the Bay area there are very few minority real estate appraisers of minority status. We presume this may also be the national situation; we found no other relevant studies. Admission to the American Institute of Real Estate Appraisers is contingent upon approval by a mail ballot sent to every member; this system clearly offers an opportunity for black-balling. The theory and interpretations of real estate appraisers strongly influence the channeling of minority loans into areas where minority families already live. Title companies, in the San Francisco Bay area, still have a very small percentage of minority work force, although one major company now has at least one black office manager (Denton, 1970).

We have sought to identify separate phases of the operation of the market for residential real estate and to report on different groups of functionaries and institutional mechanisms. It is important to remember, however, that discrimination results from the interaction of a number of attitudes and practices. Change in the total situation requires more than change in specific single factors. In a spirit similar to that pervading the Kerner Commission report, Carter (1965, p. 108–109) provides this summary of his impressions:

Discrimination against Negroes was and is a part of the fabric of American life in New York, Chicago, and San Francisco, as well as in Jackson, Mississippi; Little Rock, Arkansas; and Birmingham, Alabama. It inheres in the housing market and service of real estate brokers, landlords, builders, developers (private and public), city planners, banks, and mortgage loan companies. . . . Past practices have virtually solidified housing segregation in the North, and as yet no major break in the iron ring enclosing the Negro ghetto has been effected.

Denton pessimistically concludes (1970, p. Jb40) ". . . that by preventing the minority person from being able to shop for housing in the way that is normal for his white peers, a permanent barrier to residential desegregation has been created which may be beyond the power of positive law to reach."

Public Institutional Practices in Urban Planning and Land Use Controls, in Urban Renewal, and in the Financing, Development, and Management of Housing

We must necessarily be selective in discussing the many governmental policies and practices that affect the housing choices open to minority families. Our main presentation will be in this order: (a) land use plans and general development policy; (b) zoning and other precise land use and building regulations; (c) urban renewal; (d) support or incentives for private housing; (e) public housing; (f) fair-housing regulations; and (g) public taxation.

Certain very broad questions rise out of these facets of governmental institutional practices. The first question is whether residents and citizens get from their local governments what they want. This is not easy to determine, but there are few signs of serious dissatisfaction. Ironically, perhaps, our system of suburban government tends to give its residents a remarkably direct voice in policy determination (Wood, 1958; Davidoff *et al.,* 1970).

A second question is whether each local government can take into account regional considerations as well as its own more provincial interests. The general conclusion is that it can not. This raises difficult problems as to providing a broader policy framework and establishing review procedures. Planning and fiscal issues, in particular, call for vigorous exploration of possible regional government and for the determination of appropriate state and federal roles in urban and regional affairs. Until recently, at least, there has been a tendency to assume the validity of local self-determination, but this is increasingly coming under legislative and judicial review (Douglas Commission, 1968; Hawley & Zimmer, 1970).

A third question, and the one that probably relates most directly to our inquiry, is how the rights of minorities can be fully protected and, equally important, how the twin objectives of dispersal from inner-city minority areas and integration into other areas within the metropolis can be carried into effect. We conclude that to account for these urgent social objectives, traditional public institutional mechanisms must be changed (Kerner Commission, 1968; Kaiser Committee, 1968).

We are not certain how helpful social scientific knowledge about public institutional practices can be in bringing about attitudinal changes and political changes. In situations where the practices (e.g., exclusionary zoning or an unwillingness to create a public housing authority) are what the residents want, it will take far more than knowledge of institutional practices to bring about basic changes. Ironically, citizens and politicians may appropriate institutional practices introduced at earlier times by civic reformers and change them into mechanisms for preserving majority and status-quo interests. This has particularly been true of zoning (Babcock, 1966; Piven, 1970; Brooks, 1970; Toll, 1969; Ylvisaker, 1970). Indeed, it must be recognized that urban planning has sometimes become a hand-maiden for the stabilizers. On the other hand, urban planning has been caught squarely in the middle of battles among irreconcilable parties and interests—aggressive developers, ambitious elected officials, career-concerned professional staff members, and a diverse citizenry. City planners have often sought valiantly to control development under heavy pressures and within a political setting reflecting all of the crossfires of contemporary America (Scott, 1969; Fraser, 1970). In such a context, the vigorous introduction of changes designed to open up suburban communities adds a further set of pressures to the political battlefield (Lilley, 1970).

LAND USE PLANS AND DEVELOPMENT POLICY

The land use plan of a municipality, a county, or a metropolitan-level government or quasi-government identifies certain community or regional goals (possibly social and political as well as physical) and presents a maplike diagram of the arrangement of future land uses that will foster or incorporate these goals. It may suggest a program and time table for working toward the goals (Kent, 1964). As of 1968, there were within U.S. metropolitan areas the following local governments with planning boards and with plans as presented in Table 1. About 65 percent of suburban governments have fewer than 5,000 residents. Of communities with 5,000 or more population,

TABLE 1 Local Governments—Planning Boards and Plans (within Metropolitan Areas as of 1968)

Governments within SMSA's (1960 population)	No. of Governments	Percent with Planning Boards	Percent with Land Use Plans	
			Of All Governments	Of Governments with Planning Boards
Total	7,609	65.2	n.d.	n.d.
County governments	404	80.0	n.d.	n.d.
Municipalities				
50,000+ population	314	98.4	87.6	89.0
5,000–49,999	1,303	92.9	65.8	70.8
Under 5,000	3,360	54.9	n.d.	n.d.
New England-type townships				
5,000+ population	765	79.1	58.7	74.2
Under 5,000	1,463	45.7	n.d.	n.d.
Total municipalities and New England-type townships				
5,000+ population	2,382	89.2	66.4	74.4

[a]Source: Adapted from Manvel (1968, p. 24, 31).

about 9 out of 10 have planning boards, and 2 out of 3 have land use plans. The smaller communities are less apt to have planning boards.

There is relatively little careful research on the character and impact of suburban land use plans, and it would seem particularly relevant to the purposes of this paper that systematic studies of these plans be undertaken. We conclude from such studies of land use plans as have been made (whether or not suburban communities) that, except for unusual and recent examples, these plans have focused almost completely on physical objectives, and that social and political presumptions and goals have not been openly stated or related to the physical plans (Altshuler, 1965; Gans, 1967). Further, most metropolitan planning efforts have not been any more explicit in openly identifying social policy objectives or in working toward them (Downs, 1970; Dunleavy and Associates, 1970). We also conclude that many plans suffer from undue generality, jargon, and lack of specific proposals about how they might be carried out (Spatt, 1970; Altshuler, 1965). Land use plans may not be taken seriously by most residents, since the plans appear to be advisory in tone and sometimes not even submitted for the approval of the city council or other elected body (Denton, 1970).

Most land use plans appear to represent established interests and to take either a conserving or preserving approach. Land use plans may concentrate on the major goal of "orderly development" and such further subgoals as the control of residential densities, the preservation of open space, and the deliberate containment of commercial and industrial land uses (Davidoff, 1965; Marcuse, 1969). Either deliberately or by default, the plans have rarely sought to contend with the serious housing situation confronting disadvantaged families. This may reflect various reasons: (a) community sentiment and leaders' commitment to prevent the influx of minority households or, perhaps more common, to discourage the influx of low- and even moderate-income households; (b) the structure of local government in which a housing authority and a renewal agency may be operating relatively independently from the planning department— in such a situation, the planning department may leave it to the other agencies to promote or introduce appropriate housing; (c) a tendency of land use plans to be more concerned with the elimination of blight than with the positive provision of housing for families not well served by the private housing market (Altshuler, 1965).

As a result of these shortcomings in land use plans, the Housing and Urban Development Act of 1968 required all local communities to identify and to take into account "the housing needs of both the region and the local communities," with a subgoal of encouraging each community to do its share in providing housing for disadvantaged households. It will be particularly important to examine whether the preparation of these housing element reports brings substantial change to the land use plans and, subsequently, to the outlook and programs of the community. There is some initial evidence that suburban communities will continue to protect the status quo (Denton, 1970). It will also be important to pay careful attention to HUD-sponsored research that is coordinated by the National Association of Housing and Redevelopment Officials (NAHRO) (Nenno, 1969; Spicer, 1970; Beckman, 1970).

ZONING AND OTHER PRECISE REGULATIONS

Zoning is unquestionably at the very center of the process of land use control (Leary, 1968). It is thus at the center of major value conflicts, for, as some gain what they seek, others must lose (ASPO, 1968). Zoning has been so completely incorporated into the local political process and has become so well understood by the citizenry (at least with respect to its broad possibilities) that it is probably the major mode of land use regulation relied on by politicians and residents (Table 2).

A slightly larger number of communities have zoning ordinances than have planning boards and a considerably larger number have zoning ordinances than have land use plans. Of those local governments with population 5,000 or more that do have zoning ordinances, 42.9 percent passed their first zoning ordinance after 1950, 33.0 percent have at least some use districts prescribing residential lots with minimum size of one acre or more, and 14.8 percent do not permit any new apartments (of three units or more).

Zoning is certainly the suburban community's perfect tool if it wants to maintain essentially single-family housing and if it wants to exclude other land uses (and, as we shall discuss, to exclude various types of households) (Babcock, 1966). Zoning purports to control the character of physical development and to ensure orderly development on behalf of the community as a whole. Thus it regulates type of land use, lot size, set-back, parking requirements, etc. Indirectly, it controls density of development and thus assists in

TABLE 2 The Extent of Zoning, as of 1968, among Local Governments in Metropolitan Areas in the United States[a]

Governments within SMSA's (1960 population)	No.	Precent with Zoning Ordinance	Percent with First Ordinance since 1950	Percent with Any 1-Acre Minimum Lot Size	Percent Not Permitting Any New Apartments
Total	7,609	68.3	n.d.	n.d.	n.d.
County governments	404	49.3	n.d.	n.d.	n.d.
Municipalities					
50,000+ population	314	98.7	16.7	24.2	3.5
5,000–49,999	1,303	97.0	45.2	24.0	11.0
Under 5,000	3,360	54.0	n.d.	n.d.	n.d.
New England-type townships	765	81.0	51.4	54.6	28.2
5,000+ population					
Under 5,000	1,463	44.8	n.d.	n.d.	n.d.
Total municipalities and townships					
5,000+ population	2,382	92.1	42.9	33.0	14.8

[a]Source: Adapted from Manvel (1968, p. 24, 31–32).

meant that its zoning could be completely local in outlook [Anderson (1970) quoted in Brooks (1970, p. 18)].

The cases are rare which expressly require that the zoning municipality consider the extraterritorial effect of a zoning restriction. Indeed, the very propriety of such consideration may be questioned. . . . [M]ost courts have respected the power of each municipality to seek its own solutions, to fashion its own character, and to prescribe its own exclusions, without regard (or with small regard) to the needs of its neighbors of its larger community. . . .

It may also be difficult (Raymond and May Associates, 1968, p. 47) for individual suburban communities to

. . . deal effectively with social problems of a metropolitan scope. The problem is the result of general housing discrimination against Negroes in the metropolitan area. In the few suburban areas where housing, such as these apartments [in the case study of authors present] , is open to Negroes the rapid influx of Negroes creates massive fears and resentments, as expressed in some of the interviews.

As we have noted, an acknowledged problem is how to create the intergovernmental arrangements by which a broad policy framework can be established into which local community zoning could be expected to fit.

Another important type of land use control used by local governments is subdivision regulation. The planning commission must approve of the proposed design of a subdivision; thus, it can exercise control over the process by which land is converted into building sites (Green, 1968). Something over 80 percent of the communities having zoning also have subdivision regulations (Table 3).

TABLE 3   The Extent of Subdivision Control, as of 1968, among Local Governments in Metropolitan Areas in the United States[a]

Governments within SMSA's (1960 population)	No.	Percent with Subdivision Regulations
Total	7,609	59.3
County governments	404	62.9
Municipalities		
50,000+ population	314	92.7
5,000–49,999	1,303	90.0
Under 5,000	3,360	47.7
New England-type townships		
5,000+ population	765	74.0
Under 5,000	1,463	44.0

[a]Source: Adapted from Manvel (1968, p. 24).

Although it is recognized that subdivision regulations are part of the family of regulations controlling new subdivision and construction, there is little direct research evidence on the impact of subdivision regulations, as such, on housing opportunities for minority families. As noted by Green (1968, p. 449), restrictive covenants or deed restrictions

... are of interest to the agency regulating subdivisions, because they are customarily filed with the plat of a subdivision. Knowing this, the plat approval agency may through a process of negotiation persuade a developer to include detailed regulations governing the siting of structures, landscaping, architectural design, and so forth, tailored to the particular needs of his subdivision, which it could not easily require in its general [public] regulations.

We need to research the attitudes of local officials and planning staffs, in particular, toward covenants that restrict ownership or tenancy to majority whites and how these covenants have been handled in the process of subdivision control.

Literature identifying regulations contributing to discrimination against minority families typically mentions building and housing codes. Probably their main impact is to promote economic discrimination. Codes may prevent or discourage the greatest possible economies in housing construction and maintenance. It is alleged that inspectors are in a position to block construction. Banfield and Grodzins (1958, p. 97) concluded:

Local [building] inspectors sometimes use the [building] code as a weapon against builders who do not "play ball" with a political machine, who sell to Negroes or other "undesirables," or who are felt to be outsiders creating unwarranted or unfair competition. The inspector's unquestioning acceptance of the canons of the local community and especially of its dominant builders is as likely as venality to be the problem here.

Schermer and Levin reported (1968, p. 14) more recently that:

[L]arge city zoning and licensing officials were not found to be particularly obstructive because of racial policy. But there is almost universal feeling that such officials in white suburban areas can and do effectively impede developments that are likely to be integrated.

The Manvel–U.S. Census Bureau survey (Manvel, 1968) showed in considerable detail the recency of codes and the proportion of local jurisdictions that have adopted various standardized codes. The direct bearing on discrimination against minorities is, however, unclear.

URBAN RENEWAL

Urban redevelopment and, later, urban renewal have acquired greater responsibility in their two decades of operation. Until 1967, the criticism was that little attention was paid to the effective relocation of displaced households in the project areas or elsewhere (Greer, 1965; Anderson, 1964; Wilson, 1966). Since the HUD regulations of 1967 and the Housing Act of 1968, *new* projects must focus on provision of housing for low- and moderate-income families.

Other aspects of the urban renewal program bear on the question of housing choice for minority families. The published research literature does not bring us completely up to date on these, and some points made here may be out of date by now.

Urban renewal has been aimed chiefly at large blighted areas, and the projects have been disproportionately located in larger cities, particularly in central cities (Douglas Commission, 1968). Urban renewal has had various stated objectives, not necessarily compatible, and local communities have had considerable leeway in calculating relative priorities. Communities have chosen to get taxable real estate back on the rolls, to recapture the city center, to reattract upper-middle-income households, and to combat physical blight. Direct concern for disadvantaged households has been a low-priority objective. As of 1967, only 8 percent of families housed on urban renewal sites were low income (Grigsby, 1964; Greer, 1965; George Schermer Associates, 1968; National Housing and Development Law Project, 1969–70).

The process by which dispossessed households—a preponderance of which housed minority-group persons—are rehoused in good, reasonably priced housing is central to open-housing. More often than not, judging from research reports, this has been an inequitable if not brutal process. And yet, along with relocation from private development and other public programs—highway construction, public housing construction—relocation in the course of urban renewal could have been the point of opening housing opportunities. It now seems to be recognized that a dislocated household should, if possible, be given a choice of staying in the immediate area or of moving to another area. This opportunity for the constructive use of relocation has not been utilized to full advantage. The most critical studies have judged the relocation process to be woefully inadequate and particularly hard on minority families already caught in a discriminatory market situation where their opportunities are, in any event, severely limited (Watts *et al.*, 1964; Hartman, 1964; Schorr, 1963). A minority of research findings suggests that the relocation process has not been so demoralizing (Key, 1967).

A number of cities are reported to be making successful uses of centralized (i.e., consolidated) relocation service (Groberg, 1969). If this service could include cooperative arrangements with various suburban communities, it might open up a greater geographic range of housing choice. [In Britain, for example, such a pattern exists, known as "over-spill" housing, with central city (sender), outer community (receiver), and central government (sponsor); the central city and the central government pay a negotiated sum to the outer community for provision of the agreed-upon housing.]

Most studies report that an increase in racial concentration has resulted from the relocation caused by urban renewal. In some instances, urban renewal has been reported as a deliberate means of resegregation (Lowi, 1970). Only for Columbus, Ohio, and Topeka, Kansas, have reports suggested that displacement from urban renewal projects may have contributed to desegregation (Redwood, 1970). The desegregation described in these two studies took place within the cities rather than into the suburbs.

PUBLIC INCENTIVES FOR PRIVATE HOUSING

The most widespread governmental support for housing (apart from tax policy, treated in a later section) has been through FHA and VA mortgage insurance. From 1935 to 1967, "more than 2,750,000 new one-family dwellings, and 4,600,000 existing one-family dwellings have been purchased with the assistance of FHA financing" (Gold & Davidoff, 1968, p. 381–382). We need not recount the overwhelming impact of FHA-devised procedures and policies on metropolitan America. The Federal Housing Administration has also contributed systematically to residential discrimination against minority families. FHA not only recognized the place of restrictive covenants, but it openly recommended them during early years. Even during the period between 1948 (the *Shelley v. Kraemer* decision) and 1962 (the Executive Order on Equal Opportunity), the FHA was granting mortgage insurance in situations where it knew minorities were being excluded from purchase. Miller notes (1964, p. 68) that, until 1962,

FHA had played a major role in setting a style that resulted in ringing every American city with a necklace of white suburbs, some of them great cities in their own right, all of them bearing eloquent witness to the efficacy of governmental sanction and support of popular prejudice.

The Veterans' Administration, too, in its post-World War II program, tolerated written restrictive covenants until 1950. Even after this, VA never took steps to eliminate discriminatory practices by homebuilders. As a result, projects were segregated, either white or Negro, the latter characteristically "on the edges of existing Negro Ghettos" (Miller, 1964, p. 68). Because of its somewhat more liberal provisions, VA mortgage insurance enabled more veterans with lower incomes to buy homes than did FHA mortgage insurance. At its peak in 1955, VA insurance covered one fourth of all mortgage loans, but the program subsequently declined rapidly in coverage. As of 1967, FHA insurance covered 11 percent and VA insurance 5 percent of all new nonfarm housing units.

In recent years, the FHA has greatly liberalized its policies; this has been followed by a marked increase in defaults, so that by 1964 (the peak year for defaults) losses amounted to three fourths of FHA income (Douglas Commission, 1968, p. 102):

... a group of financially conservative Members of Congress ... demanded greater caution in insuring. On the other hand, Congressional liberals ... wanted FHA to take more chances. ... FHA was caught between two fires. It was damned if it did and damned if it didn't.

Recently, Congress has broadened the scope of FHA insurance, and by 1969 there were nearly one million applications for FHA mortgages (some five times the volume of VA mortgage applications). Inexorably, the mortgage loan programs of both FHA and VA are seeking broader coverage, both in reaching families of minority status and of lower income and in reaching into geographic areas (e.g., inner-city districts) that formerly would have been considered ineligible for mortgage insurance.

There apparently remains some gap between acceptance of nondiscrimination and positive leadership in the direction of integrated housing in the FHA and VA organizations. The following reactions to FHA officials from developers seeking to build integrated projects illustrate this point (Schermer & Levin, 1968, p. 12, 13):

It was one long contest between FHA wanting to conform people to a narrow and fixed formula on the one hand and our wanting to adapt the formula to the needs and abilities of people who needed housing, were earnest in their desire to live in a real community, and prepared to accept integration. ...

I wouldn't say FHA is opposed to open occupancy—they are just afraid of innovation. They didn't understand the co-op. They couldn't understand open occupancy. . . .

The FHA ought to take some leadership in this kind of thing, but it doesn't. There is no commitment there. They are neutral. The developer has to have all the ideas, ask all the questions, dig out all the answers. They deal in stereotypes. Negroes and whites are supposed to behave in certain ways, so they make their decisions accordingly. . . .

Unsympathetic treatment by FHA local officials in dealing with proposals for moderate-income housing, under such newer programs as Sect. 221(d)(3), has been reported (Douglas Commission, 1968, p. 150–151):

Some [sponsors of this housing] were repelled by what they regarded as cold, bureaucratic, and at times actually hostile treatment at the hands of FHA.

We are confident that this was not the intention of top FHA officials. They seem to have tried to be helpful. But as testimony before our Commission revealed, the rank and file officials in district and local offices were, in many cases, highly unsympathetic. They were accustomed to dealing with the conservative real estate and financial community. They did not feel at home in having business dealings with churches and philanthropists whom they tend to regard as soft and impractical. Nor did they welcome having the poor as their constituents. This was a social class whom they have never served and who seemed alien to their interests and associations. After these attitudes were increasingly revealed by our hearings, the head of FHA reacted vigorously. He called his field representatives together and instructed them to pay special attention to such applications. . . . This produced a decided change of attitude in many offices, although the old indifference and antagonism linger among many of the personnel.

Despite liberalization of policy, FHA regular financing does not help low- and moderate-income families. As of 1965, only 8 percent of new FHA homes and 24 percent of existing FHA homes were priced below $12,000, and only 5 percent of the new-home fixed monthly costs and 4 percent of the existing-home monthly costs were less than $125. These figures indicate an economic discrimination, which indirectly affects the availability of homes for minority families (George Schermer Associates, 1968).

Various federally subsidized housing programs (in addition to public housing per se, which we treat later) were begun during the 1960's. These have included rent-supplement programs for families in the public-housing-income range and have aimed, particularly, at providing housing for families in the range between the upper-income limits of public housing and the lower-income limits of decent private housing. Notable among these programs has been the Sect. 221(d)(3) program, which provided rental and cooperative housing for low- and moderate-income families and individuals by subsidizing mortgage rates above 3 percent; about 74,000 housing units were approved from 1961 through 1967, and over 100,000 housing units were approved January 1968 through September 1970. The Sect. 235 program subsidized mortgage rates on home purchase, and about 90,000 housing units were approved November 1968 through September 1970. For 1969, these median characteristics were reported as shown:

Annual gross income of purchaser	$ 5,669
Assets of purchaser	$297
Age of household head	32 yr
Family monthly adjusted income	$371
Acquisition cost of home	$15,110
Mortgage	$14,954
Mortgagor's share of mortgage payment	$80
Mortgagor's monthly subsidy	$55

The Sect. 236 program subsidized rental and cooperative housing so that monthly rentals could be brought to a level no less than 25 percent of the tenant's adjusted monthly income; nearly 140,000 housing units were approved April 1969 through September 1970. For 1969, the median rent paid by tenants was $124 (U.S. Department of Housing and Urban Development, 1970a,b; Douglas Commission, 1968). Some of these programs, being very recent, probably deserve more time to get under way before being submitted to research.

A few preliminary generalizations can be made about these new federal programs: The construction of new housing has been slow. Delays are common. Local resistance to housing for low- and moderate-income families, particularly by immediate neighbors, has been formidable. For obvious reasons, the programs are more heavily concentrated in the cities than in the suburbs. The Douglas Commission report stated (1968, p. 149):

One of the basic, though unavowed, purposes of the rent-supplement program was to promote in a constructive fashion a greater degree of economic and racial integration. . . .

It was also hoped that these buildings, with their mixed occupancy, could be diffused through a city and not confined to the slums or gray areas.

These latter purposes were not explicitly avowed but were soon detected. Those who were generally hostile to racial integration were therefore successful in persuading the House to require that the consent of a locality was necessary before rent supplements could be put into effect there. Unfortunately, this virtually barred the program from the suburbs.

We find little, if any, current research literature reporting on these varied, but mainly recent, housing programs, especially on their operation in suburban areas. We need answers to questions like these: Have the local suburban governments and their planning, renewal, and housing agencies taken any initiative? What particular points of resistance have emerged? How effectively have the programs worked? Do small scattered-site developments prove more susceptible than large single-site projects? We should ascertain which types or patterns of subsidized housing are turning out to be the most acceptable and the most effective.

PUBLIC HOUSING

The distinctively American version of public housing, dating from the late 1930's, has been governmentally built and managed rental housing, usually in project form, and often separated and architecturally different from its community setting. Such housing projects were built in both central cities and other smaller cities, the latter presumably independent cities rather than suburbs. Partly because the initial purpose was interlocked with slum clearance and partly because the projects tended to be built in areas already inhabited by the poor, the projects came to be associated with run-down areas, with the poor, and increasingly, with black or other minority occupants. Public housing in the United States, in contrast to that in Britain and the Scandinavian countries, tends to bear a stigma (Huttman, 1970). Friedman (1967, p. 362–363) writes of this anathema, public housing.

...[P]ublic housing in the big cities is more and more the home of the most despised and dispossessed group in America: the urban, problem-family Negro. The more this happens, the more others abandon public housing—physically, by moving out, and politically, by despising it. The worst thing about big-city public housing is not that it is shoddy and dreary. The worst thing is that it is despicable to live there, and that degraded, hopeless people, the victims of weakness, fate, and prejudice, make their homes there. And the more this is true, the more the white community reacts with hostility. The very mention of public housing in the suburbs or in middle class areas is political death. . . .

Significant variations in the shape of public housing have been introduced during the past few years. New large projects are rarely built. Scattered-site housing is being substituted where feasible. Under Turnkey and leased-housing schemes, housing authorities are turning to private construction and to the leasing of newly built or older housing in order to provide housing for individual eligible families. Housing exclusively for elderly persons has become more important.

Scattered public housing, however, brings new difficulties. This is true even in the central city, and certainly far more so in suburban communities. Meyerson and Banfield (1955) provided the classic study of an earlier situation in Chicago where each alderman could, through log-rolling politics, gain support for the "veto" of public housing in his ward. The opportunity for veto is enhanced by the prevalence of local referenda. A federal law, the "Phillips Amendment," of 1954 (National Housing and Development Law Project, 1969–70: Ch. IV, Pt. II-13 and 14)

purports to permit any local governing body in the nation to authorize a referendum in the community to determine whether a public housing project is needed in their community. . . . [in addition], referendum requirements exist in at least thirteen states. . . .

The most common form of referendum requirement is illustrated by Article 34 of California's state constitution . . . , which prohibits any local governing body or housing authority from constructing or acquiring a federally financed low-income housing project without a majority vote to the population in the affected area. The effect of requiring majority approval has been to sharply curtail the construction of decent and adequate low-income housing units. Such voter approval is required for housing for low-income persons but not for any other income group.

Leased housing has been excepted from the referendum requirement by the California Attorney General.

Whatever the intent of the Congress or the administrative officers in HUD, the local housing authority exercises considerable initiative and judgment of what is best for the local community. One recent study of the make-up and attitudes of housing authority commissioners concludes that local authorities are "a principal hindrance to increased activity in the housing field." Hartman and Carr (1969, p. 49) elaborate further in their portrait:

This survey gives a picture of housing commissioners as male, white, in the middle and upper-middle income ranges, well educated, heavily weighted toward business and professional occupations, and with even distribution among the middle and elderly age ranges.

In reply, commissioners explained that more public housing had not been built in their communities partly because of their own evaluation of need; other "reasons given were neighborhood hostility to public housing, community reluctance to use scarce land and lack of support from public officials (Hartman & Carr, 1969, p. 50).

One highly significant datum that we failed to uncover was the quantitative distribution of public-housing authorities, projects, and housing units in suburban areas. Published Department of Housing and Urban Development summaries do not show this, and even the Douglas Commission was unable to report this information. This gap could readily be closed, and the Department of Housing and Urban Development should release and feature such information as a way of documenting the situation within metropolitan areas.

A major consideration in the introduction of public housing into suburban communities is the degree to which it is associated simultaneously with low income, with heavy concentration of minority persons, and with likely inclusion of problem families. This combination of associations ensures greater resistance than might occur if the potential tenants did not differ from the rest of the suburban population in so many ways.

Traditional public housing has been shifting toward housing for the elderly. By the mid-1960's, about half of all new public housing was in this category. Significant questions arose as to the suitability of suburban sites for such housing, and, yet, restriction of housing for the elderly mainly to central cities may reinforce social demographic segregation between central city and suburb.

A suburban community that does not want public housing has available several lines of defense (or inaction). It can refuse to establish a housing authority. Many suburban communities do just that; nationwide, half of the cities in the 25,000–50,000 class have no housing authorities. Even if it had a housing authority, it could "fail to" complete and submit a workable program for many years, so that it disqualified itself from eligibility for public housing. All this has changed, however: A workable program is no longer required as a prerequisite for eligibility. If the suburban community has an authority and goes through the motions of keeping it active, it can take a conservative, custodial view and plan for little additional housing.

As is the case with zoning, the local housing authority can settle for its interpretation of its own local needs. Generally, we lack a metropolitan arrangement for identifying the full complementarity that could exist between a suburban community and the central city. The recent cooperative agreement among suburban communities in the Dayton, Ohio, area was newsworthy, precisely because this had not previously happened elsewhere in the United States (Herbers, 1970; Miami Valley Regional Planning Commission, 1970). But, until there are governmental mechanisms at the metropolitan or state level and until such mechanisms beget metropolitan-wide housing policy, it remains unlikely that separate suburbs will feel obligated to consider broader needs than their own. As of 1968, the Douglas Commission was able to conclude (1968, p. 130):

... [T]he public housing program has been slowed to a faltering walk largely by economic-class and racial antagonisms. Other conditions and influences have played considerable parts, but they have been and are relatively secondary. Only more confusion and frustration can come from evading this fact. It would be equally futile either to pretend that some new twist or gimmick in the subsidy formula would make much difference or to condemn out-of-hand all changes in law or administrative procedure. . . .

The Commission reported that a noticeable improvement seemed to be taking place. But the acceptance of public housing in the suburbs remains in doubt.

Some studies conclude that future efforts to provide housing for low-income families must place primary reliance on income maintenance or a system of subsidies to the families in question, rather than dependence on an institution such as public housing, which, however able its architecture, may be caught up in bureaucratic management (Glazier, 1967; George Schermer Associates, 1968). Schermer Associates have argued (1968, p. 83):

A great many low-income families are quite capable of being good tenants and many can benefit from purchasing and owning homes. All that is required is provision for rent supplements, interest subsidies, or other arrangements through which the family is assisted in meeting the cost of the shelter. . . .

Such systems place much greater responsibility upon the private sector of the housing industry and upon the individual family, reduce the need for institutional-type public housing, and would probably stimulate the rehabilitation and maintenance of the existing housing stock. . . .

FAIR-HOUSING LEGISLATION AND FAIR-HOUSING GROUPS

As we have already stated, and as Eley and Casstevens (1968, p. 6–7)
describe, residential segregation reflects deep-seated and complex
attitudes and prejudices.

Most whites simply do not want Negroes living next door or in white neighborhoods. Buttressing this prejudice is the traditional American view of the rights
of private individuals to own and control the use and disposition of property.
. . . Americans have historically thought of the authority of the state as ceasing
at the doorstep of the home. . . . Reinforcing white America's dedication to the
abstract principle of property rights—and perhaps underlying it—has been the
firm belief that racial integration in housing depresses property values. And
pervading the entire issue are considerations of social status—the belief on the
part of many whites, especially those in the lower and lower-middle classes,
that their status is seriously diminished if Negroes move into the neighborhood.

In this social and political context, the introduction and halting
spread of fair-housing legislation from 1957 to the present has represented a logical expansion of civil rights from earlier efforts to curb
governmental discrimination in housing and to ensure governmental
integration in schools. But there is an essential difference: Fair-housing
legislation bears on the "private" decisions of the sellers and renters
of housing, clearly a highly sensitive area, whereas the earlier focus
was on "public" (governmental) decisions.

The spread of fair-housing legislation has been accompanied by
many local campaigns; some legislation has been fought through
and supported, and some has been resisted and defeated. Until very
recently, the real estate interests have been stubbornly opposed to
such laws. The voter approval of Proposition 14 in California was, of
course, a major setback for fair-housing proponents; Proposition 14
reversed the Rumford open-housing act and ensured that no further
open-housing laws would be enacted. The recent situation seems to
be that more support has been available for fair-housing laws, perhaps partly because this permits a token support of the idea but does
not commit individual homeowners (Eley, 1969, p. 60):

The ironic political fact of fair-housing legislation at this time [as of 1969]
seems to be that such laws have won lukewarm public acceptance, but most
whites are still unprepared to change their housing practices to permit real integration. At the same time, the decreasing momentum of the civil-rights revolution and the surging Negro drive for independent black power reinforce Negro
and white separation, at least in the short run. One may speculate that fair-

housing laws are being passed with greater ease and frequency today mainly because their supporters want them for psychological and symbolic reasons, and opponents and moderates are now persuaded that such laws do not threaten present practice. The function of a fair-housing law is today mainly symbolic and ritualistic. Its existence holds aloft the explicit standard of equal opportunity in housing, confirming the American creed for all of us; but parties on both sides tacitly realize that provisions will not be enforced in a way that basically threatens white neighborhoods. Supporters have the public policy they desire, and opponents have the practice they want to preserve. . . .

Circumstantial evidence supporting this gloomy verdict is not difficult to find. For one thing, and most important, social scientists and other careful observers have found no direct relationship between the presence or absence of a fair-housing law and the extent of racial integration in a given community or state. Other factors such as the general economic health of the community seem to have greater influence. At the same time, the movement for fair-housing legislation has helped to make integrated housing a subject of attention and concern. The public agitation has apparently improved the general climate in much of the country for acceptance of black families in white neighborhoods. Upper- and middle-class whites seem increasingly disposed to accept black neighbors of similar socioeconomic status. This is still token integration, however, and does not relieve the ghetto conditions in which most Negroes live.

This compromise character of fair-housing legislation, and the discrepancy between what is declared illegal and what can in practice continue, is further analyzed by Friedman (1967, p. 366–367):

. . . [G]overnment faces a real dilemma. Negroes demand integrated housing. Many white liberals agree, with varying passion and commitment. Other whites violently disagree, particularly small householders in the suburbs and in urban ethnic enclaves. From the standpoint of government, the best solution is to place an ordinance or statute on the books which proclaims the rights of Negroes to live everywhere; and to do nothing further. Actually, the form of these ordinances represent a quite typical compromise. Those in favor are not strong enough to ram through fair housing laws which really sting; those against are not strong enough to block passage. The compromise takes the form of a ringing symbolic declaration, coupled with flabby enforcement provisions. . . .

One difficulty in enforcing fair-housing legislation is that each case must be brought to trial separately, except for those situations in which class actions can be brought. A minority family seeking housing may decide that the cost and delay of going to court are not worth the effort. There are ways in which the laws can be made more effective, such as by sharpening the definition of "discrimination" to include provisos that the applicant qualifies as having an appropriate income, a reasonable credit rating, and a family size within the current housing laws for the space involved (Kolben, 1969). But this is a matter of legal tactics and beyond the purview of social science research.

The courts have played an important part in the extension of civil rights. In *Jones v. Mayer* (1968), the Supreme Court, applying an 1866 civil rights law, provided a basis for a more extensive coverage of fair housing than has been achieved by the 1968 Civil Rights Act. We do not know if judicial leadership in the sphere of fair housing will continue. The Court's role may change with changes in their composition.

It is difficult to assess the extent to which changes can be brought about by fair-housing legislation. Optimistically, attitudes, with time and the rise of a new generation, will, indeed change. The pessimistic view, perhaps not inconsistent, suggests that "It is evident that discrimination in housing, as well as in other areas of life, operates subtly and cannot be stopped by legislation alone" (Watts *et al.*, 1964, p. 35).

A considerable number of local nonprofit fair-housing groups have been seeking to carry fair housing beyond antidiscrimination into effective positive action. The national organization for this purpose is the National Committee against Discrimination in Housing (NCDH). Studies vary in their assessment of the effectiveness of these local organizations. Many fair-housing organizations achieve some small successes, in the sense that they operate house-listing services, run tests of discriminatory practices, and lobby for stronger enforcement procedures.

But observers are far less convinced of the broader effectiveness of these organizations. The following self-evaluation by a strong fair-housing organization in the San Francisco Bay area is illustrative (Midpeninsula Citizens for Fair Housing, 1969, Appendix B, p. 9–10).

It is clear that the housing market cannot be opened by fair-housing groups. The local fair housing group is the largest and most effective . . . in the Bay Area and appears to be among the top local groups in the nation. Yet five years of persistent and often imaginative work have failed to produce a perceptible improvement in housing market discrimination practices, although many of the local, fair housing leaders believe that the community climate is more favorable to fair housing than it was five years ago.

After reviewing activities by fair-housing groups in the Bay Area, Denton concluded (1970, p. Jb65):

Most local fair housing groups are trying to *reduce the effects* of institutional racism but are not trying to initiate major social change to *eradicate its causes*. Given this ameliorative outlook, their goals are necessarily limited to information campaigns and placement of token minority persons in white neighborhoods.

Some observers have particularly emphasized the importance of authentic real estate brokerage service and reassuring salesmanship and have questioned whether this can be offered by amateurs.

Based on our research on the fair housing groups we are more than ever convinced that the location service offered by them is not an adequate substitute for the services of a broker; that most buyers need the services [furnished by a bona fide broker] and cannot obtain them other than through [a real estate] agent. Of course one might think that a really neutral adviser—such as a worker in a Fair Housing Project—would be preferable to an interested intermediary such as an agent. This, however, overlooks the need of most buyers for the application of straightforward salesmanship. [Denton (1970, p. Ja32)]

It is true that suburban fair housing groups have been promoting sales and rentals of houses to Negroes, with moderate success. Some such groups have said that response from Negroes has been disappointing, causing them to wonder whether Negroes really are interested in suburban locations. However, this is a great deal of difference, psychologically, between being wooed by a salesman who wants to sell a product and being urged by an ideological group to become a pioneer and examplar. There are too few instances in which homes in suburban developments have been affirmatively merchandized to Negroes to permit any generalizations. [Schermer & Levin (1968, p. 20–21)]

LOCAL TAXATION AND FISCAL POLICY

Some scholars have noted that, particularly within metropolitan areas, separate municipalities or other local governmental units deport themselves like business firms. That is, their officials weigh public actions on behalf of these communities so as to create the most favorable balance between returns from revenue and expenditures for services. It has also been suggested that the municipalities ensure a range of choice for metropolitan residents, who can choose the particular level and character of services they want and can afford (Duggar, 1956; Tiebout, 1956; Mace, 1961). Some communities offering high levels of service may have such a favorable property tax base (e.g., high valuation of commercial, industrial, or residential property) that they can maintain relatively low tax rates. Where tax disparities exist between local communities, the ones with low taxes sometimes succeed in attracting even more economic activity, thereby reinforcing their favorable situation

(Netzer, 1968; [U.S.] Advisory Commission on Intergovernmental
Relations, 1969).

Since local communities depend heavily on local taxes, particularly the property tax, they may, for fiscal reasons, seek to limit the
loads imposed on expensive programs. For example, prospective increases in loads on the community's school and welfare systems may
be avoided. Thus, the local community may inevitably be led to discriminatory policies. Policies purporting to preserve the character of
the community and to order its physical arrangement subtly fuse
into less openly stated policies designed to keep out low-income or
minority families.

In other words, the culture of local governments equates respect
for fiscal considerations with responsible leadership. This may enable
a local community to use fiscal reasoning to justify exclusion of
families against whom there may also exist prejudices. Given the
current pattern, it may be extremely difficult to disentangle fiscal
responsibility from prejudice against unwanted newcomers.

Under such conditions, we may ask how communities can be encouraged or forced to alter such policies. Margolis (1961) has observed that voters, "rather than acting as hard-headed shoppers,
adopt ideological positions" toward public programs in question.
Thus they are open to political persuasion; in effect, this permits
the substitution of a sense of public responsibility for self-interest.
Various researchers (Brazer, 1964) have studied the impact of increasing governmental size and complexity and the imposition on
localities of political judgments made by state or federal government.

Some of the most pressing and expensive local services (e.g., education and welfare) could be more fully financed by states or the
federal government according to formulas that would take into
account both the total population of a community and the burdens
placed upon it by its income distribution, its property base mix, and
the numbers of children to be educated (U.S. President's Task Force
on Urban Renewal, 1970). Revenue sharing is currently proposed,
but unless it were to incorporate compensatory fiscal support, observers argue that it could be used by local communities to fortify
their discriminatory policies.

The burden of residential property taxes has been extensively
studied. In brief, such taxes fall heavily on housing consumers.
Further, these taxes are regressive in character, taking a larger percentage of income from lower-income families than from higher
and falling proportionately more heavily on renters (as increased

rents) than on home owners who may be able to take offsetting income-tax deductions (Netzer, 1968; Douglas Commission, 1968).

Income taxes are not typically used by local governments, although there is a trend toward their use, especially by cities. Income taxes, by whatever jurisdiction levied, have an impact on housing. They favor owners of housing; conversely, they discriminate against renters. Because of the depreciation formulas permitted, income tax provisions also favor the owners of rental property. Gains in property transactions can be taxed at capital-gains rates, and losses can be fully deductible. In his report to the Douglas Commission, Slitor (1968) outlined various proposals for tax reform, while still respecting the overall value of the income tax. A major consideration for local communities is the extent to which the income tax can be used to supplement the property tax (Douglas Commission, 1968; [U.S.] Advisory Commission on Intergovernmental Relations, 1969).

In general, fiscal and tax policies relate directly to economic discrimination and only indirectly to discrimination against minority families as such. However, one study of assessment practices for one-family residences in Forth Worth found that Negro-owned homes were assessed for a greater percentage of sales prices than were white-owned homes (Hendon, 1968).

Other institutional practices affect housing choices. Incorporation and annexation are important ways by which local areas exercise their options, often in ways closely related to fiscal policy (Denton, 1970). School policies are significant as is police behavior. It must be continuously kept in mind that specific practices are directed by community attitudes and values, however subtle the dictums.

Local communities presumably have great freedom in determining their own affairs. Even the courts are reluctant to question local prerogatives. The federal government, to an increasing extent, and some state governments (the situation varies strikingly from state to state) are assuming responsibility for guiding the actions of local governments. The strongest actions are those implied by suggestions, such as that by the U.S President's Task Force on Urban Renewal (1970, p. 7) "that federal aids *of all sorts* be withdrawn from communities unless they undertake a program to expand the supply of low and moderate housing within their boundaries." More moderate proposals include schemes for fiscal assistance, review of development and zoning policies, and increased incentives for participation in programs. There is great need for research on federal and state program guidelines. Much of it should be closely linked to the programs being observed in order to foster thorough and objective observation, evaluation, and reporting.

The Community Context: Employment, Community Services, and Transportation

This section is brief partly because it is assumed that the Schnore paper deals with changing ecological patterns and partly because we chose to place our main stress on those private and public institutional practices that seem to bear most directly on the degree of housing choice open to minority households. Our coverage is selective.

It is convenient and tempting to oppose "central city" and "suburb," and, as a heuristic device, it has merit. But we should exercise great caution: Both a central city and a suburban ring may exhibit internal heterogeneity. Central cities may have their problem-laden inner-city districts; they may also have other types of districts with different characteristics. Suburbs, too, deserve to be differentiated. Some older suburbs are now running into problems similar to those confronted in the central cities (Labovitz, 1970). Such older suburban cities, for obvious reasons, may provide housing for minority families. In any literal sense, such movement from the central city constitutes dispersal; but, by different measures, it can also represent an expansion of the central city itself rather than dispersal and thus be construed as a continuation of an already established pattern of residential segregation. It has been suggested that age and growth rate of a community (or, for closer analyses, of a residential district) be used as major classificatory devices rather than to rely on only a central city–suburb dichotomy (Foley *et al.,* 1965; Duncan *et al.,* 1962).

EMPLOYMENT DISTRIBUTION

A great deal of evidence has been published on the shift in the distribution of employment within metropolitan areas. In every area studied, almost all employment growth has taken place in the suburban ring and not in the central city (Newman, 1967; NCDH, 1970; Kain, 1968; Mooney, 1969; Dunleavy and Associates, 1970). Close analysis shows serious imbalance results from this shift (Chinitz, 1964, p. 28–29).

As many types of jobs move into the periphery, the central cities are becoming more and more specialized in functions which require chiefly professional, technical and clerical workers—a skilled and literate labor force. But the skilled and literate groups are precisely those segments of the population which are increasingly choosing to live outside the urban center. The slum dwellers, on the other hand, are poorly suited to fill the city's office and service jobs; the jobs for which they are suited—the less skilled occupations involved in many types of manufacturing, wholesaling, and household service operations—are moving farther and farther away from them.

The importance of one's housing as the locational base from which one has access to employment and other services is stressed by various reports. As the Kaiser Committee (1968, p. 13) put it:

The location of one's place of residence determines the accessibility and quality of many everyday advantages taken for granted by the mainstream of American society. Among these commonplace advantages are public educational facilities for a family's children, adequate police and fire protection, and a decent surrounding environment. In any case a family should have a choice of living as close as economically possible to the breadwinner's place of employment.

One researcher (Weber, 1964, p. 80) has concluded: "There is little doubt . . . that segregated residential patterns impair the effective operation of the labor markets."

WELFARE POLICIES

Various features of welfare policy have direct bearing on housing choices of low-income families. These features may be widespread or imposed differentially, local area by local area. They include the amount and categories of benefit, the residence requirements, the duration of benefits, and the degree to which the welfare recipients are openly known as such. It would be important to understand the interplay between welfare policies and housing policies, especially housing for welfare families.

SCHOOLS

There are various relations between the nature of schools and the opening of housing opportunities for minorities. Various researchers stress the great importance of high quality of public education to both minority and majority-white families. It is essential to the success of any program to promote racial or ethnic residential integration. It can help draw minority families to new areas, and it can help keep white families in areas into which minority families are moving (Potomac Institute, 1968; Simpson & Yinger, 1965).

The attitude of the school administration toward integration also affects residential integration. Desegregration of a school system may reinforce a trend toward integration of residential areas (U.S. Commission on Civil Rights, 1967). One study has suggested that the Negro families seeking desegregated schools for their children are similar to those shown by Bullough (1969) and Weinstein and Geisel (1962) to seek desegregated housing (see p. 162).

Whether suburban schools should be granted specific subsidies as incentives for taking in larger numbers of minority-family students remains to be researched. We should also examine whether the use of tracks or ability groups in schools has a direct bearing on residential integration.

TRANSPORTATION

Transportation is an integral feature of the spatial structure of a community, providing both services within the community and links to more distant points. In recent years, it has become clear that transportation facilities do not offer equal services to advantaged and disadvantaged persons. The advantaged either have automobiles for their own use or are situated as to take advantage of public commuter systems; the systems have traditionally been geared to bring people from outer residential districts to the metropolitan center. It is the disadvantaged who must rely on public transportation systems that do not serve their needs. In particular, commuter systems that satisfactorily bring people into the metropolitan center are not geared to take people in the opposite direction with equal effectiveness. This discrepancy is largely due to the spatial spread of possible destinations, such as places of employment, in the suburban area (Kain & Meyer, 1970; Foley et al., 1970; Oakland City Planning Department, 1970).

Some studies suggest that in suburban areas where the density is too low to support a conventional public transit system, or in some inner areas where automobile ownership is unusually low, there is evident need for new systems of service. An interview study of residents of poverty areas in Long Island counties concluded that these families deserve to "be compensated for by a more personalized type of service than a conventional bus system, if a mobility more closely allied with car ownership is to be provided" (Pignatoro & Falcocchio, 1969, p. 525).

Residential dispersal, then, would be advantageous to minority families by enabling workers to live near their jobs, thus lessening dependence on an inadequate and expensive transportation system. Once such dispersal takes place, however, it is important that adequate public transportation become available in suburban areas and thus reduce dependence on the automobile.

Access to transportation points to the importance of conveniently located residences in the suburbs, and not unnecessarily isolated residential sites (unless the family deliberately seeks other amenities in lieu of accessibility). Residential dispersal, in turn, points to the advantage of integration, if it can mean sharing accessibility to good schools and other community services.

INTANGIBLES OF COMMUNITY SETTING AND SERVICES

The obvious considerations—access to work, access to shopping, quality of stated services—can only partially account for what one actually takes into account in making a residential location decision. Status may be a consideration, so may be the amenities of the area. As Smith (1970, p. 26) has put it,

It is in the nature of housing . . . that the immediate physical environment and the society about the household qualifies the kind of enjoyment which the household can expect from its dwelling. The appearance of neighboring houses, the activities of neighbors, and the reputation of the neighborhood within the larger community may add to or detract from the ultimate housing satisfactions to be enjoyed by the occupant household. The expectations of change in any of these factors must also be significant for the household's own evaluation of the dwelling.

Researchers have stressed the fact that considerations relating to the character and convenience of the setting may be more important to minority members faced with a housing-location decision than philosophy about residential integration (Potomac Institute, 1968, p. 79):

Persons who would prefer integration and those who would prefer segregation tend to place physical considerations and convenience ahead of their racial preferences.

Convenience of location, quality, price, and safety, in that order, are the major factors in attracting white families to racially inclusive center city developments. Next in importance are attractive design and community amenities which set a given neighborhood apart and give it character. In the suburbs, physical factors are less relevant to integration than affirmative marketing and community relations.

It remains to stress the pivotal role of leadership in the local community. Since the governmental process, however central, radiates to include the operation of varied interest groups, the research net must be broadly spread. We need to understand where support for or resistance to residential dispersal and integration is most likely to be generated—whether from elected governmental officials, governmental staff members, nongovernmental organizations, or selected individual citizens.

We have already dealt at some length with the gatekeeper roles of realtors. It would also seem very important to examine thoroughly the role of the realtor in reflecting and shaping community opinion. A study of Kalamazoo (although not a suburban city) showed that realtors were able to exercise a degree of influence—in defeating a proposal to create a city housing commission—beyond their presumed legitimated place (Bouma, 1970). What other key groups are in a position to "make or break" programs that would liberalize housing choices for minority families?

The metropolitan level of political leadership constitutes a particularly challenging situation. Councils of government, havine spread rapidly during recent years, characteristically lack political muscle and may, in fact, be better geared to vetoing potentially more powerful metropolitan governments than to asserting leadership. We have alluded to the Dayton housing plan as a great exception. Yet the allocation of housing responsibility to all suburban communities is a metropolitan matter. The federal and state governments may initiate programs and provide financial support, but the allocation within a given metropolitan area remains a local, albeit metropolitan, matter.

Conclusions and Implications

Our final observations are impressionistic, in view of the volume of research examined. We have some reactions about the character of the problem faced by those who seek to widen the opportunities for minority families to disperse their residences, and we have some re-actions about the state of knowledge bearing on this problem. Several conclusions can be drawn from the research literature:

1. Institutional practices that serve to limit or block housing op-portunities are impersonal and weblike in character. Any single rep-resentative of some part of this web can pass blame to another and does not have to accept direct, open responsibility himself for block-ing opportunities.

2. It is difficult to disentangle deliberate discriminatory practices from a larger fabric of practices and purported reasons why decisions are made. For example, it is particularly difficult to separate certain physical development controls, like zoning, from discrimination.

3. The planning, actual production, and subsequent sale and re-sale or rental of housing is a complex set of subprocesses with in-numerable constraints, regulations, and negotiations among various parties at sequential points. Given this complexity and the number of points at which behind-the-scenes negotiations and decisions may occur, it is difficult to pinpoint discrimination, as such, in order to take steps to eliminate it.

4. The most visible spot at which discrimination can take place is the actual point of sale or rental of the housing. A real estate broker or a management agent may become a crucial gatekeeper at that point, and it is the point at which fair-housing laws seek to eliminate discrimination. But for all of its importance, it is merely the most visible step in a much larger institutional structure.

5. Available research literature does not show clearly the most effective points at which discrimination can be attacked and sub-urban communities encouraged or forced to admit minority house-holds. There are no simple strategies. The web of discrimination is so complex that a multifaceted attack—using fiscal, legal, and political means—must be made.

6. Fair-housing (antidiscrimination) legislation must be bolstered by concerted enforcement programs. Political officials and enforce-ment personnel will need to bring positive commitment.

7. Other approaches are needed that go well beyond antidiscrimi-nation. These programs, positive in character, must be carefully thought out and patiently put into effect. Many aspects must be taken into account; minority households must be sold on the ad-vantages of participating; plans must be laid to prepare for success-ful adjustments between newcomers and earlier residents. The

programs must be carried forward with enthusiasm and determination. The alternative is continued apathy.

8. The social psychology of housing choice deserves attention. Selectively, minority families may bring themselves to the point where they are ready and willing to seek dispersed housing and to cope with the frustrations and inequities of the institutional mechanism by which housing is provided.

9. Open information—about the institutional system, about housing openings, about the hows of homeowning, about financing, etc.— is an important ingredient in the successful dispersal of minority households. If a real estate listing system is not completely open, alternative information systems should be developed with government assistance.

10. Inevitably, local leadership is essential in moving a community off dead center from apathy or resistance to positive, even enthusiastic, support. Metropolitan leadership, characteristically urgently needed, is a particularly difficult challenge.

11. Given the strong place of fiscal rationales in local community management, two general approaches bear consideration: (a) Some major functions such as education and welfare should perhaps be financed directly by state or federal governments so as to ease the need for reliance by local communities on discrimination for fiscal reasons; (b) the state or federal governments should offer local communities direct financial incentives to provide more housing for minority and moderate- or low-income families.

12. Despite some impatient interest in achieving rapid results in the fight to widen housing opportunities and to eliminate discrimination, we must realize that there remains a long and discouraging struggle to change attitudes and to affect thorough institutional change. Indeed, success may not come until a fresh generation moves into positions of responsibility.

In general, it is difficult to locate comprehensive, up-to-date research on the institutions that provide or block housing opportunities. The more scholarly the research, the greater the likelihood that it is selective in coverage, unsustained over time, and only questionably representative of the heterogeneous and changing situations comprising the American scene. More current and comprehensive reports come from governmental review commissions and from those advocate organizations with research capabilities, but one cannot rely on the disinterestedness of such groups or their desire to make a scholarly contribution to social science knowledge. A fascinating facet of this problem is the growing literature produced by legal scholars and advocates, in which the presentation may be an integral part of a brief.

Events have been moving with such force and rapidity in the United States that one must question the value of reports written a half-dozen years ago, which have been based on research done a decade before. The question is precisely what changes have occurred. In some cases old values and attitudes may still be applied to new situations. In that diverse patterns and responses may co-exist simultaneously, in what proportions and under what conditions may we expect these alternate practices?

A further problem lies in the difficulty of conducting sophisticated research on institutional practices. The researchers must be very familiar with the institutions and have access to behind-the scenes operations and decisions. In such research, it may be extremely difficult for others to appraise the researcher's objectivity and comprehension.

We probably need more analyses of situations where we are carefully shown the divergent roles and viewpoints of varied participants. Interestingly, Babcock's *The Zoning Game,* although written in a breezy style and not purporting to be social science, comes as close as any of the research literature to being a deliberate report of how one phenomenon, zoning, is viewed from different vantage points. Bullough's *Social–Psychological Barriers to Housing Desegregation* provides insights on the outlook of minority persons who have sought housing. The Northwood–Barth study also reports, from the vantage points of various participants, the process in which Negroes pioneered into white residential areas.

The Denton consultant report to the San Francisco regional office of NCDH, from which we have quoted at length, is a remarkable study of the workings of real estate institutions. It does have its limitations: It is, admittedly, mainly descriptive; it deals with the San Francisco Bay area (so that we are not sure of its national applicability); and it may reflect Denton's own biases and his role as consultant to NCDH.

Some dispersal of minority households will inevitably occur as suburbs continue their vigorous growth. However, very serious blockages will persist—reflecting economic disadvantage and social-status gaps, the outlook and preferences of minority persons, the dearth of homes within reach of moderate- or low-income families, and deeply rooted institutional practices that provide an intricate web of discrimination. This web, as we have seen, results from actions of many people—homeowners; developers; real estate brokers and others associated with the sale, rental, and financing of housing; government officials (elected and staff); and the citizenry at large.

In such a situation it may prove exceedingly difficult to measure degree of success in dispersal efforts. One is tempted to rely on quantitative measures of the size of the group induced to move. But we must also assemble qualitative evidence, so as to determine how successful the experience has been for the participants. In the long haul, it may be the favorable feedback from successful experience that will most effectively catalyze sustained institutional and attitudinal change.

Acknowledgments

The author gratefully acknowledges assistance from many persons, particularly in the form of criticism of a first draft. Included are Elliott A. Medrich, William L. C. Wheaton, Wallace F. Smith, Michael B. Teitz, William H. Hastie, Jr., Chester W. Hartman, Kenneth F. Phillips, Alvin Hirschen, Peter Labrie, Del Green, and George R. Swanson. Judith Riggs provided valuable editorial assistance. Vincent P. Rock, Amos H. Hawley, and members of the Social Science Panel of the Advisory Committee to HUD were at all points encouraging and cooperative.

References

Abrams, C. *The city is the frontier.* New York: Harper & Row, 1965.
Altshuler, A. A. *The city planning process: A political analysis.* Ithaca: Cornell University Press, 1965.
American Society of Planning Officials (ASPO). *Problems of zoning and land-use regulation.* Research Report No. 2 for the U.S. National Commission on Urban Problems. Washington, D.C.: U.S. Government Printing Office, 1968.
Anderson, M. *The federal bulldozer.* New York: McGraw-Hill Paperbacks, 1964.
Babcock, R. F. *The zoning game: Municipal practices and policies.* Madison: University of Wisconsin Press, 1966.
Babcock, R. F., & Bosselman, F. P. Suburban zoning and the apartment boom. *University of Pennsylvania Law Review,* June 1963, 3, 1040–1091.
Banfield, E. C., and Grodzins, M. *Government and housing in metropolitan areas.* New York: McGraw-Hill, 1958.
Beardwood, R. The new Negro mood. In [the editors of] *Fortune, The Negro and the city.* New York: Time-Life Books, 1968.
Beckman, N. Legislation review—1968–1969: Planning and urban development. *Journal of the American Institute of Planners* (AIP), Sept. 1970, 36, 345–359.

Bernstein, B. The distribution of income in New York City. *The Public Interest,* Summer 1970, (No. 20), 101–116.

Billingsley, A. [with assistance of Amy Tate Billingsley]. *Black families in white America.* Englewood Cliffs, N.J.: Prentice-Hall, 1968.

Biochel, M. R., Aurbach, H. A. Bakerman, T., & Elliott, D. H. Exposure, experience and attitudes: Realtors and open occupancy. *Phylon,* Winter 1969, 30, 325–337.

Birch, D. L. *The economic power of city and suburb.* Supplementary paper No. 30. New York: Committee for Economic Development, 1970.

Bouma, D. H. Issue-analysis approach to community power: A case study of realtors in Kalamazoo. *American Journal of Economics,* 1970, 29, 241–252.

Brazer, H. E. Some fiscal implications of metropolitanism. In B. Chinitz [Ed.], *City and suburbs: The economics of metropolitan growth.* Englewood Cliffs, N.J.: Prentice-Hall, 1964. Pp 127–150.

Brooks, M. *Exclusionary zoning.* Chicago: American Society of Planning Officials, 1970.

Bullough, B. *Social-psychological barriers to housing desegregation.* Los Angeles: Graduate School of Business Administration, University of California, July 1969.

Carter, R. L., Kenyon, D., Marcuse, P., & Miller, L. *Equality.* New York: Pantheon Books, 1965.

Chintz, B. [ed.], *City and suburbs: The economics of metropolitan growth.* Englewood Cliffs, N.J.: Prentice-Hall, 1964.

Clark, K. B. *Dark ghetto: Dilemmas of social power.* New York: Harper & Row, 1965.

Daniels, R., & Kitano, H. H. L. *American racism: Exploration of the nature of prejudice.* Englewood Cliffs, N.J.: Prentice-Hall, 1970.

Davidoff, P. Advocacy and pluralism in planning. *Journal of the American Institute of Planners,* Nov. 1965, 31, 331–338.

Davidoff, P., Davidoff, L., & Gold, N. N. Suburban action: Advocate planning for an open society. *Journal of the American Institute of Planners,* Jan. 1970, 36, 12–21.

Denton, J. H. *Report of consultant.* San Francisco: National Committee against Discrimination in Housing, 1970. Appendix J of summary report by NCDH.

Douglas Commission. *See* [U.S.] National Commission on Urban Problems.

Downs, A. Alternative forms of future urban growth in the United States. *Journal of the American Institute of Planners,* Jan. 1970, 36, 3–11.

Drake, St. C. The social and economic status of the Negro in the United States. *Daedalus,* Fall 1965, 94, 771–814.

Duggar, G. A framework for the analysis of urban development policy: Some financial factors in local programs and some implications. *Regional Science Association Papers and Proceedings,* 1956, 2, 210–224.

Duncan, B., Sabagh, G., & Van Arsdol, M. D., Jr. Patterns of city growth. *American Journal of Sociology,* Jan. 1962, 47, 418–429.

Dunleavy, Hal, and Associates. *Research report: Population, housing, jobs.* San Francisco: National Committee against Discrimination in Housing, 1970. Appendix H of summary report by NCDH.

Eley, L. W. Fair housing laws—Unfair housing practices. *TransAction,* June 1969, 6, 56–61.

Eley, L. W., & Casstevens, T. W. [Eds.] *The politics of fair-housing legislation: State and local case studies.* San Francisco: Chandler, 1968.

Foley, D. L., Drake, R. L., Lyon, D. W., & Ynzenga, B. A. *Characteristics of metropolitan growth in California: Vol. I, Report.* Berkeley: Center for Planning and Development Research, University of California, Dec. 1965.

Foley, D. L., Lee, D. B., & Appleyard, D. Social and environmental impacts of the BART system. In *Impact of the bay area rapid transit system on the San Francisco metropolitan region.* Washington, D.C.: Highway Research Board, 1970. Pp. 13–19.

Fraser, J. B. In Santa Clara Valley: The debris of development. *City,* Aug/Sept. 1970, 4, 21–30.

Fried, M., & Levin, J. Some social functions of the urban slum. In B. J. Frieden & R. Morris [Eds.], *Urban planning and social policy.* New York: Basic Books, 1968. Pp. 60–83.

Friedman, L. M. Government and slum housing: Some general considerations. *Law and Contemporary Society,* Spring 1967, 32, 357–370.

Friedman, L. M. Government and slum housing: A century of frustration. Chicago: Rand McNally & Co., 1968.

Funnyé, C. Zoning: The new battleground. *Architectural forum,* May 1970, 132, 62–65.

Gans, H. J. *The Levittowners.* New York: Pantheon Books, 1967.

George Schermer Associates. *More than shelter: Social needs in low- and moderate-income housing.* Research Report No. 8 for U.S. National Commission on Urban Problems. Washington, D.C.: U.S. Government Printing Office, 1968.

Glazer, N. Housing problems and housing policy. *The Public Interest,* Spring 1967, 7, 21–51.

Gold, N. N., & Davidoff, P. The supply and availability of land for housing for low- and moderate-income families. In *The report of the President's Committee on Urban Housing. Vol. 2. Technical Studies.* Washington, D.C.: U.S. Government Printing Office, 1968. Pp. 287–409.

Grebler, L., Moore, J. W., & Gusman, R. C. *The Mexican-American people.* New York: The Free Press, 1970.

Green, P. P., Jr. Land subdivision, In W. I. Goodman & E. C. Freund [Eds.], *Principles and practice of urban planning.* Chicago: International City Managers Assoc., 1968. Pp. 443–484.

Greer, S. *Urban renewal and American cities: The dilemma of democratic intervention.* Indianapolis: Bobbs-Merrill, 1965.

Grigsby, W. G. Housing and slum clearance: Elusive goals. *Annals of the American Academy of Political and Social Science,* March 1964, 352, 107–118.

Groberg, R. P. *Centralized relocation: A new municipal service.* Washington, D.C.: National Association of Housing and Redevelopment Officials, April 1969.

Grodzins, M. *The metropolitan areas as a racial problem.* Pittsburgh: University of Pittsburgh Press, 1958.

Gwartney, J. Discrimination and income differentials. *American Economic Review,* June 1970, 60, 396–408.

Haggstrom, W. C. On eliminating poverty: What we have learned. In W. Bloomberg, Jr., & H. J. Schmandt [Eds.], *Power, poverty, and urban policy.* Beverly Hills: Sage Publications, 1968. Pp. 509–530.

Hartman, C. Social values and housing conditions. *Journal of Social Issues,* April 1963, 19, 113–131.

Hartman, C. The housing of relocated families. *Journal of the American Institute of Planners,* Nov. 1964, 30, 266–286.

Hartman, C., & Carr, G. Housing the poor. *TransAction,* Dec. 1969, 7, 49–53.

Hastie, W. H., Jr. A relic of slavery: A study of the causes, effects, and parameters of American residential discrimination. Unpublished term paper, Department of City and Regional Planning, University of California, Berkeley, 1970.

Hawley, A. H., & Zimmer, B. G. *The metropolitan community: Its people and its government.* Beverly Hills: Sage Publications, 1970.

Helper, R. *Racial policies and practices of real estate brokers.* Minneapolis: University of Minneapolis Press, 1969.

Hendon, W. S. Discrimination against Negro homeowners in property tax assessment. *American Journal of Economics and Sociology,* April 1968, 27, 125–132.

Herbers, J. Suburbs accept poor in Ohio housing plan. *The New York Times,* December 21, 1970.

Huttman, E. D. Stigma in housing: International comparisons. Paper presented at American Sociological Association meeting, Sept. 1970.

Kain, J. F. Housing segregation, Negro employment, and metropolitan decentralization. *Quarterly Journal of Economics,* May 1968, 82, 175–197.

Kain, J. F., & Meyer, J. R. Transportation and poverty. *The Public Interest,* Winter 1970, 18, 75–87.

Kaiser Committee. *See* [U.S.] President's Committee on Urban Housing.

Kent, T. J., Jr. *The urban general plan.* San Francisco: Chandler, 1964.

Kerner Commission. *See* [U.S.] National Advisory Commission on Civil Disorders.

Key, W. When people are forced to move. 1967. Cited by R. P. Groberg, *Centralized relocation: A new municipal service.* Washington, D.C.: National Association of Housing and Redevelopment Officials, April 1969. Pp. 177–178.

Kolben, A. A. *Enforcing open housing: An evaluation of recent legislation and decisions.* New York: New York Urban League, 1969.

Kristof, F. S. Housing policy goals and the turnover of housing. *Journal of the American Institute of Planners,* Aug. 1965, 31, 232–245.

Labovitz, P. C. Racial change comes to the suburbs. In *Planning 1970.* Chicago: American Society of Planning Officials, 1970. Pp. 145–152.

Lansing, J. B., Clifton, C. W., & Morgan, J. N. *New homes and poor people: A study of chains of moves.* Ann Arbor: Institute for Social Research, University of Michigan, 1969.

Leacock, E., Deutsch, M., & Fishman, J. H. *Toward integration in suburban housing: The Bridgeview study.* New York: Anti-Defamation League of B'nai B'rith, 1965.

Leary, R. M. Zoning. In W. I. Goodman & E. C. Freund [Eds.], *Principles and practice of urban planning.* Chicago: International City Managers Assoc., 1968. Pp. 403–442.

Lilley, W., III. Housing report: Romney faces political perils with plan to integrate suburbs. *National Journal,* Oct. 17, 1970, 2, 2251–2263.

Lowi, T. J. Apartheid U.S.A. *TransAction,* Feb. 1970, 7, 32–39.

Mace, R. L. *Municipal cost–revenue research in the United States: A critical survey of research to measure municipal costs and revenues in relation to land uses and areas, 1933–1960.* Chapel Hill: Institute of Government, University of North Carolina, 1961.

Mack, R. W. [Ed.] *Our children's burden: Studies of desegregation in nine American communities.* New York: Random House, 1968.

Manvel, A. D. *Local land and building regulation: How many agencies? What practices? How much personnel?* Research Report No. 6 for the U.S. National Commission on Urban Problems. Washington, D.C.: U.S. Government Printing Office, 1968.

Marcuse, P. Integration and the planner. *Journal of the American Institute of Planners,* March 1969, 35, 113–117.

Margolis, J. Metropolitan finance problems: Territories, function, and growth. In National Bureau of Economic Research, *Public Finances: Needs, sources, and utilization.* Princeton: Princeton University Press, 1961. Pp. 229–293.

McEntire, D. *Residence and race.* Berkeley and Los Angeles: University of California Press, 1960.

Mercer, N. A. Discrimination in rental housing: A study of resistance of landlords to non-white tenants. *Phylon,* Spring 1962, 23, 47–54.

Meyer, J. R., Kain, J. F., & Wohl, M. *The urban transportation problem.* Cambridge, Mass.: Harvard University Press, 1965.

Meyerson, M., & Banfield, E. *Politics, planning, and the public interest.* New York: The Free Press, 1955.

Miami Valley Regional Planning Commission. *A housing plan for the Miami Valley region.* Dayton: July 1970.

Midpeninsula Citizens for Fair Housing. Racial Discrimination in the Midpeninsula housing market. Palo Alto: circa 1969. Appendix B of a proposal entitled, "Industry Subscription Services."

Miller, L. Government's responsibility for residential segregation. In J. Denton, [Ed.], *Race and property.* Berkeley: Diablo Press, 1964. Pp. 58–76.

Miller, S. M., & Roby, P. A. *The future of inequality.* New York: Basic Books, 1970.

Mooney, J. D. Housing segregation, Negro employment, and metropolitan decentralization. *Quarterly Journal of Economics,* May 1969, 83, 299–311.

National Committee against Discrimination in Housing (NCDH). *Jobs and housing: A study of employment and housing opportunities for racial minorities in suburban areas of the New York metropolitan region.* New York: NCDH, 1970.

National Housing and Development Law Project. *Handbook on housing laws.* Vols. I and IA. *Guide to Federal Housing, Redevelopment and Planning Programs.* Berkeley: Earl Warren Legal Institute, University of California, 1969–1970.

Nenno, M. K. Planning and programming for housing and community development. In *Planning 1969*. Chicago: American Society of Planning Officials, 1969. Pp. 59–66.

Netzer, D. *Impact of property tax: Its economic implications for urban problems*. Washington, D.C.: U.S. Government Printing Office, 1968. (Supplied by National Commission on Urban Problems to the Joint Economic Committee, U.S. Congress)

Neutze, M. *The suburban apartment boom*. Washington, D.C.: Resources for the Future, 1968. (Distributed by Johns Hopkins Press)

New York City Rand Institute. *Rental housing in New York City*. Vol. 1. *Confronting the crisis*. New York: 1970.

Newman, D. K. The decentralization of jobs. *Monthly Labor Review,* May 1967, 90, 7–13.

Northwood, L. K., & Barth, E. A. T. *Urban desegregation: Negro pioneers and their white neighbors*. Seattle: University of Washington Press, 1965.

Oakland City Planning Department. *Travel from West Oakland*. Oakland: Jan. 1970.

Pascel, A. H. The analysis of residential segregation. In J. P. Crecine [Ed.], *Financing the metropolis: Public policy in urban economics*. Beverly Hills: Sage Publications, 1970. Pp. 401–434.

Pettigrew, T. F. Racially separate or together? *Journal of Social Issues,* 1969, 25, 43–69.

Pignataro, L. J., & Falcocchio, J. C. Transportation needs of low-income families. *Traffic Quarterly,* Oct. 1969, 23, 505–525.

Piven, F. F. Comprehensive social planning: Curriculum reform or professional imperialism. *Journal of the American Institute of Planners,* July 1970, 36, 226–228.

Raymond and May Associates. *Zoning controversies in the suburbs: Three case studies*. Research Report No. 11 for U.S. National Commission on Urban Problems. Washington, D.C.:U. S. Government Printing Office, 1968.

Redwood, J., III. Relocation in the context of urban development: Another look at the physical, economic, social and psychological costs and benefits of forced displacement. Unpublished term paper, Department of City and Regional Planning, University of California, Dec. 1970.

Riessman, F. *Strategies against poverty*. New York: Random House, 1969.

Robinson, N. Civil rights and property rights re-examined. In J. Denton [Ed.], *Race and property*. Berkeley: Diablo Press, 1964. Pp. 35–41.

Rossi, P. H. *Why families move*. Glencoe, Ill.: Free Press, 1955.

Schermer, G., & Levin, A. J. *Housing guide to equal opportunity: Affirmative practices for integrated housing*. Washington, D.C.: Potomac Institute, 1968.

Schorr, A. L. *Slums and social insecurity*. Washington, D.C.: U.S. Department of Health, Education, and Welfare, 1963.

Scott, M. *American city planning since 1890*. Berkeley and Los Angeles: University of California Press, 1969.

Simpson, G. E., & Yinger, J. M. *Racial and cultural minorities: An analysis of prejudice and discrimination*. (3rd ed.) New York: Harper & Row, 1965.

Slitor, R. E. *The federal income tax in relation to housing*. Research Report No. 5 for U.S. National Commission on Urban Problems. Washington, D.C.: U.S. Government Printing Office, 1968.

Smith, W. F. *Housing: The social and economic elements.* Berkeley and Los Angeles: University of California Press, 1970.

Spatt, B. M. A report on the New York plan. *Journal of the American Institute of Planners,* Nov. 1970, 36, 438–444.

Spicer, R. B. Housing elements are taking shape. *ASPO Planning,* Aug. 1970, 36, 95–96.

Sudman, S., Bradburn, N., & Gockel, G. The extent and characteristics of racially integrated housing in the United States. *Journal of Business,* Jan. 1969, 42, 50–87.

Tiebout, C. M. A pure theory of local expenditures. *Journal of Political Economy,* Oct. 1956, 64, 416–424.

Tobin, J. Raising the incomes of the poor. In K. Gordon [Ed.], *Agenda for the nation.* Washington, D.C.: Brookings Institution, 1968. Pp. 77–116.

Toll, S. I. *Zoned America.* New York: Grossman Publishers, 1969.

U.S. Advisory Commission on Intergovernmental Relations. *Urban America and the federal system.* Washington, D.C.: U.S. Government Printing Office, 1969. Prepared by Allen D. Manvel.

U.S. Bureau of the Census. Trends in social and economic conditions in metropolitan and nonmetropolitan areas. *Current Population Reports, Series P-23,* Sept. 3, 1970b, (No. 33).

U.S. Bureau of the Census. Income in 1969 of families and persons in the United States. *Current Population Reports, Series P-60,* Dec. 14, 1970a, (No. 75).

U.S. Commission on Civil Rights. *Racial isolation in the public schools.* Washington, D.C.: U.S. Government Printing Office, 1967.

U.S. Commission on Civil Rights. *For all the people . . . by all the people: A report on equal opportunity in state and local government employment.* Washington, D.C.: U.S. Government Printing Office, 1969.

U.S. Department of Housing and Urban Development (HUD). *1969 HUD statistical yearbook.* Washington, D.C.: U.S. Government Printing Office, 1970a.

U.S. Department of Housing and Urban Development (HUD). *Housing and Urban Development Trends.* Washington, D.C.: November 1970b.

[U.S.] Housing and Home Finance Agency (HHFA). Changing a racial policy, Levittown, N.J. In *Equal opportunity in housing.* Washington, D.C.: HHFA, 1964. Pp. 17–27.

[U.S.] National Advisory Commission on Civil Disorders [the Kerner Commission]. *Report.* Washington, D.C.: U.S. Government Printing Office, 1968.

[U.S.] National Commission on Urban Problems [the Douglas Commission]. *Building the American city.* Washington, D.C.: U.S. Government Printing Office, 1969.

[U.S.] President's Committee on Urban Housing [the Kaiser Committee]. *A decent home.* Washington, D.C.: U.S. Government Printing Office, 1968.

[U.S.] President's Task Force on Urban Renewal. *Urban renewal: One task among many.* Washington, D.C.: U.S. Government Printing Office, 1970.

Warner, W. L., et al. *Social class in America.* Chicago: Science Research Associates, 1949.

Watts, L. G., et al. *The middle income Negro family faces urban renewal.* Boston: Research Center of the Florence Heller Graduate School for Advanced Studies in Social Welfare, Brandeis University, 1964.

Weaver, R. *The Negro ghetto.* New York: Harcourt Brace, 1948.

Weber, A. R. Labor market perspectives of the new city. In B. Chinitz [Ed.], *City and suburb: The economics of metropolitan growth.* Englewood Cliffs, N.J.: Prentice-Hall, 1964.

Weinstein, E. A., & Geisel, P. N. Family decision making over desegregation. *Sociometry,* March 1962, 25, 21–29.

Werthman, C., Mandel, J. S., & Dienstfrey, T. Planning and the purchase decision: Why people buy in planned communities. Berkeley: Center for Planning and Development Research, University of California, 1965.

Wilson, J. Q. *Urban renewal: The record and the controversy.* Cambridge, Mass.: MIT Press, 1966.

Wood, R. C. *Suburbia: Its people and their politics.* Boston: Houghton Mifflin, 1958.

Ylvisaker, P. N. Utter chaos or simple complexity. In *Planning 1970.* Chicago: American Society of Planning Officials, 1970. Pp. 6–16.

Factors Affecting Racial Mixing in Residential Areas

JAMES S. MILLEN

ABSTRACT: What conditions favor continuing movement into a neighborhood by members of different racial categories and what proportions are necessary to retain a neighborhood that is racially mixed? There is only limited sociological research in the area of housing and mixed neighborhoods. Insofar as many mixed housing situations have appeared to be without acute problems, they have not commanded attention. Existing research provides useful, but limited knowledge of the totality of the racially mixed housing experience.

There is considerable evidence that racial mixing in any given neighborhood is most easily achieved when residents are of similar socioeconomic status. In a mobile society, considerable instability is to be expected. However, there is no consistent evidence of a particular ratio or "tipping point" at which whites will move out of a neighborhood or refuse to enter. Stability depends on the total constellation of local circumstances. In some situations, instability may ensue at very low levels of nonwhite occupancy, in others, stability may persist with nonwhite occupancy approaching 50 percent.

This paper is based on a survey of sociological evidence on racial mixing in residential areas. Its chief concern is to identify the factors

James S. Millen is with the Department of Sociology, University of North Carolina at Chapel Hill.

that influence the appearance and stability of racially mixed neighborhoods and to assess their relative importance. It is directed toward the issues that must be considered by those who wish to facilitate racial mixing in the future. Accordingly, it is not primarily concerned with the present distribution of minority group residence, except insofar as this offers clues to continuing influences on racial mixing. Attention is concentrated on the housing market and the actions of those who may be directly concerned with it, whether as buyers, sellers, tenants, managers, or administrators. The actual progress of racial integration in housing will be greatly affected, on a national level, by economic and political conditions outside the housing market. It may well be that income levels and job opportunities among minorities and local or national political circumstances will have a great impact on integration in housing, but the focus here is narrower. At the same time, it is recognized that racial mixing in housing is seen by many as one means by which more general racial equality can be pursued, though its effectiveness in that respect is not examined.

The central problem dealt with can be stated briefly as follows: What conditions favor continuing movement into a neighborhood by members of different racial categories in such proportions that it will remain racially mixed? These conditions include social interaction and the degree of racial harmony in mixed neighborhoods, but these are considered mainly as they may affect stability as defined above in the narrower sense of multiracial entry. The reason for this emphasis is that the chief concern of public policy in the area of race and housing is taken to be the assurance of equal rights and opportunities for the acquisition of satisfactory homes. Our interpretation of what must be done to secure equal rights to different races must be influenced by observation of the apparent consequences of segregated and integrated living patterns, as the problem of equal educational opportunity has demonstrated. However, it would probably not be widely regarded as practicable or even desirable for the government to try to determine the patterns of residence or interracial association that may result from equality of opportunity in housing. Hitherto, the formal and informal operations of the housing market have restricted freedom of choice for minority group members. To enlarge their freedom is to permit greater diversity, not to seek a new uniformity in interracial living patterns. This is not to deny the need for affirmative action to overcome the effects of past inequality, but it does seem that the greatest scope for action is in

creating opportunities for individuals to choose homes, without
giving primary attention to the racial factor.

There has been a great deal of sociological research in the area of
race relations, and much of it has an indirect bearing on the problems of racial mixing in housing. The amount of systematic research
directly concerned with these problems, and in particular with the
question of entry into mixed housing areas, however, is much smaller.
The acute social problems of predominantly black urban neighborhoods have compelled the attention of government and of scholars
by their visible costs in violence, crime, and poverty. The growing
self-consciousness of black communities has drawn interest to programs designed to increase the resources of those communities. The
possibility of reversing the modern trend toward residential concentration of the black population (Taeuber & Taeuber, 1965) through
efforts to promote individual opportunities in the housing market
may seem small, while economic inequality remains so great. Moreover, the residential dispersal of blacks could hamper the growth of
their political resources on the basis of communal organization.
Finally, the opportunities for federal government action in the housing market may, in practice, be too restricted for programs in this
area to offer a quick route to improving the situation of racial
minorities.

Racial mixing in housing is, by its very nature, a dispersed process
less easy to focus on than the concentrated problems of the ghetto,
which helps account for the limitations of the literature on the subject. Many mixed housing situations have appeared without acute
problems and, as a result, have not demanded attention. Where these
situations have been studied, their small scale and diversity inhibit
generalization. Furthermore, what has been written is often descriptive, impressionistic, and strongly committed to particular policies.
Hence, it is cumulative only to a limited extent. Another difficulty
is that many factors that influence mixed housing have not been
stable. Laws forbidding discrimination in housing have been introduced, national and local government policies have been modified,
the policies and conduct of many groups engaged in the housing
market have changed, and the attitudes of buyers and residents
toward racial mixing have changed (Hecht, 1970). Although there
is a good deal of evidence concerning these changes, especially the
more formal ones, their impact on behavior in regard to mixed housing has not been studied systematically on a large scale. The diversity
and complexity of the issues make this far from simple, but more

could certainly be done, particularly in comparing the situation in different areas and types of communities and in studying the progress of racially mixed areas over time.

Three examples of the kind of research that is helpful for informal policy-making can be cited in this area. The first is the series of studies carried out for the Commission on Race and Housing in the late 1950's and summarized in McEntire's *Residence and Race* (1960). These studies, several of which are cited in this paper, cover a wide range of issues, though not always on a systematic national basis. The second example is the more recent survey of racially integrated neighborhoods—using a national sample, though concentrating on private housing—undertaken by Sudman and his associates (Sudman & Bradburn, 1966; Sudman *et al.,* 1969). Sudman's work is a guide to the national situation at one point in time, the result of factors operating over a long period in the past. It is thus of limited value as a clue to recent changes or the prospects of further racial mixing of residence. But, like the studies done for the Commission on Race and Housing, it does emphasize the range of situations and variables in racially mixed housing. This is important, whatever the gaps or defects of particular studies. Finally, the work of the Taeubers (1965), though not concerned mainly with the problems of racially mixed housing, deserves notice because it does examine the development of the Negro housing situation over time as well as nationally, using data from the 1940, 1950, and 1960 Censuses.

These comments are not intended to belittle the competence of many more restricted studies or the need for intensive treatment of single issues or neighborhoods. They are simply made to emphasize that broad generalizations of the kind made in this paper must be regarded as very tentative in view of our limited knowledge of the whole universe of racially mixed housing situations to which they apply.

The factors affecting residential mixing of racial categories will be dealt with here under a number of general headings. These represent an effort to distinguish the main issues or problem areas, though in practice the issues are interrelated. Under these headings a number of propositions or conclusions are offered, but these are not very specific, being rather an attempt to indicate the general trend of findings on each point. It should perhaps be emphasized that, in focusing on the topic of racial mixing in housing, one imposes a somewhat artificial unity and exclusiveness on a series of problems and situations that need not be experienced or conceived of as predominantly racial in character. In particular, the process of racial differentiation in the housing market overlaps that of differentiation on the basis of income and social status. Although it cannot be explained solely on economic grounds, without regard to race, the character of many housing choices would not be drastically altered by the elimination of racial prejudice and discrimination.

Definition and General Character of Racial Mixing in Residential Areas

Discrimination in housing, as well as segregation based on occupation and economic status, has affected members of all non-Caucasian groups living in the United States. In addition, Mexican-Americans, Puerto Ricans, and some ethnic groups of European origin have suf-fered in the past and often continue to suffer from racial discrimina-tion (McEntire, 1960, Ch. 4). The effects of racial discrimination, economic status, and voluntary clustering in an alien environment are intertwined. Americans of European origin have generally been able to exercise free choice in housing as their economic status and assimilation to the larger society increased, although attachment to ethnic identity and communities has often persisted through several generations (e.g., Gans, 1962).

Widespread discrimination and, hence, enforced limitation of racial mixing in housing have continued to affect some groups even when they are far removed from immigrant status and in spite of improvements in economic status. The situation of Jews and of Japanese-Americans reveals the operation of continuing discrimina-tion in the face of economic success. However, the most serious obstacles to racial mixing in housing, in view of their pervasiveness, rigidity, and the numbers involved, have affected black Americans. Most of the evidence dealt with in this paper concerns the mixing of blacks with whites of all ethnic groups. Nonetheless, the factors that affect this process apply for the most part to the residential mixing of any group commonly identified as a minority and possessing in-ferior social status in some degree. The extent to which individuals can be identified as members of a minority group and the nature of majority stereotypes applicable to that group vary widely. Individ-uals of many minority groups may "pass" as members of some larger or more acceptable category if their appearance is not too distinctive and they choose to suppress the cultural traits of their group.

Defined rather broadly to include any situation in which members of white and black America are so distributed that no visible or imaginary boundary can be drawn on the ground so as to separate the residences of each category into a distinct neighborhood, racial mixing of these categories has always been widespread in the United States. This does not mean that members of different racial categories have ever been similarly distributed. In their study of Negroes in American cities, the Taeubers found, using census tract data, that in every city studied a majority (usually a large majority) of Negro residents would have to shift from one block to another in order to achieve an even, unsegregated distribution. More crucially, the segregation of other ethnic groups and of different occupational groups, measured in the same way, has been found to be much less than that of Negroes (Taeuber, 1965, Ch. 3). Similarly, the degree of racial mixing defined by any spatial definition tell us little about the nature of social contacts between neighbors.

The survey by Sudman *et al.* did identify a sample of neighborhoods, defined as such by residents and local leaders, in which racial mixing of residents existed. Generalizing from this sample to the whole population, they estimated that, in April 1967, 19 percent of all U.S. households lived in racially mixed neighborhoods. However, the majority of these racially mixed neighborhoods contained quite small proportions of Negroes and so were integrated only in a very limited, though still important, sense. Of all households estimated to be living in racially mixed neighborhoods, 42 percent lived in neighborhoods with less than 1 percent Negro households and another 26 percent in neighborhoods that were 1–5 percent Negro. Because of this prevalence of slightly integrated neighborhoods, a smaller percentage of all Negro than of white households was estimated to be living in integrated neighborhoods in the nation as a whole. Eighty percent of the white households living in integrated neighborhoods were in ones containing less than 10 percent Negro households; two thirds of all Negro households living in integrated neighborhoods were to be found in those containing over 10 percent Negro residents. Less than 1 percent of white households living in integrated neighborhoods were living in those with majority Negro occupancy (Sudman *et al.*, 1969).

In spite of problems of definition and sampling, these figures do suggest some important points to be borne in mind when specific instances and problems of racial mixing are considered:

1. Most whites who "experience" racial mixing by living in a neighborhood containing nonwhites are in overwhelmingly white neighborhoods. They may have no contact with nonwhite neighbors and in some cases may not acknowledge their neighborhood as mixed. Very few whites live in neighborhoods containing more than 10 percent nonwhites.

2. Most nonwhites who experience racial mixing do so in neighborhoods with substantial, often predominantly, nonwhite occupancy.

3. Token integration is probably more widely accepted than the troubles of some pioneers would suggest, but it cannot provide racially mixed residence for many nonwhites. This would require that many more white households be willing to enter and remain in neighborhoods where 10 percent or more of the residents are nonwhite. This is particularly true of those metropolitan areas where much of the nonwhite population now lives.

The level of racial mixing between 10 and 30 percent of nonwhites in a neighborhood—which many proponents of integrated housing have seen as ideal because it would permit dispersed nonwhite residences while encouraging whites to remain, it is hoped, by preserving their numerical predominance—is therefore an uncommon experience, even for those living in racially mixed neighborhoods. If we add the requirement of stability—the continuation of both whites and nonwhites to enter the neighborhood in such proportions as to keep the racial balance of residents relatively stable—this "ideal type" of integrated neighborhood becomes even more unusual. It is, however, on this type of neighborhood that attention must be concentrated.

Token integration is a necessary stage in the enlargement of minority group opportunities. Although token integration appears to have made considerable progress, it is not an adequate solution and does not assure swift or smooth advance to more substantial integration. Racial mixing in neighborhoods with 50 percent or more nonwhite occupancy but including a substantial and stable white minority offers considerable potential for integration. It could be achieved by whites entering previously black neighborhoods, especially in the inner cities, a form of redistribution that would account for present economic limits on black movement. It would preserve the communal institutions and political strength of black people, while reducing their isolation and perhaps upgrading neighborhoods physically. Unfortunately, the widespread experience of racial transition and the tendency for whites to move out of public housing where non-white demand is high (McEntire, 1960, Ch. 18) do not suggest that such mixed neighborhoods will attract enough white residents. The exceptions to this are in limited categories, especially the young or old without children, in some older inner city areas with special social or physical attractions, or at high rental or subsidy levels. These possibilities deserve to be pursued, as they have been in some cities, but they cannot provide a substitute for racial mixing in those suburban areas, of varying price level and social character, where a large proportion of white America now lives. Such areas have attracted white people for positive reasons (better housing, more space, new communal facilities, access to employment), not predominantly as a refuge from black invasion of the cities. It must be expected that they will appeal to many more black people for the same reasons. In the strength of this appeal to members of different racial cate-gories lies both the need and the hope of success for more substan-tial racial mixing.

The "ideal" type of stable, substantially mixed neighborhood must then become quite common if equal opportunity in housing is to be realized. The ideal, however, should not be defined too narrowly. The dynamism of the housing market, continuing diversity of income and individual needs and tastes, and the maintenance of racial identity must all limit the stability and uniformity of neigh-borhoods.

The process of "filtering," wherein homes successively meet the needs of less affluent occupants as the more affluent move into new property, is widespread, though not universal (Smith, 1964). As long as there is inequality of income between races, this process must be expected to result in a changing racial mixture in some neighbor-hoods. Elimination of discrimination against nonwhites may make racial transition slower and less complete in these instances, but it cannot entirely prevent it. Areas undergoing social or racial transi-tion cannot be expected to display as much social cohesion as some more stable neighborhoods. The process of transition may indeed be marked by loss of the former identity of the neighborhood and modification of the boundaries recognized by residents, especially if racial transition is occurring.

Individual variations in attitudes and style of life will influence entry and social interaction in racially mixed neighborhoods. They must also be expected to permit neighborhoods with very different ratios of white to nonwhite occupancy. Consequently, no single ratio can properly be regarded as ideal, assuming—and this will not usually be the case—that anyone is really in a position to fix the ratio. The wide dispersal of black people into predominantly white neighborhoods is something that white people have the greatest power to promote or resist, hence the weight of attention given to white behavior in this paper and elsewhere in the literature on residential mixing. It represents, though, a more demanding social readjustment for blacks and a possible sacrifice of communal solidarity that many may not be willing to make. It is right that white people should seek to provide more opportunities for nonwhites to live where they choose, but the response that most nonwhites will make to those opportunities remains problematic and may alter the future character of racially mixed neighborhoods.

Racial mixing in residence is therefore feasible; it exists quite widely and can be expected to increase, provided the reduction of discrimination and economic progress and differentiation in the nonwhite population continue. However, substantial increase will require considerable readjustment by both whites and nonwhites and will produce a great variety of outcomes for reasons already indicated. How factors more specific to the housing situation may operate to channel this increase will be discussed in the remainder of this paper.

Type of Housing as a Factor in Racial Mixing

1. *Stable racial mixing is more easily achieved in rental housing than in areas of entirely owner-occupied housing, provided that management supports it.*

Two general arguments appear to support this proposition. First, the influence of central management of a group of rental properties can be used to facilitate entry by members of different racial groups, to help create an atmosphere in which racial mixing is regarded as normal and initial prejudices or frictions are overcome, and to maintain a housing environment that will attract different races on grounds of quality or value for money. Second, the fact that occupants of rental housing do not have to undertake a large financial investment makes it easier for both whites and nonwhites to overcome the element of risk or uncertainty that many are likely to feel in entering a mixed neighborhood. Whites, in particular, are often deterred from ownership in a mixed neighborhood by fears about property value. Nonwhites are more likely to be deterred from ownership by shortage of capital and by discrimination in the selling and financing of housing.

The proportion also requires qualification. First, the policy of management in rental housing has frequently been hostile to racial mixing. Such a policy, applied on a large enough scale, has helped create almost totally segregated neighborhoods. Information discrimination is still widely prevalent in the letting of rental property. Even where some mixing is accepted, racial quotas or selectivity, "benign" or otherwise, is common (McEntire, 1960; Potomac Institute, 1968). Second, the turnover of occupants in rental property is usually greater than in owner-occupied housing so that, where demand is racially unbalanced, where management is dispersed or ineffective, or where management decides to promote a transition from white to nonwhite occupancy, extreme instability is more likely than in an owner-occupied area. Management policy is thus a crucial factor, and the affirmation of this proposition rests on the expectation that an increasing proportion of managements will be persuaded to accept racial mixing because of legal requirements, social climate, and economic interest. Managers of rental property are more open to persuasion and pressure than the multitude of home owners, and once racial mixing is accepted they can do much to make it stable. Some of these arguments require further comment and illustration.

The potential effect of management and the fact that high turnover can be used to restore racial balance are illustrated by one of the studies carried out by the Griers (1960, Ch. 13). "Hillview," a private rental tract in California, was let from the start on an open-occupancy basis, but was not filled and became almost entirely Negro in occupancy. Under new management, following financial difficulties, however, white tenants were attracted in large enough numbers to fill the tract with two thirds white and one third Negro tenants, a considerable degree of physical and social mixing being achieved. Such a turnaround gives no assurance of stability (the tract was only 5 years old when studied), but the management planned to maintain this ratio. Their success in restoring racial mixing suggests that this could be achieved, as it has been for quite long periods in other well-managed rental developments (Potomac Institute, 1968).

The Griers do stress some other important elements in the situation: The area as a whole contained only 6 percent nonwhites so that demand from that group was limited; there were numerous white in-migrants to the area, who sought rental accommodation and were ignorant of the past history of the tract; the tract was well located and offered good value for money in a medium price range. These factors will affect the stability of any mixed housing area, rental or owner-occupied. Central management, either in rental housing or in developments newly built for sale, can manipulate the above stated factors, but not with complete freedom.

Much of the recorded experience of racial mixing in rental housing has been in public housing. Public-housing authorities in the North and West adopted open-occupancy policies in many places before legally required in private housing (McEntire, 1960). Public housing for low-income tenants has been concentrated in central city areas and has been exposed to heavy nonwhite demand. Therefore, substantial nonwhite entry has followed from open occupancy, not token representation of nonwhites resulting from high rents or in-formal selectivity as in some private rental developments (Grier & Grier, 1960, Ch. 9). Finally, the policies of public-housing authorities have attracted attention because of their visibility and potential influence. Consequently, some of the earliest and most systematic studies of reactions to racial mixing were made in public-housing projects (Deutsch & Collins, 1951; Wilner *et al.*, 1955).

These studies compared segregated to fully integrated projects containing a minority of nonwhites. In both studies, it was found that integration led to more interracial contact and to more favorable attitudes toward racial mixing. Wilner *et al.* (1955) noted the effect of management policy in promoting a social climate that legitimized and aided racial mixing. In spite of such findings, public housing has not in the past contributed as much as it might have to racial inte-gration in housing. Many projects have been formally or informally segregated, others have become predominantly or entirely nonwhite under the pressure of nonwhite demand and accelerated white with-drawal. The concentration and limited scale of public housing, re-sulting from local pressures and low national priority, indicate that racial mixing has not been spread very widely. Its potential impor-tance remains high, though, as a source of housing for low-income groups and so for many nonwhites, who are ill placed to seek new housing on their own. The subsidized rents of public housing can make it exceptional value for money and so attract low-income whites to mixed developments, particularly if these are dispersed in predominantly white or mixed neighborhoods.

The role of management as an aid to racial mixing in rental housing can be matched to some extent in new housing developments built for sale. These are often large and controlled by a single management, subject to the support of planning and financial agencies, which have often obstructed racial mixing. If the obstacles are overcome and the builder decides to sell on an open-occupancy basis, large sources of new housing will open up to minority group members who can afford to buy. This is now happening in many areas, and the volume of housing thus made available for mixed occupancy should help to overcome the problem of concentrated demand from middle-income nonwhites who faced pioneer developers of private mixed neighborhoods in some instances (Grier & Grier, 1960). The influence of the large developer as a maker and an executor of policy in this area is shown in the case of Levitt and Sons. In the sale of homes in Levittown, Pennsylvania, this very large builder maintained a policy of excluding nonwhites, but decided, under legal pressure, to sell to them in its next development in the suburbs of Philadelphia, Levittown, New Jersey. The influence of the developer on white residents who had opposed the efforts of nonwhites to enter the Pennsylvania development, careful planning, and public relations work resulted in the peaceful integration of the newer Levittown (Gans, 1967, Ch. 14). Nonetheless, the developer claimed to have lost white customers, in spite of the fact that the cost of the houses restricted nonwhite entry to a low level and ensured that those nonwhites who did enter were of relatively high economic and occupational status.

This example leads us back to the questions of property value, cost, and value for money as they are perceived by potential and actual residents in racially mixed neighborhoods.

The expectation that property values would decline steeply as a consequence of nonwhite entry in a neighborhood was long the common view among those professionally engaged in the housing market (Laurenti, 1961, Ch. 2). There is widespread, though scattered, testimony to its currency among homeowners. This orthodoxy has been attacted by a number of studies (Laurenti, 1961; Rapkin & Grigsby, 1960; Smith, 1964) and by many less systematic but well-informed observers, including professional real estate men. The circumstances of nonwhite entry are so various, as are the fluctuations of races, that precise conclusions are hard to draw. It appears, however, that in comparison to all-white neighborhoods of otherwise similar character (age, location, housing quality, etc.), property values in neighborhoods entered by nonwhites do not generally fall and have sometimes risen because of the concentration of nonwhite demand. In many instances, of course, neighborhoods entered by nonwhites have been old and declining in physical attractiveness; investment in property in such areas is likely to be insecure, whether or not their social and physical decline is linked to the race of occupants. Furthermore, sharp fluctuations in house prices have occurred following nonwhite entry in some instances. The fears of some white residents and the efforts of some unscrupulous real estate salesmen have led to panic selling and individual losses (turned most often to the middle man's profit, not the eventual buyer's). This is not the inevitable pattern, though; panic selling has not been general, even in those areas where racial transition has been progressing (Rapkin & Grigsby, 1960; Wolf & Lebeaux, 1969).

The argument that white people will be less willing to buy than to rent in racially mixed areas does not, therefore, rest on the certainty of declining values and should not be pressed too far. Clearly, whites do remain in areas entered by nonwhites and sell without panic or loss; some buy property in older mixed areas (Rapkin & Grigsby, 1960), and many buy in new developments entered by some nonwhites. Nonetheless, white entrants appear to be extremely sensitive to the presence of a substantial number of nonwhites in an area; and, where the alternative of buying in all-white areas exists, a moderate degree of sensitivity or uncertainty about the safety of so large an investment as a house can dry up or divert white demand. Rental property is not immune to such sensitivity, but the factors noted here of low investment by occupants, higher turnover, and central management appear to make it less vulnerable and therefore an important channel for the spread of mixed occupancy. In the long term, the property value issue, whose effect on potential buyers has not been examined on a large scale, should be reduced to its proper perspective. White buyers and residents (or nonwhites) will neither cease to be anxious about property values, nor are they likely to be convinced by academic studies of the subject; real estate brokers and other professionals, however, can have much more influence. However, the spread of some nonwhite residents to a larger proportion of neighborhoods of all age and price levels will reduce the possibility of white choice on purely racial grounds and encourage judgment of value on a variety of criteria, even though racial proportions may continue to be one of these.

The advantage of rental housing from the point of view of non-whites seeking to live in mixed neighborhoods can be expected to decrease with the elimination of discrimination in sales and financing policy and with improvements in their economic circumstances. In the past, the unwillingness of most financial institutions to advance money to nonwhites for the purchase of homes in mainly white areas has created a second barrier beyond the reluctance of most owners and their agents to sell. The claimed experience of those who did lend to nonwhites has varied (McEntire, 1960, Ch. 13; Helper, 1969). Apart from racial prejudice and the desire of whites to maintain segregation, the difficulty of nonwhites in raising capital for house purchases, and sometimes in meeting repayments, springs from the level of nonwhite incomes, shortage of assets and credit records, insecurity of employment, and reliance on more than one earner in a family. Increasing numbers of nonwhites are able to compete effectively with whites for financing, and large numbers have, in the past, bought homes, though mostly older and cheaper houses in areas already nonwhite or undergoing transition. It remains true, though, that rental housing can provide an accessible way for many nonwhites to obtain newer homes in mixed neighborhoods. This view gains some support from the finding of Sudman *et al.* (1969) that integrated neighborhoods have a higher proportion of renters than segregated ones and that nonwhites are more likely than whites to be renters in these neighborhoods. The integrated neighborhoods located in Sudman's survey tended to be older than segregated white areas and were not necessarily stable. However, in the narrower field of planned racially mixed housing developments, the survey carried out by Schermer and Levin found 91 rental projects and a number of mixed rental and owner occupied areas in a total of 154 developments. [This survey was wide ranging and claimed to be representative of successful, substantially mixed developments, but was not a systematic national example (Potomac Institute, 1968).]

2. Racial mixing is feasible at all price or rental levels, but stable and substantial mixing is most likely in the middle price range.

In the higher price range, minority group residents tend to be few at present; because of this and the likelihood that they will not fit white stereotypes, acceptance by whites should be easier. There are, however, many examples of resistance to nonwhites buying high priced homes (Hecht, 1970; Rosen, 1962), which cannot anyway satisfy mass demand. In low-cost housing, especially in the larger cities, nonwhite demand is much greater and white fears of declining amenities, crime, and racial conflict likely to be sharper. These obstacles to the maintenance of racial balance in demand can be overcome if the supply of new low-cost housing is sufficient and dispersed in location and if management of housing and neighborhoods is effective. The studies of private interracial housing by the Griers (1960) and the Potomac Institute (1968) both describe developments at a variety of price levels, and reference has already been made to racial mixing in low-rent public housing. The Potomac Institute study (Potomac Institute, 1968, p. 67) concludes that: "Partially subsidized moderate income housing seems to offer the best prospects for integration. It is at this level that the greatest overlapping of the white and non-white market occurs."

In addition to stressing the importance of those sections of the housing market in which strong demand from majority and minority groups can be sustained, this conclusion points to a further proposition.

3. Good quality and value for money are means of overcoming resistance to racially mixed housing.

An underlying theme of this paper has been that the effects of prejudice and discrimination in the housing market cannot be overcome by appealing to the ideals of tolerance and racial equality. These ideals exist and can be used to break down formal and informal barriers to racial mixing. However, they are not alone in most people's minds when they make decisions about housing, anymore than is prejudice, and they are balanced by strongly held values concerning freedom of choice and property rights, which apply more immediately to members of the majority group. Therefore, more material sanctions are needed to secure acceptance by the great majority who have not been exposed to substantially integrated housing situations. Law and official policy, firmly applied, can influence the professional "gatekeepers" of the housing market through negative sanctions. The positive inducements of housing and neighborhood quality are more easily applied to the mass of individual customers for housing. Since they apply to members of all racial categories they can be the basis of common interests where mixed neighborhoods have been established (Northwood & Barth, 1965; Wolf and Lebeaux, 1969).

Value for money is, of course, a major factor in the success of any housing development, but in the past discrimination and pressure of demand have compelled nonwhites to pay more than whites for comparable accommodation (Duncan & Hauser, 1960). If mixed housing areas are to attract white as well as nonwhite demand, it is important that they offer better and not worse than average value for money. In this way, both racial mixing and the improvement of minority group housing can be pursued. Studies of white buyers of housing in racially mixed areas indicate that they are attracted by the suitability of location, price, and quality to their requirements and not generally distinguished by unusual attitudes toward racial mixing. This was true of those who bought in the unpromising situation of older neighborhoods of Philadelphia entered by nonwhites (Rapkin & Grigsby, 1960, Ch. 8). It also applied to white buyers in the interracial developments studied by the Griers (1960), where white demand threatened to outbalance nonwhite demand in some instances, although the policy of racial mixing was uncommon at that time.

4. Location and neighborhood facilities are a major factor in housing choices and will influence the success of racial mixing.

The issue of location and neighborhood quality is in many instances linked to the presence or proximity of racial minorities, but it plays a large part in individual housing choices for reasons other than race and status. Customers will judge locations on the basis of physical appearance, proximity to work, friends, shops, and public facilities. They will also be concerned with the quality and cost of public services, especially the quality of education and, in some areas, the level of crime (Potomac Institute, 1968, Ch. 3 and 6; Wolf & Lebeaux, 1969; Grier and Grier, 1960). The association between low neighborhood quality in these respects and the presence of large numbers of nonwhite residents has probably done as much to deter whites from entering or staying in mixed neighborhoods as any distaste for interracial contacts, which are common in other contexts. While low neighborhood quality does not necessarily result from nonwhite or mixed occupancy, and can be avoided in such neighborhoods in inner-city areas, mixed developments in the suburbs do offer positive attractions of location to both whites and nonwhites; further, they enjoy some advantage in remoteness from the stereotyped image of the black neighborhood.

Proximity to existing nonwhite areas will also tend to influence nonwhite demand for housing and the expectations of white people concerning nonwhite demand. The effects of discrimination are hard

to disentangle from those of choice, but the pattern of nonwhite
movement into neighborhoods, adjoining those they already occupy,
will not be altered quickly by a wider range of choice, especially in
the face of economic inequalities. While this is true, the social character of such areas may change enough to discourage white entry,
even where the quality of property and public services is well maintained and many white residents stay (Wolf & Lebeaux, 1969). On the
other hand, nonwhites may hesitate to move to neighborhoods remote from existing nonwhite communities and their social institutions, even if they do not face active discrimination (McEntire, 1960,
p. 187–188).

The force and uniformity of these attitudes is by no means clear,
though, since the opportunities open to members of different racial
categories have been shaped by institutions responsible for the construction and sale of most housing. The choice of location by developers, generally influenced by the attitude of planning authorities
and sources of finance in favor of segregated housing (Grier & Grier,
1960, Ch. 6 and 7; McEntire, 1960, Part 3), has reinforced discriminatory marketing practices (Helper, 1969; McEntire, 1960, Part 3;
Hecht, 1970). Deliberate efforts to attract occupants from different
racial categories can succeed both in the suburbs and in inner-city
areas (Potomac Institute, 1968, Ch. 3). The question then becomes,
who are these people and in what numbers will they live together?

Social Characteristics of the Market for Racially Mixed Housing

*1. The market for racially mixed housing is not restricted to those
with very distinctive social characteristics or racial attitudes.*

This view has been implied by the preceding discussion that argued
that positive advantages in a home or neighborhood can outweigh
any negative expectations linked to racial mixing. Discrimination
and economic inequality have commonly distorted the balance between these positive and negative factors. Where the positive advantages of housing and neighborhood quality do coexist with racial
mixing, they are neither ignored nor destroyed; but the balance can
only operate fairly if demand from minority group members is not
artificially concentrated. Thus problems in attracting demand from
all racial groups tend to be experienced most strongly, while racial

mixing is spreading but still not general. Even at this stage, the experience of pioneering mixed developments indicates that efforts to appeal to customers with specially favorable attitudes to racial integration—through organizations favoring such policies—are neither successful nor required (Grier & Grier, 1960, Ch. 9 and 10). Although a few individuals will avoid or leave mixed areas because of strong prejudice, most will evaluate nonwhite neighbors on a less stereotyped basis and make pragmatic judgments of their impact on the area, without making any special effort to seek interracial friendships (Northwood & Barth, 1965; Williams, 1964; Wilner *et al.,* 1955). In established neighborhoods where minority group members have entered, a small number of residents who are particularly hostile or sympathetic to the minority group can, however, guide the reaction of the hesitant majority and so impede or facilitate racial mixing (Rosen, 1962; Hecht, 1970).

Entry into a mixed neighborhood is more demanding in some respects for nonwhites than for whites, since the former are more likely to be a small minority of residents and have to face discrimination and hostility. Nonwhites entering new mixed developments are also likely to differ more from the average member of their racial category than do whites in this situation. In a study that compared Negroes in mixed to those in segregated areas in the Los Angeles region, Bullough (1969) found that those who lived in the mixed neighborhoods ranked considerably higher than the rest of the nonwhite population in income, education, and occupation. This is to be expected in view of the gap between average nonwhite and white rank on these criteria. Bullough (1969) also found that nonwhites in mixed neighborhoods scored lower on measures of anomie, powerlessness, and feeling of social distance from other ethnic groups than nonwhites of similar socioeconomic status living in segregated neighborhoods. If this is true, then persuasive marketing and efforts to spread information about mixed neighborhoods will be needed if nonwhites are even to take full advantage of the opportunities that their current economic status allows them.

Evidence concerning the effects of education and social status on racial prejudice and discriminatory behavior is complex (Williams, 1964). Though there is evidence that prejudice declines with increased educational attainment and that discrimination is low in some high status contexts, the housing market allows those of higher socioeconomic status to avoid contact with nonwhites more easily than those of lower status. Thus, in a study of white attitudes in a racially changing area of New Jersey, Fishman (1961–1962) found that, although high status whites expressed more favorable attitudes to nonwhites, they were also more likely than lower status whites to move out of the area; they saw its relative quality and social standing declining, and they had the money to move elsewhere.

It should be noted that any type of housing, mixed or not, will attract residents with distinctive social characteristics in respect to age, family compositoin, income, and other criteria. Insofar as particular types of housing are suited to stable racial mixing at present, and this was argued above, then the market among whites and nonwhites for each development will be socially distinctive. The emphasis, though, is on the appeal and accessibility of these types of housing, not on the appeal of racial mixing.

2. Stable racial mixing is most easily achieved where residents from the different racial categories are of corresponding socioeconomic level.

This proposition does not rest on the assumption that homogeneity in respect to the socioeconomic status of residents is a desirable characteristic of all neighborhoods. Although many areas accommodate residents of disparate status as close neighbors, the trend in modern developments has been away from this. Individual attitudes to this factor vary, and, for some, heterogeneity, including racial heterogeneity, in a neighborhood is an attraction (Sudman & Bradburn, 1966). Nonetheless, to the degree that sensitivity about the effect of racial mixing on the quality and status of a neighborhood remains widespread, it can be reduced by homogeneity in other social characteristics. A number of studies of the reactions of white residents to nonwhite entrants in a neighborhood record the effect of perceived similarity of status and life style in overcoming initial reserve (Grier & Grier, 1960; Meer & Freedman, 1966–1967; Northwood & Barth, 1965; Wilner *et al.*, 1955; Wolf & Lebeaux, 1969). Direct observation of the status characteristics of other entrants of a different race is less easy for customers evaluating a new development; uniformity in the cost of housing units can have the same effect here in allaying anxiety about association with low-status neighbors.

It is possible that resistance by whites to racial mixing would be lowest where nonwhite neighbors were of higher socioeconomic status than themselves; this is a characteristic of some nonwhite pioneers (Northwood & Barth, 1965). However, it would be unrealistic to expect this to be true of any large-scale movement of nonwhites into mixed housing. Given equal opportunity, nonwhites are likely to evaluate neighborhoods according to the same criteria as whites and to choose the best housing they can afford. Racial mixing for its own sake is not the chief goal of either group and dual racial standards will become increasingly unacceptable. In the past, nonwhites of relatively high socioeconomic status have been compelled to accept such a dual standard. In search of better housing, they have entered mixed neighborhoods, but these have mostly been in areas whose attraction for higher status whites was declining. Consequently, these neighborhoods have not been homogeneous in respect to the socioeconomic status of the two racial groups, nonwhites often outranking white residents (Taeuber & Taeuber, 1965, Ch. 8). Heterogeneity in such circumstances is a situation forced on both racial groups. Desired improvements in race relations will follow from mixing on an equal basis in all cultural areas, not just from contact as neighbors on the restricted basis of proximity and concern for the neighborhood.

Influence of Racial Proportions on the Stability of Mixed Housing

It has already been stated that the stability—and so in the long run the existence—of racially mixed neighborhoods depends on the relation between racial proportions among existing residents and among new entrants. If a higher percentage of new entrants than of residents come from one racial category the neighborhood is, in this crucial sense, unstable. Racial transition is not inevitable where such a situation exists. The prospect of stabilization at a new level depends on the balance of demand from different racial groups over a long period. The important factor here is the reaction of residents and, even more, of prospective entrants belonging to the racial category that formerly provided most entrants. The establishment of equal access to housing for nonwhites, growth of the nonwhite population in many areas, and improvements in its economic status must lead to many unstable situations of the kind defined above. Complete racial transition can only occur if the demand for homes from the entering group is large enough to absorb all the property in the neighborhood; for this to occur when the entrants come from a minority group, their demand must be concentrated. Substantial transition has taken place in many inner-city neighborhoods in the past, but it must become less frequent as nonwhite demand is dispersed over more areas and price levels. Eventually, therefore, stability in racially mixed neighborhoods should be achieved at many different proportions of nonwhite occupancy.

This outcome requires that white customers should not avoid housing that represents good value for money just because of nonwhite entry. In the study of changing neighborhoods in Philadelphia quoted earlier, Rapkin and Grigsby (1960, Ch. 4) found that white purchases, though not stopped, fell off sharply in most cases in comparison with the level of demand a few years earlier. The difficulty in evaluating this and other examples of white response is that many factors other than the racial situation affect demand. If the overall weight of these factors of housing quality and competing supplies does not ensure continuing white demand at a reasonably high level, then even moderate nonwhite demand can take up all housing units coming on the market, create even less favorable expectations among whites, and so accelerate the transition process. This can occur, as Rapkin and Grigsby show, at very low levels of nonwhite occupancy. Accordingly, it seems that no level of occupancy by the minority group is low enough to ensure stability. On the other hand, if demand from the minority group falls off, is diverted elsewhere, or is controlled, then stability can ensue with any racial proportions. Demand from whites may often drop as the proportion of nonwhites rises, but no proportion of nonwhites is so large as to make social harmony within a development impossible, and there is no consistent evidence to identify a particular "scare point" at which whites will flee or refuse to enter; too much depends on local circumstances (Grier & Grier, 1960, Ch. 4).

Theoretically, it can be suggested that whites will respond differently to levels of minority group occupancy approaching 50 percent than to low levels. Low levels of minority group presence represent mainly a status threat to whites, and this type of threat can be overcome, as suggested above, by interpersonal contact and by evidence that the quality of the neighborhood is not likely to decline. However, if the minority group approaches the point of being a majority in the neighborhood, then it is more likely to be seen as representing a corporate power threat to local whites (Blalock, 1967). How far this proves true depends on the political organization of the area and of the racial groups in it and on the importance of the local institutions that may be threatened with take-over. In a small housing develop-

ment, the perceived threat need not be great, especially if some outside management of the housing exists. In a larger neighborhood,
given the current political climate, it may be very strong.

As a numerical minority, black people (and other racial minorities)
must accept an inferior power position in many situations, insofar as
these are defined on racial lines. They cannot, however, be expected
to discard the advantages of communal social and political organization that other ethnic groups have exploited. Consequently, strategies
for controlling racial proportions to ensure that neighborhoods remain mixed must be politically as well as ethically controversial. Even
if legal equality of access to all housing is ensured to different races,
the policies of those who sell or manage housing and of public agencies
will greatly influence racial proportions in different neighborhoods.

Control of racial proportions appears to be commonplace in mixed
rental developments. It can be maintained without the use of formal
quotas by the screening of applicants, or, more acceptably, by varying the level of promotion to different racial groups (Potomac Institute, 1968). When a policy of this kind merely involves the reversal
of the more usual practice of marketing to only one racial category,
no objection is likely. More deliberate manipulation of demand may
be accepted by members of all racial categories if they are anxious to
maintain racial mixing (Grier & Grier, 1960). However, such practices may well be unresponsive to the demand for housing from different races and too responsive to doubtful generalizations about
the effect of minority group presence. Their use in small numbers of
pioneer interracial projects is not a serious limitation on equal opportunity; their general use would be.

A stronger case can be made for the dispersal, not of racial minorities as such, but of publicly supported low-income housing outside the central city areas in which it has generally been concentrated.
This would, in practice, lead to more racial mixing in suburban neighborhoods and would involve some control of racial proportions in
these neighborhoods through the price mechanism that will operate,
in any case, as long as racial economic inequality persists. A further
gain for racial mixing might be that these developments would prove
more attractive to white families who qualified for such housing than
those in some inner-city neighborhoods. Limitation of the size of
such projects would reassure existing local residents and help maintain high quality public services, especially education, while spreading tax burdens widely. This argument, which has been stated co-
gently by Anthony Downs (1970), depends on the assumption that

low-income whites and nonwhites aspire to a middle-class suburban life style. This is uncertain, though suburbs are diverse and not all middle class; moreover, many nonwhites have entered them in recent years. Implementation of this policy would face serious political obstacles as well, but it has the strong appeal of linking efforts to deal with racial and socioeconomic inequality.

References

Blalock, H. M., Jr. *Toward a theory of minority-group relations.* New York: John Wiley, 1967.

Bullough, B. *Social-psychological barriers to housing desegregation.* Los Angeles: Graduate School of Business Administration, University of California, 1969.

Deutsch, M., & Collins, M. E. *Interracial housing: A psychological evaluation of a social experiment.* Minneapolis: University of Minnesota Press, 1951.

Downs, A. Testimony presented before the Select Committee on Equal Educational Opportunity of the United States Senate. Washington, D.C., September 1, 1970.

Duncan, B., & Hauser, P. M. *Housing a metropolis—Chicago.* New York: Free Press, 1960.

Fishman, J. A. Some social and psychological determinants of intergroup relations in changing neighborhoods: An introduction to the Bridgeview study. *Social Forces,* 1961–1962, 40, 42–51.

Gans, H. J. *The Urban villagers: Group and class in the life of Italian Americans.* New York: Free Press, 1962.

Gans, H. J. *The Levittowners.* New York: Pantheon Books, 1967.

Grier, E., & Grier, G. *Privately developed interracial housing.* Berkeley and Los Angeles: University of California Press, 1960.

Hecht, J. L. *Because it is right.* Boston: Little Brown, 1970.

Helper, R. *Racial policies and practices of real estate brokers.* Minneapolis: University of Minnesota Press, 1969.

Laurenti, L. *Property values and race.* Berkeley and Los Angeles: University of California Press, 1961.

McEntire, D. *Residence and race.* Berkeley and Los Angeles: University of California Press, 1960.

Meer, B., & Freedman, E. The impact of Negro neighbors on white home owners. *Social Forces,* 1966–1967, 45, 11–19.

Northwood, L. K., & Barth, E. A. T. *Urban desegregation: Negro pioneers and their white neighbors.* Seattle: University of Washington Press, 1965.

Potomac Institute. *Housing guide to equal opportunity.* Washington, D.C.: Potomac Institute, 1968.

Rapkin, C., & Grigsby, W. G. *The demand for housing in racially mixed neighborhoods.* Berkeley and Los Angeles: University of California Press, 1960.

Rosen, H. M., & Rosen, D. H. *But not next door.* New York: I. Obolensky, 1962.

Smith, W. F. *Filtering and neighborhood change.* Berkeley: University of California Press, 1964.

Sudman, S., & Bradburn, N. *Social–psychological factors in inner-group housing.* Chicago: National Opinion Research Center, 1966.

Sudman, S., Bradburn, N. M., & Gockel, G. The extent and characteristics of racially integrated housing in the United States. *The Journal of Business of the University of Chicago,* 1969, 42, 50–92.

Taeuber, K. E., & Taeuber, A. F. *Negroes in cities.* Chicago: Aldine Press, 1965.

Williams, R. M., Jr. *Strangers next door.* Englewood Cliffs, N.J.: Prentice-Hall, 1964.

Wilner, D. M., Walkley, R. P., & Cook, S. W. *Human relations in interracial housing.* Minneapolis: University of Minnesota Press, 1955.

Wolf, E. P., & Lebeaux, C. N. *Change and renewal in an urban community.* New York: Praeger, 1969.

Social Stratification in Urban Areas

CORA B. MARRETT

ABSTRACT: In general, the evidence supports the view that urban areas tend to be segregated by socioeconomic status. Incomes, for example, do tend to increase as one moves toward the urban fringe. At the same time, considerable hetero- geneity among suburbs exists. Not all outlying areas are uniformly of higher eco- nomic status than the city they surround. Yet disparities between the central city and suburb persist for virtually all large metropolitan areas. Moreover, the degree of social class heterogeneity lessens as the unit under study is reduced.

Five different rationales have been advanced in support of action to reduce socioeconomic stratification in urban areas. First, such action, some argue, would serve to increase the possibility of racial integration. Racial segregation, however, occurs for blacks at all economic levels; it is not the plight of low-income blacks alone. Reducing socioeconomic stratification need not facilitate racial integration. In fact, it might tend to increase it. Second, socioeconomic integration would improve job opportunities for the poor. Movement of low- and moderate-income families closer to job opportunities in the suburbs is persuasive, but it may not necessarily result in economically mixed neighbor- hoods. Proximity to jobs does not inevitably require neighborhood diversity, although it could mean greater heterogeneity among suburbs. Third, disper-

---

Cora B. Marrett is Associate Professor of Sociology, Western Michigan State University.

sion of low-income families will facilitate educational and social upgrading of lower socioeconomic groups. Research findings, though limited, suggest, on the one hand, that some low-income groups adjust more easily to middle-class ways and, on the other hand, that socioeconomically mixed communities do not necessarily upgrade the poor. Fourth, reducing stratification may be necessary to increase the supply of low- and moderate-income housing. While the supply of low-cost housing is below the level of need, the issue is territorial rather than social. Production is impeded by lack of availability of suitable sites. Space for low-income housing may require municipal heterogeneity, not necessarily socioeconomic mixing at the neighborhood level. Fifth, social class balance has been proposed as a means of improving interpersonal relationships in society. However, research indicates that neither home purchasers nor tenants seem to want heterogeneity. Moreover, a few studies point to the strains likely to become evident in mixed communities. Socioeconomic classes may differ in life styles and values, as well as income. In sum, a close examination is needed of the assumption that communication is improved and social relations are strengthened by heterogeneous residential areas.

One conclusion, however, is evident. The various ends sought in mixed socioeconomic developments imply different strategies. For example, action to stabilize inner-city neighborhoods may require emphasis on improved services and facilities for middle-class residents. The character of the schools, for example, may be a major concern. Alternatively, appropriate financial incentives may be essential to open up sites in the suburbs for low- and moderate-income housing. For attainment of some objectives, there is also need to explore mechanisms through which neighborhood homogeneity and suburban heterogeneity can be simultaneously accomplished. Recognition that low-income residents have not consciously chosen to live in homogeneous communities is essential. Measures that widen their options may disclose a rather different pattern of preference than that presently evident. It cannot be assumed that greater heterogeneity would produce a more tolerant society.

In recent years a substantial body of literature has appeared on the "urban crisis." Generally, the crisis referred to involves the concentration of low-income and minority groups in declining central cities and an attendant dispersal of the more affluent throughout other parts of the metropolis. According to a number of observers, efforts must be made to redress the racial and economic imbalances characteristic of many metropolitan areas. The call has been for a greater mixture of socioeconomic and racial segments in urban communities.

The movement against racial segregation can be easily understood given the heightened sensitivity to race in the society. An attack on the exclusion of low-income persons from particular communities, however, is a somewhat different matter, because there are no strong historical and judicial precedents opposing such exclusion. In fact, socioeconomic segregation in residential patterns has been an accepted fact in American life. In view of the support such patterns have received, it is pertinent to review the current attempts to alter the distribution of socioeconomic groups. A central question in the present discussion is: What are the ends to be accomplished through mixed community development? Although this presentation is by no means an exhaustive analysis of a very complex subject, some of the reasons why socioeconomic integration has been proposed are examined. The inquiry further discusses the social science knowledge relevant to the stated objectives, laying particular stress on those findings that may be appropriate to evaluating the given objectives.

The metropolis as portrayed in many discussions consists of a central city, heavily populated by the dispossessed, and a series of outlying areas that are politically independent of and economically different from the central city. Although the residents of these suburban jurisdictions have access to the facilities and resources of the city, the inhabitants of the inner core find their own geographic mobility strictly limited. This is the picture often given. To what extent is it consistent with the demographic analyses of urban America? What is the historical development of residential patterns by social class?

Social Class Distribution

In general, urban areas do tend to be segregated by socioeconomic status. Indeed, studies of social stratification have often used place of residence as both an indicator of and appendage to social class. As Schnore reports (1965a,b), income levels tend to increase as one moves toward the urban fringe. This patterning of incomes does not deny the heterogeneity that may be seen among suburbs. As Berger (1960) and Dobriner (1963) have found, not all outlying areas are uniformly of higher economic status than the city they surround.

There is some disagreement on whether the current socioeconomic distribution has always been characteristic of American cities.[1] Several references (Burgess, 1925; Warner, 1962) depict the pre-auto,

---

[1]The Pinkerton (1969) article is the primary source for this section.

pre-streetcar period as one in which the central city was rather heterogeneous. With the advent of improved transportation systems,
middle-income persons left the inner city to the indigent, and the
suburbs tended toward increased homogeneity. A second perspective
challenges that portrayal, however. Greer's study (1962), which asserts that suburban homogeneity was characteristic before the transportation revolution, argues that the greater mobility of the population has tended to produce more suburban diversity.

What inferences can be drawn from this research? Are urban areas,
especially suburban locations, becoming ever more homogeneous? Or
has the outward movement of the entire population made the urban
fringe more diverse than ever? The research, Pinkerton (1969) notes,
may appear contradictory and hence unclear until several circumstances are considered. First, different time periods have been used
in the historical analyses. Thus, the findings need not be inconsistent,
but may reflect instead change over time. Second, the unit of analysis
has not always been the same. Some studies have been of an entire
metropolitan area; others have centered on portions of that area.
Moreover, the definition of metropolitan area is not identical throughout the studies. Third, some incongruity may be a function of different approaches to social class. Although there is convergence toward
the use of income, education, and occupation as measures of social
class or socioeconomic status, not all research uses the same dividing
lines for each of these measures. Also, the number of class levels reported has been variable.

While there are undoubtedly some irreconcilable differences in the
research on urban class patterns, the material does tend to support the
conclusion offered in a 1965 report from the U.S. Advisory Commission on Intergovernmental Relations: The social and economic disparities between central city and suburb do not hold true throughout
the country, but they do apply to virtually all the large metropolitan
areas and to northeastern urban areas. The present patterns have not
always obtained for all locales, although they seem firmly established
in many. It also appears as if the degree of social class heterogeneity
lessens as the unit under study is reduced. When the entire metropolitan area is the scale for analysis, then notable diversity may be seen.
But tendency has not been toward a mixed class situation within a
given neighborhood (Pinkerton, 1969, p. 503).

It is against this background that attempts to increase socioeconomic mixture are being launched. Although social class "balance"
could be attained by a reciprocal move of suburbanites into the core

and the inner-city residents to the outer communities, greater emphasis has been placed on the latter movement than on the former one.

Objectives of Social Class Balance

The assault on socioeconomic segregation is being waged from very different vantage points and for markedly different reasons. One cannot assess fully the costs and benefits of socioeconomic integration without understanding the variety of goals with which it has been associated. The discussions on the topic suggest that greater income integration should serve to (a) increase the possibility of racial integration in the society; (b) improve the job opportunities of the poor; (c) upgrade low-income people educationally, socially, and culturally; (d) increase the supply of low- and moderate-income housing; and (e) improve interpersonal relations in the society.

As will be seen in the subsequent analysis, mechanisms other than socioeconomic integration may be more appropriate for achieving some of these objectives. Moreover, it is doubtful whether certain of the aims would be accomplished even if more economic integration were to occur.

RACIAL AND SOCIOECONOMIC INTEGRATION

It is frequently maintained that socioeconomic segregation exacerbates the problem of racial segregation in the society. Because disproportionate numbers of blacks are poor, policies and practices that limit the mobility of the poor are thereby seen as circumscribing opportunities for black Americans. Discussions on restrictive land use controls propose that since the vast majority of Negro families are part of the low-income housing market, only token racial integration will occur as long as no change occurs in the economic factors affecting housing. The challenge to zoning ordinances typifies the view that economic discrimination, whether intentionally or not, is highly similar to racial discrimination. As an opinion handed down in a recent court case holds (cited in Plager, 1970, p. 340):

Zoning ordinances have long been used to contain particular racial groups inside the ghetto. This has been true in school zoning as well as property zoning. . . . It is critically important to classify these zoning practices for what they are: sophisticated means of invidious racial discrimination; invidious because racial discrimination is difficult to prove in this otherwise acceptable means of city planning.

Efforts to link problems of poverty with those of race are understandable given the inferior economic status of many blacks and the attentiveness in the society to problems of racial discrimination. Undoubtedly, racial and economic factors can and do converge. Frieden (1968) contends that income segregation would probably have become weaker had it not joined forces with attitudes about race. Since World War II, large numbers of migrants to the central city have not only been poor but also have been black.

For many purposes racial and class analyses need not be separate. But the effect of both on residential patterns is not necessarily consistent. From their study of residential segregation in cities, the Taeubers (1965, p. 94–95) conclude:

. . . the net effect of economic factors in explaining residential segregation is slight. . . . Clearly, residential segregation is a more tenacious social problem than economic discrimination. Improving the economic status of Negroes is unlikely by itself to alter prevailing patterns of racial residential segregation.

The basis for these assertions is their finding that racial segregation occurs for blacks at all economic levels; segregation is not the plight of low-income blacks alone. Research on the ten largest metropolitan areas by Kain and Persky (1969) confirms the Taeubers' conclusion. That research shows that existing patterns of residential segregation cannot be explained by socioeconomic status alone. In Detroit, one of the cities included in the analysis, the researchers found that 45 percent of the poor white families lived in the suburbs, but only 11 percent of the poor blacks.[2]

In moving from studies of residential segregation to programs designed to achieve neighborhood integration, the need for distinguishing between class and race is again made evident. Based on a nationwide examination of attempts to attain racial balance, a recent report from the Potomac Institute (1968) reasons that moderate-income housing seems to offer the best prospects for integration. That assertion is consistent with Nathan Glazer's (1967) contention that the mixture of races of the same economic level may be workable,

[2]Zelder (1970) is highly critical of studies such as the Taeubers' and Kain and Persky's in which tract data are basic. The conclusions of these studies, he posits, are more pessimistic than the facts would warrant.

but integration across economic lines is enormously difficult. In the same vein Wolf and Lebeaux regard efforts to reduce racial and class segregation as often diametrically opposed. "The most stable, and [to the participants] the most satisfactory instances of racial mixture are those where social class is fairly uniform and comfortable" (Wolf & Lebeaux, 1967, p. 111).

Taeuber (1968, p. 11) points out that altering low-income residential patterns without eliminating racial discrimination could tend only to increase racial segregation: "Income improvements or housing subsidies enable additional white families to emulate the segregated residential patterns enjoyed by middle- and high-income whites." Similarly, if racial discrimination and any other race-connected factors that affect housing choice were removed, segregation along economic lines could still persist.

It appears, then, as if socioeconomic integration need not facilitate racial integration, nor is racial desegregation, if taken as a goal, dependent on the attainment of an economically mixed community. Resolving problems of economic segregation would not simultaneously reduce racial discrimination.

EMPLOYMENT AND SOCIOECONOMIC INTEGRATION

The isolation of the poor is thought to have serious economic as well as racial implications. From this perspective, the current pattern of income stratification "deprives the poor and members of minority groups from living within a reasonable distance of jobs" (Romney, 1970, p. 8). The problem has been made acute by the increasing tendency of industries to locate their plants in outlying regions. During the 1960's, more than 50 percent of all new jobs created in the standard metropolitan areas were outside the central city (*Michigan Law Review*, 1970, p. 340).

The view that the impoverished should have the chance to reside in the areas where jobs are emerging is a highly persuasive one. Those unmoved by the contention that socioeconomic segregation is undemocratic may well be affected by the argument that, unless housing patterns are changed, the vicious cycle of poverty in which so many are caught is not likely to be broken. The need to locate near job opportunities is a compelling reason for dispersing the poor, rather than improving the physical environment of the inner city.

This movement of low- and moderate-income families closer to job opportunities, however, would not inevitably produce economically mixed neighborhoods. If access to jobs is the sole intent, such could be attained through income-segregated neighborhoods. For advocates of mixed suburban development who base their position on the need for more employment opportunities, improved job possibilities could take precedence over social class balance. If the desire is for the opening of suburban housing chances to the nonaffluent, then it matters little if the housing is so situated that interaction among diverse groups occurs.

Heterogeneity within suburban communities, although not necessarily within each suburban neighborhood, is the aim of those who stress the importance of greater accessibility to jobs. Thus, this perspective differs from those for which success is indicated by the interchange of different groups within a neighborhood. Greater social class balance in suburban communities could improve job opportunities for the poor, but the attainment of greater proximity to jobs does not inevitably call for neighborhood diversity.

UPGRADING THE LOWER CLASS AND INTEGRATION

Closely related to the notion that the economic improvement of low-income families is dependent on their residential dispersion is the view that dispersion is also likely to result in the educational and social upgrading of the lower class. The view is indicated by Frieden (1968) who asserts that economic segregation into low-income neighborhoods produces social and cultural isolation into an environment that fosters defeatism and perpetuates poverty. From this standpoint, continued socioeconomic segregation can only aggravate current social problems; polarization will increase as long as opportunities for contact between different income groups are restricted.

In a paper that regards some of the tendencies toward income stratification in communities as legitimate, Downs (1970) emphasizes the injurious effects such stratification has on the poor. He remarks (1970, p. 21) that "major improvements of the conditions and characteristics of the socially, economically, and culturally most deprived households in our society require their removal from neighborhood environments where certain highly deleterious influences predominate." His supposition that the upgrading of the lower class requires the interaction of various income groups is a popular one among some scholars.

The social and cultural improvement of the lower class as seen from this point of view does not make the suburbanization of the nonaf-

fluent mandatory; interaction could be achieved if the more prosperous could be attracted to the central city. Whatever the direction
of the movement, the position indicates that low-income households
must be mixed with middle- and higher-income ones if the life chances
of the lower class are to be bettered. Downs proposes that within these
mixed areas low-income neighborhoods should not predominate since
that would drive out the upper-income households and diminish the
likelihood that a middle-class way of life would prevail.

In an essay highly critical of Downs' thesis, McKinney (1970) sets
forth an alternative to the scattering of low-income families as advanced by Downs. "This alternative road is the development and
evolution of the indigenous minority neighborhood sub-community
within a cohering larger minority community where the reality of
achievement, prestige, and power come into being and are recognized
both by the minority community and the majority community"
(McKinney, 1970, p. 9). What McKinney is opposed to is the seem-
ing cultural imperialism of an approach that imposes on the upper
classes the task of uplifting their inferiors. The improvement of the
ghetto, favored by McKinney and others, is supported because of
the belief that the interaction of lower- and upper-income groups
cannot, and indeed should not, compel the former to different life
styles.

Although not extensive, there are some social science findings
relevant to this issue. First, the research suggests that some low-
income groups adjust more easily to middle-class ways than do
others. In fact, in some instances the only difference between two
families will be an economic one, not one of life style. Success in
socioeconomic integration may be achieved through the selection
of lower-class families who are socially compatible with the more
affluent. Hartman suggests that this is essentially what has occurred
in some of the newer housing programs. After describing programs
involving leased housing and rent supplements, Hartman (1969,
p. 439) concludes: "In virtually all cities where these newer programs have been tried, the amount of meaningful social and economic integration has been minimal, and in some cases non-existent."
Where mixing has occurred, "the utmost care has been taken in tenant selection. . . ." The programs "skim the cream off the top of the
public housing population and in effect provide no information. . .
about the impact of and prospects for this kind of mixing."

Second, the research suggests that whether planned or unplanned,
socioeconomically mixed communities do not necessarily upgrade

the poor. Form (1951, p. 121) questions whether geographical proximity enhances social interaction and improves social life: "The hope to encourage interaction and cooperative experiences among socially heterogeneous people is not likely to be realized anywhere." The current state of knowledge on this problem is summarized by Keller (1966, p. 504):

The evidence gathered from new towns and housing estates throughout the world suggests that mixing groups may actually lead to hostility and conflict rather than to a more interesting and varied communal life, that the better off, no matter how defined or measured, refuse to live side by side, not to say cooperate in community clubs and projects, with those they consider inferior to them, and that those whose conceptions of privacy and friendship, sociability and neighbouring are opposed will soon find themselves pitted against each other in resentment or withdrawing into loneliness. Social contrasts do not, apparently, automatically foster either creative self- or community-development.

If it is a change in the life style of the nonaffluent that is the goal, then evidently some means other than social class balance must be sought. Balance could aggravate the very problems many wish to obliterate from communal life.

INCREASED HOUSING AND INTEGRATION

It is a well-established fact that the supply of low-cost housing is far below the needed level. Although a number of technological and labor breakthroughs may improve the potential for constructing more low-cost housing, actual construction cannot occur if sites cannot be obtained. The problem of site selection explains the support for mixed economic development issuing from certain sectors. As Stegman (1971, p. 5) notes:

... at the very time that a number of factors have combined to produce a supportive climate for initiating and sustaining high levels of production, difficulties in obtaining adequate and/or appropriate sites for proposed developments seem to be increasing in geometric proportion to output.

The ruling in *Gautreaux v. Chicago Housing Authority* has in some ways compounded the site selection problem, for it suggests that the courts are inclined to look with disfavor on the choice of locales in racially compacted central cities.

The need to enlarge the housing market, while simultaneously meeting the actual or potential demands of the courts, has resulted in a challenge to the socioeconomic homogeneity of suburban America. The appropriate locations, if they are to be outside areas of minority concentrations, are in suburban jurisdictions. But these are the very areas that have resisted the intrusion of the city's problems. In order to enlarge their base of support, those whose need is, in fact, territorial join in the cry against homogeneity. Apparently, greater interest is likely to be engendered if the struggle is against segregation than if it is for low-cost housing.

But this objective does not require the mixing of the rich and the poor; nonaffluent islands within prosperous suburbs could prove the much needed space. The scale at which socioeconomic integration would be observable, were this objective to be reached, would be the entire municipality, not the neighborhood. Although socioeconomic integration could be attained with a substantial in-migration of suburbanites, without some modification in suburban housing patterns, the results could be an even more limited housing market for the poor. Thus, the achievement of mixed neighborhoods is not, in fact, the central thrust of the argument among some who challenge suburban exclusiveness: The goal is space for low-income housing.

IMPROVED RELATIONSHIPS AND INTEGRATION

Social class balance has also been proposed as a means for improving interpersonal relations in the society. The physical separation typical of metropolitan areas has supposedly decreased the ability of people from different backgrounds "to communicate with each other about the problems which clearly affect everyone" (Romney, 1970, p. 4). In contrast to the concern for uplifting the lower class, this objective postulates mutual benefits of integration. As Gans (1961, p. 177) points out, those who support this view see socioeconomic heterogeneity as promoting tolerance of social and cultural differences, thus reducing political conflict and encouraging democratic practices. Bauer (1951, p. 23) sees segregation along economic lines as problematic, not just for the low-income person shut off from employment opportunities or inadequately housed, but for the society as a whole. Socioeconomic segregation is to her objectionable because it is "alien both to our traditions and our concept of social progress."

Research suggests that mixed communities are difficult to achieve. Gans (1961) states that neither home purchasers nor tenants seem to want heterogeneity, and the housing market is not organized to provide it. He reports an instance in which, once the difference of about 20 percent in the cost of adjacent homes was passed, the developers found unsalable homes on their hands. It may be difficult to build the kind of neighborhood that can attract the full spectrum of socio-economic groups found in the metropolis.

A few studies also point to the economic strains likely to become evident in mixed communities. In his analysis of the Levittowners, Gans found that the upper-middle-class residents desired extensive school facilities while the working class rejected these as expensive frills (cited in Michelson, 1970). The low-income family may incur a number of added costs by its move to the suburbs. Moreover, the facilities it regards as adequate may be thought totally unsatisfactory by the other residents.

Socioeconomic status does not tend to be purely a matter of income; classes may differ in their life styles and values as well. It is this contrast that apparently renders heterogeneity problematic. Keller (1966) notes that unequal groups tend to pull apart; the better-off, more respectable, or more ambitious shun contact with those they regard as their inferiors. Michelson (1970, p. 79) cites a study that supports Keller's view. In a mixed-class suburb, the research found that the working-class wives had difficulty adjusting, for they lacked the social skills necessary for informal interaction with the middle-class women. Similarly, Gans reports (cited in Michelson, 1970) that the working-class residents of Levittown withdrew to themselves, feeling uncomfortable in interaction with their more affluent neighbors.

Despite continued support for mixed communities, the efforts have not been impressive. Thus, a very close examination of the assumption that communication is improved and social relations strengthened by the establishment of economically heterogeneous communities is needed. It is not concluded here, however, that nothing can be accomplished through the alteration of neighborhood patterns. Rather, this paper argues that we must be clear on the disadvantages as well as on the advantages that mixed communities might bring. Heterogeneity is not totally good or bad.

Mixed Communities: Remaining Issues

Throughout, the discussion has submitted that a variety of motives exist for greater socioeconomic heterogeneity. Some of the motives are concerned primarily with improving the life of the nonaffluent.

Consequently, they neither inevitably require the intermixture of different social classes within a given neighborhood, nor do they necessitate the outward flow of inner-city residents. But other motives would be thwarted were the ghettos rebuilt, rather than obliterated. Kain and Persky (1969, p. 77) remark that two possibilities currently exist: the improvement of the ghetto—or "ghetto gilding"—and ghetto dispersal. Of the two, "only the latter is consistent with the stated goals of American society." Kain and Persky argue for dispersal on a pragmatic basis: "As long as the ghetto exists, most of white America will write off the central city." Thus, their opposition to ghetto gilding is not ideological; it is based on the position that, given current conditions, the ghettos will not be gilded.

Evidently, the various ends sought in mixed development require different strategies. If it is an improvement of opportunities for the nonaffluent that is envisioned, then the attraction of upper-income groups to the central city may be as critical as the suburban migration of the poor. Thus, the problem would become: How can the central city become more heterogeneous? Relevant here would be the social science findings on the factors affecting housing choice among population groups. The programs that have been undertaken to stabilize inner-city neighborhoods may be particularly insightful. These efforts stress the importance of good services and facilities to middle-class residents. The flight to the suburbs has often taken place because of the deterioration of neighborhood services.

The nature of the schools is likely to be a major concern. As the Potomac Institute study (1968, p. 18) observes, "If family-type housing is involved, neither white nor Negro middle-class families will remain in an area that does not provide high quality schools." Wolf (1965) reviews the data on school and residence and reports that parents with high educational aspirations for their children would like to avoid classroom situations where teachers must spend time compensating for educational deficiency. Middle-class parents, she notes, are reluctant to have their children in classrooms with too many children from lower social strata.

If the problem is that of bringing back to the city those with substantial economic resources, not the interaction of the rich and the poor, then the community may have to be so structured as to meet the interests of the more prosperous. This could result in the isolation of the middle- and upper-income residents from the other inhabitants. The consequence would be heterogeneity at the tract level, but little interaction among the various socioeconomic groups.

Different strategies would be required if it is assumed that low-income residences must be created on the urban periphery. The argument has been made that the poor are desired by neither the central city nor the suburb. Changes in residential patterns are not likely if the appeal is only to the suburbanite's sense of fair play. Instead, various incentives may be needed to induce outlying jurisdictions to admit low- and moderate-income housing. In order for dispersal to occur, financial arrangements must be made in which the expenses incurred in a middle-class suburb as the result of low-income migration would be shared by the city.

Although the available evidence does not tend to show greater harmony resulting from heterogeneity, it does not deny that economic and housing improvements may accompany changed patterns of suburbanization. Moreover, there are other qualifications that should be borne in mind. First, the scale of development is significant. Michelson (1970) concludes that heterogeneity within the city block is difficult to sustain, for it is among neighbors that social interaction is likely to occur and that social evaluations are made. A homogeneous block need not require total community uniformity, however. Keller (1966) suggests that there may be certain mechanisms through which neighborhood homogeneity and community heterogeneity could be simultaneously accomplished. Facilities and services could be so arranged as to necessitate some social class interchange. For this to succeed, however, the services must be essential to all groups.

Second, as Gans (1961, p. 182) acknowledges, the acceptance of economic homogeneity should not serve as justification for racial discrimination. Persons with economic resources cannot be denied residence in a neighborhood because they differ in skin color from most of the residents. But is racial heterogeneity any more justifiable than economic diversity? Should not the desire for a racially homogeneous area be as seriously regarded as an interest in maintaining economic exclusivity? Gans argues that there is a difference, that there is governmental support for the individual who chooses to move into a neighborhood where the residents are of a different racial background. If his move disturbs the community's life, "it is an unfortunate but irrelevant consequence. Freedom of choice, civil rights, and the protection of minority interests are of higher priority than peaceful social life or consensus" (Gans, 1961, p. 182). Gans' statement implies that, in many instances, policies cannot be based on the stated preferences of segments of the population: Some larger good must be considered. There are those who have applied this argument to the economic situation, maintaining that the society can ill-afford to regard only the wishes of the more affluent.

At present, Gans' position is well-founded, because economic integration has low priority in the society. This is not so for racial integration.

Third, it should be noted that the homogeneity that occurs voluntarily in suburban areas is not equivalent to the enforced homogeneity in dilapidated areas. After citing some of the factors retarding mixed communities, Michelson proceeds to discuss some of the social class similarities that exist. Such an analysis is a worthwhile corrective to the position that maintains that the poor are as desirous of retaining their current situation as are the rich. Low-income persons may not aspire to be pioneers in middle-income neighborhoods, but this does not connote total satisfaction with their circumstances. It must be continually recognized that low-income residents have not consciously chosen to live in homogeneous communities; they have not deliberately selected as neighbors those who reflect their own values and concerns.

Continued homogeneity at the level of the city block should not spell inadequate housing for the impoverished. The quality of housing is a different issue from the composition of the neighborhood.

Some final remarks are in order on the nature of social science research in this area. At present, many of the arguments both for and against mixing are based more on ideology than on concrete evidence. More intelligent policies can be made and more informed decisions reached when substantially more study is given to the issue. Analyses of the nature of interaction in mixed communities, as well as of the changes individuals have undergone as they move into heterogeneous areas, could be highly significant. The arguments have been notably stronger than the empirical data. Unquestionably, balance is a complex issue, and persons would be misled if they assumed that heterogeneity would necessarily produce a more tolerant society. Failure to attain a given end through mixing does not mean that none of the goals associated with mixing are unrealistic. The selection of attainable ends would be greatly facilitated if the current work on socioeconomic diversity were to be augmented.

References

Bauer, C. Social questions in housing and community planning. *Journal of Social Issues*, 1951, 7, 1–33.

Berger, B. M. *Working class suburb.* Berkeley: University of California Press, 1960.

Burgess, E. W. The growth of the city: An introduction to a research project. In R. E. Park, E. W. Burgess, & R. D. McKenzie [Eds.], *The city*. Chicago: University of Chicago Press, 1925. Pp. 47–62.

Dobriner, W. *Class in suburbia*. Englewood Cliffs, N.J.: Prentice-Hall, 1963.

Downs, A. Testimony presented before the Select Committee on Equal Educational Opportunity of the United States Senate. Washington, D.C., September 1, 1970.

Frieden, B. J. Housing and national urban goals: Old policies and new facilities. In J. Q. Wilson [Ed.], *The metropolitan enigma*. Cambridge, Mass.: Harvard University Press, 1968. Pp. 159–204.

Form, W. Stratification in low and middle income housing areas. *Journal of Social Issues*, 1951, 7, 116–117.

Gans, H. J. The balanced community: Homogeneity or heterogeneity in residential areas? *Journal of the American Institute of Planners*, August 1961, 27, 176–184.

Glazer, N. Housing problems and housing policies. *The Public Interest*, Spring 1967, 7, 21–51.

Greer, S. *Governing the metropolis*. New York: John Wiley, 1962.

Hartman, C. W. The politics of housing. In A. Shank [Ed.], *Political Power and the Urban Crisis*. Boston: Holbrook Press, 1969. Pp. 433–447.

Kain, J. F., & Persky, J. J. Alternatives to the gilded ghetto. *The Public Interest*, Winter 1969, 14, 74–87.

Keller, S. Social class in physical planning. *International Social Science Journal*, 1966, 18, 494–512.

McKinney, H. C. Observations on residential desegregation and/or minority community/sub-community development, 1970.

Michelson, W. *Man and his urban environment*. Reading, Mass.: Addison-Wesley Publishing Co., 1970.

Michigan Law Review. Constitutional law: Snob zoning. *Michigan Law Review*, Dec. 1970, 69, 339–359.

Plager, S. J. Judicial review: Recent decisions in planning law: 1969. *Journal of the American Institute of Planners*, Sept. 1970, 36, 335–344.

Pinkerton, J. R. City–suburban residential patterns by social class: A review of the literature. *Urban Affairs Quarterly*, June 1969, 4, 499–519.

Potomac Institute. *Housing guide to equal opportunity*. Washington, D.C.: Potomac Institute, 1968.

Romney, G. Statement before the Select Committee on Equal Education Opportunity of the United States Senate. Washington, D.C., September 1, 1970.

Schnore, L. F. On the spatial structure of cities in the two Americas. In P. M. Hauser & L. F. Schnore [Eds.], *The study of urbanization*. New York: John Wiley, 1965a. Pp. 347–398.

Schnore, L. F. Social class segregation among nonwhites in metropolitan centers. *Demography*, 1965, 2, 126–133.

Stegman, M. National housing and land use policy conflicts: The social significance of Operation Breakthrough. Unpublished paper prepared for Division of Behavioral Sciences, National Academy of Sciences. 1970.

Taeuber, K. The effect of income redistribution on racial residential segregation. *Urban Affairs Quarterly*, Sept. 1968, 4, 5–14.

Taeuber, K., & Taeuber, A. F. *Negroes in cities.* Chicago: Aldine, 1965.

U.S. Advisory Commission on Intergovernmental Relations (ACIR). *Metropolitan social and economic disparities: Implications for intergovernmental relations in central cities and suburbs.* Washington, D.C.: ACIR, 1965.

Warner, S. B. *Streetcar suburbs.* Cambridge, Mass.: MIT and Harvard University Press, 1962.

Wolf, E. The Baxter area: A new trend in neighborhood change? *Phylon*, Winter 1965, 26, 344–353.

Wolf, E., & Lebeaux, C. Class and race in the changing city. In L. F. Schnore [Ed.], *Social science and the city.* New York: Sage Publications, 1967. Pp. 99–129.

Zelder, R. Residential segregation: Can nothing be accomplished? *Urban Affairs Quarterly*, March 1970, 5, 265–277.

Social Classes
in Cities
and Suburbs

LEO F. SCHNORE

ABSTRACT: City–suburban differentiation represents another manifestation of
the three dimensions of segregation according to which urban Americans have
sorted themselves out in space—that is, color or ethnicity, socioeconomic class,
and type of family. Very little work has simultaneously considered color and
class. Moreover, the research literature reflects confusion about the main trends
in the relationship of cities and suburbs. However, one important point does
tend to emerge from the material: The social class structure of our metropolitan
areas appears to be more varied and complex than many have tended to believe.
In northern metropolitan areas, for example, the percentage of higher-income
nonwhite families is found to rise with distance from central cities just as it does
for white families. Socioeconomic residential differentiation for both groups is
continuing.

The knowledge available that bears on the probable success of a policy of
socioeconomic mixing is limited. There is need for an enlarged and coherent
research effort along the following lines: replication of prior research using the
1970 Census data; longitudinal studies of historical trends; simultaneous observation of both color and class segregation; metropolitan-wide analyses; and
special attention to changes introduced by annexation. Also needed is more

Leo F. Schnore is Professor of Sociology, University of Wisconsin.

intensive examination of suburbanization of the population at large, the functions of individual suburbs, and segregation of family type.

The "urban crisis" is multifaceted; the prominent theme espoused by
policy-makers and social scientists involves a marked polarization of
cities and suburbs according to color and class. Cities, it is said, are
increasingly left to the blacks and the poor, while the white middle
class continues to abandon the center in a mass exodus to the suburbs. The Nixon administration has made it clear that these apparent
trends must be altered. In the absence of heroic measures, it would
seem, we will soon see only poverty-stricken black cores surrounded
by white rings of affluence. Urban and rural "community development" must occur, but without force or extreme measures. Even the
Congress has taken cognizance of the problem. As Representative
Ashley (1969, p. 1) observed at the first hearing (June 3, 1969) of
the *Ad Hoc* Subcommittee on Urban Growth of the House Banking
and Currency Committee,

By the end of this century our nation will have another 100 million people,
according to most demographers. . . . First we will examine the dimensions of
this growth. Where will the growth take place? In rural, inner-city, or suburban
areas? Where do people want to live? Do they move to large metropolitan areas
because they prefer them or because of job opportunites? What will be the future
of the core city, the suburban ring, the rural small towns?

The city–suburb polarization theme has received considerable attention in the urban research literature. Surveying the available
empirical material, one concludes that this city-suburban differentiation simply represents another manifestation of the three principles
of segregation according to which American urbanites have long been
"sifted and sorted" in space. These three principles are color or ethnicity, social class, and type of family. Evidently the greatest attention has been given to color and ethnicity and the least to family type.
As for socioeconomic status, a substantial amount of effort has been
directed toward describing the residential location of social classes.
Regrettably, very little work has involved simultaneous consideration
of color *and* class; it is commonly believed that a certain fraction of
segregation by color is attributable to economic (class) factors, but
it is becoming increasingly evident that this is a small fraction indeed
and that black disadvantages in educational attainment, occupational
achievement, and income account for only a modest amount of their
observable segregation in urban space. It is the force of discrimina-

tion on the basis of color that is the principal factor underlying segregation. The blacks simply have sharply limited options, with respect to housing "choices," and nothing is to be gained by ignoring or minimizing that fact.

In any event, the problem of polarization by color and class has vitally important implications. Segregation in our schools, for example, follows residential segregation wherever a "neighborhood" pattern of districts is followed. Less demonstrable is the possibility that segregation by color is a potent factor in generating the kind of racial unrest that exploded with such devastating force in Watts, Hough, Newark, and Detroit. Clearly, more careful research is needed; in the meantime, however, there is a body of facts at our disposal that cannot be dismissed.

City–Suburban Status Differences: Cross-Sectional Evidence

1950 EVIDENCE

The first hint of the fact that suburban populations are not inevitably higher in status than those of the cities they surround was presented in a doctoral dissertation based on census materials (Schnore, 1955, Ch. 3). Data for 1950, based on all three measures of status, showed a clear-cut association between city size and the direction of city–suburban status differences. When cities (roughly grouped in three size classes) and their metropolitan rings were examined, it was found that higher "suburban" status occurred only around large cities, i.e., those of 500,000 or more inhabitants in 1950. Smaller cities exhibited higher values on all three status measures than their suburbs (Table 1).

The 1950 Census materials were also useful in delineating the complications caused by color in the comparison of city and suburban socioeconomic status. Table 2 illustrates the kind of paradox that may emerge when color and class are considered simultaneously. In the Chattanooga Standard Metropolitan Area (SMA), the median family income of ring inhabitants was clearly higher than that of all city dwellers. Examination of city–suburban income differentials by color, however, revealed that city incomes were higher—on the average—for both whites and nonwhites (chiefly Negroes)! The explanation is simple: Chattanooga's "ring" was overwhelmingly white, and nonwhites were much more heavily represented in the city itself.

TABLE 1 City–Suburban Status Differences by City Size, 1950[a]

Status Measure	Large Cities (500,000 or more)(%)	Middle-Sized Cities (100–500,000)(%)	Small Cities (50–100,000)(%)
Median family income			
Ring higher	95	37	19
City higher	5	63	81
Median school years completed			
Ring higher	74	40	24
City higher	26	60	76
Proportion of employed males in professional occupations			
Ring higher	68	35	15
City higher	32	65	85
Number of SMA's[b]	19	75	74

[a]Adapted from Schnore and Varley (1955).
[b]Equals 100 percent for each panel.

Nonwhites comprised only 4.8 percent of the ring population, but 30.0 percent of the city population. The higher average income of the more numerous suburban whites raised the overall suburban average income to a point above that of the city, while the lower incomes of the city nonwhites depressed the city average.

1960 EVIDENCE

Much more detailed studies of city–suburban status differences were conducted on the basis of 1960 Census data for urbanized areas (UA). (As noted above, the outlying portion of the UA is a more satisfactory areal unit than the metropolitan ring for representing the "suburban"

TABLE 2 Median Family Income, by Color and Residence, Chattanooga SMA, 1950[a]

Color	Median Family Income, Entire SMA ($)	Median Family Income, City ($)	Median Family Income, Ring ($)
White	1,840	1,918	1,768
Nonwhite	985	1,015	819
Total	1,642	1,609	1,691

[a]Source: Schnore (1962a).

situation.) Four investigations will be summarized, the second, third, and fourth of which are more detailed studies of the first.

The first study to be summarized was entitled "The Socioeconomic Status of Cities and Suburbs" (Schnore, 1963b). It covered 200 urbanized areas, used "advance reports" from the 1960 Census, and was basically concerned with characterizing city–suburban status differences in the United States (without regard for regional location) for the total U A population (without respect for color). Beyond that, it represented an attempt to assess the role of population size and age of city in affecting the direction of city–suburban status differences, while exercising some control over the boundary problem.

The data were manipulated in two complementary ways: via simple cross tabulations and by means of multiple-regression analysis. Table 3 shows the results of the analysis for city–suburban comparisons by population size and age of city. It is clear that the popular view of the city–suburban differentials is derived mainly from the experience of larger and older areas (the upper half of the table is concerned with population size). While none of the cities in the two largest size classes exceeds its suburbs in income or educational

TABLE 3   City–Suburban Differentials in Socioeconomic Status, by Size of Urbanized Area and Age of Central City, 1960[a]

Size of Urbanized Area and Census in Which Central City First Reached 50,000	Percent of Urbanized Areas with Higher Suburban Values in:			
	Median Family Income, 1959	Those Completing High School	Those in White-Collar Occupations	Number of Areas
Size				
1,000,000 and over	100.0	100.0	87.5	16
500,000–1,000,000	100.0	100.0	86.4	22
250,000–500,000	79.3	75.9	55.2	29
150,000–250,000	72.1	62.8	48.8	43
100,000–150,000	70.3	64.9	40.5	37
50,000–100,000	56.6	49.1	30.2	53
Census year				
1800–1860	100.0	100.0	100.0	14
1870–1880	100.0	100.0	100.0	17
1890–1900	86.1	75.0	58.3	36
1910–1920	75.0	75.0	54.2	48
1930–1940	71.9	56.3	31.3	32
1950–1960	50.9	47.2	24.5	53
All areas	74.0	68.5	50.5	200

[a]Source: Adapted from Schnore (1963b).

standing, increasing proportions do so as one moves down the size
range to the very smallest areas. A similar pattern emerges in the
third column devoted to occupational comparisons. The lower half,
devoted to age of city, as determined by census year when city first
reached 50,000 yields even more clearcut patterns. A detailed analysis of this table follows (Schnore 1963b, p. 79–80):

The first column reveals that suburban fringes consistently register higher median
family income in the older areas; none of the 31 cities reaching a size of 50,000
in 1880 or earlier has a higher average income than its suburbs. In contrast, the
newer Urbanized Areas tend consistently to show larger and larger proportions
of central cities with higher income. When the measure of educational status is
employed, as in the second column, the results are generally the same. The proportion of persons completing at least a high school education is consistently
higher in the suburbs of older cities, while newer cities tend to show the opposite pattern. Similarly, the occupational measure suggests that age is clearly
associated with city–suburban differentials in socioeconomic status. Examining
the third column, we find that none of the 31 oldest cities exceeds its suburban
fringe in the proportion of white-collar workers. At the other extreme, three out
of every four of the newest cities contain higher proportions of white-collar
workers than their adjacent suburbs.

Size and age, of course, are themselves correlated, and to assess their
predictive abilities we turned to partial correlation techniques.

For each of the three measures of socioeconomic status for each
urbanized area, we assigned arbitrary numerical values—a 0 if the
central city was higher on the measure and a 1 if the suburban fringe
was higher. As an additional check, we supplemented this "dummy
variable" treatment by repeating the analysis using suburb–city ratios,
i.e., dividing the suburb's value on each of the three status measures
by the city's respective value. Besides age and size, however, we took
care to add a third "independent" variable: the percentage of the
total urbanized area's 1960 population found within the central city.
This proportion seemed to us a rough, but useful, measure of the extent to which a city had been successful in extending its official
boundaries to keep up with the physical spread of urban development within its immediate vicinity. Inspection of the data for the
200 urbanized areas under study indicated that those with a high
proportion of the total U A population in central cities tended to
show higher city values on income, education, and occupation; they
also tended to be smaller and newer. Six years later, Hadden made a
similar point (1969, 281–282):

[O]ne should be skeptical of research that indicates there is a positive relationship between the size of Urbanized Areas and the socioeconomic status of their suburbs, since the direction of this relationship is the same as the administrative boundary bias. What is apparently happening here is that the smaller Urbanized Areas have a greater proportion of the high status families living near the periphery of the city being included in the Central City, and this has the effect of systematically inflating the socioeconomic characteristics of the Central City and, in turn, reducing the differential between the Central City and "suburb."

The fact that we controlled this factor would seem to render Hadden's point moot with respect to this study.

In any case, the results were extremely clear. In sum, it was concluded (Schnore, 1963b, p. 82) that

the predictive ability of population size is substantially reduced when the other two variables—age and annexation—are taken into account. . . . By contrast, age continues to serve as a highly significant predictor of city–suburban differentials in socioeconomic status; when size and annexation are held constant, age continues to exert a large and measurable influence upon the direction of the differences between cities and suburbs.

There are unquestionably other variables worthy of consideration, and subsequent research had identified at least some of them.

COLOR AND REGION AS CONFOUNDING VARIABLES

The importance of controlling color in the course of making city–suburban comparisons has been alluded to already. Neglecting the varying balance between the whites and nonwhites, two main color groups recognized in the 1960 Census, is especially likely to complicate matters when regional location is also ignored. Consequently, a follow-up study (Palen & Schnore, 1965) looked closely at variations in city–suburban status between color groups within two broad regions—the South and the non-South. Comparisons of city and suburban status were possible for 180 urbanized areas when looking at the white populations only and for 131 areas when examining nonwhite populations separately. The same three status measures were employed, i.e., median family income, percent completing high school, and proportion of the employed labor force in white-collar occupations. We shall not show all the findings here, but we will simply illustrate the major results by reference to those concerning family income, since they are typical of the configurations discernible in the other two measures.

TABLE 4 City-Suburban Differentials in Median Family Income in 1959, by Size of Urbanized Area and Age of Central City, for Color Groups and Regions, 1960[a]

| | Percent of Urbanized Areas with Higher Suburban Median Family Income in 1959 | | | | | | | | |
| | Total United States | | | South | | | Non-South | | |
	Total	Nonwhite	White	Total	Nonwhite	White	Total	Nonwhite	White
Size of urbanized area									
1,000,000 or more	100.0	75.0	100[b]	100.0	38.5	100.0	100.0	80.0	100.0
500,000–1,000,000	100.0	59.1	100[b]						
250,000–500,000	79.3	60.7	75.9	60.0	40.0	50.0	89.5	72.2	89.5
150,000–250,000	72.1	62.1	67.5	64.7	73.3	52.9	76.9	50.0	78.3
100,000–150,000	70.3	68.4	47.1	92.3	83.3	46.2	58.3	42.9	47.6
50,000–100,000	56.6	64.7	46.2	52.9	90.0	18.8	58.3	29.6	65.2
Age of central city									
1800–1860	100.0	71.4	100[b]	100.0	60.0	100.0	100.0	87.0	100.0
1870–1880	100.0	92.9	100[b]						
1890–1900	86.1	78.3	87.1	100.0	75.0	100.0	82.1	80.0	82.6
1910–1920	75.0	50.0	76.1	70.6	58.8	70.6	77.4	40.0	79.3
1930–1940	71.9	50.0	50.0	76.5	60.0	47.1	66.7	20.0	53.3
1950–1960	50.9	60.7	33.3	60.9	86.7	18.2	43.3	30.8	50.0

[a]Source: Adapted from Palen and Schnore (1965).
[b]Largest and oldest classes collapsed in regional panels due to limited number of cases.

Table 4 shows that *whites*—in the south and non-South—continue to show the city–suburban status differences by both size of urbanized area and age of city. On the other hand, *nonwhites* in cities and suburbs manifest differences according to region. Outside the South, their patterns are very similar to those of the whites; that is, city-suburban status differences tend to be like those of the whites, with higher-status populations in the older and larger urbanized areas. *In the South, however, the pattern is precisely reversed.* In that broad region, suburban nonwhites display higher status in the newer and smaller areas. (The education and occupation measures do not display such a perfect reversal, but it is clear that the previously observed tendencies for the total population, without respect to color and region, do not operate for southern nonwhites.)

We could only speculate concerning this divergence from the dominant pattern (Palen & Schnore, 1965, p. 91):

Some of the unusual features of the Southern nonwhite findings are probably due to the effects of housing segregation, which recent research [by Taeuber and Taeuber for the 1950–60 intercensal decade] shows to be increasing in that section of the country while decreasing in the North and West. However, the most probable reason why the Southern nonwhites fail to show the usual city–suburban status differences is that in the South, as opposed to the North, the poorer and less advantaged nonwhite residents traditionally lived on the periphery of the city. Although there are indications that this pattern is changing, there still exists many nonwhite areas at the *edges* of Southern cities, large and small, old and new. This "historical survival" of low status neighborhoods on the Southern city's periphery, as well as in its central core, may be confounding the pattern of city–suburban status differentials found in other populations. The Southern nonwhite population, in short, may be in a state of transition between the traditional residential pattern of the Old South, and the contemporary American urban pattern seen in both white and nonwhite neighborhoods in the rest of the country.

CLASS SEGREGATION WITHIN THE BLACK GHETTO

Reference to "neighborhoods" in the foregoing passage reminds us that a finer areal grain than "cities versus suburbs" is sometimes necessary and useful. Segregation by color is a "fact of life" within large cities in all parts of our country (Taeuber & Taeuber, 1965). The fact that urban populations are residentially segregated according to social class (Duncan & Duncan, 1957) leads to some interesting questions: Does residential segregation according to social class exist *within* color groups? More particularly, are the social classes segregated within the nonwhite ghetto? Does the pervasive force of color segre-

gation today operate to oblige nonwhites of widely different social
status to live "side by side" in the ghetto?

The 1960 Census provided partial answers in a study of ghettos in
two dozen metropolitan centers (Schnore, 1965b, Ch. 16). Census
tract statistics were employed, from which only those tracts that contained at least 400 nonwhites *and* were contiguous to the main areas
of nonwhite concentration, i.e., the major ghettos were selected.
Then, those tracts with unusual population characteristics, such as
those with large populations in "group quarters"—people living in
"rooming houses, dormitories, military barracks, or institutions"
(U.S. Bureau of the Census, 1962, p. 3)—were eliminated. Finally,
we tabulated the data for nonwhites only—generally following a
tradition of the "Chicago school" of urban ecology and of Ernest W.
Burgess, in particular—by combining tracts within radial distance
zones based on a 1-mile interval and, except in New York City,
centered on the heart of each "central business district." Some of the
results (for family income only) are presented in Table 5 in the form
of weighted averages for the nonwhite families of the various distance
zones.

Although only income patterns are shown in Table 5, they are
reasonably representative of the results for the educational and
occupational measures of the "social class." The cell entries show
the percentage of all nonwhite families in each zone representing
an aggregate income of $7,000 or more in the calendar year preceding
the 1960 Census. Following is a descriptive analysis of this table
(Schnore, 1965b):

The various metropolitan centers have been grouped according to the broader
regions in which they are located. It will be seen immediately that these are
not the "regions" traditionally recognized in census publications over the years.
Note that a "border" region is designated in the tables. The "border" cities are
those which have been repeatedly identified as "way stations" in the literature
dealing with northward migration of southern Negroes over the years, or as
cities "caught between North and South" as far as social and cultural influences
are concerned. The four main quadrants have been arranged in a way that permits a quick grasp of the major findings. In each column of figures—zonal
percentages for each named metropolitan center—the highest percentages have
been underscored.

As expected, the Burgess pattern was found to be quite general as far as
Northern metropolitan centers were concerned. . . . In general, there is an
upward-sloping gradient with increasing distance from the center. If we ignore
minor deviations, it is safe to say that the nonwhite ghettos in large northern
cities still tend to display the pattern observed earlier in considering Chicago.

That is, *as distance increases from the center of the city, the socioeconomic status of nonwhite neighborhoods goes up. Nonwhite family income is higher, nonwhite educational levels mount, and the relative number of nonwhite males in "white-collar" employment increases.*

If we turn now to the data for the "border" cities—represented in the lower-left quadrant—we see the Burgess pattern manifested again. In five out of the six cities, the highest value appear in the outermost distance zones. Again, there is generally an upward-sloping gradient. Washington, D.C., is a clear-cut exception, showing three out of three deviations from the pattern found in the other five border cities. In general, however, *nonwhite ghettoes in large border cities tend to resemble those in cities of the North, insofar as internal "class segregation" is concerned.*

As for Washington itself, the widely noted influx of nonwhites into the city, especially since World War II, is apparently the main cause of the deviation from a perfect zonal pattern. Nonwhites have spread from "traditional Negro neighborhoods" into formerly white neighborhoods through much of the city. The changes that have occurred there do not represent a steady progression away from the center and toward the periphery in only one or two directions, as in most other Northern and border cities.

When we turn to the large cities of the South, where most nonwhites are Negroes, quite a different pattern appears. Examination of the lower-right quadrant . . . reveals that four out of five cities display a certain consistency: *moving away from the center of the city, nonwhite areas show a rise in socioeconomic status, followed by a decline. . . .*

Up to this point, we have talked only about "southern" *versus* "northern" patterns of class segregation within nonwhite subcommunities, noting that "border" cities tend to resemble cities in the North. We should probably be surprised if clear-cut differences *didn't* exist between North and South. But some of the dangers attending easy and casual "explanations" of such materials as these are suggested by the remaining quadrant in the table.

The upper-right quadrant shows data for five metropolitan centers. The first two are in the "Southwest"—Dallas and Houston. In both cases, the patterns of class segregation within nonwhite areas are clearly more similar to comparable areas in Southern cities than to Northern nonwhite ghettos. Perhaps this will come as no surprise to those who are familiar with these two cities, but the results do tend to contradict assertions to the effect that developments of the 'forties and 'fifties had made both Dallas and Houston much less "Southern" and more "Northern" and/or "Western."

As for the metropolitan centers of the Far West, the same upper-right quadrant gives a summary characterization of Los Angeles and the San Francisco–Oakland "Bay Area." Superficially, they would appear to resemble the southwestern and southern cities as far as class segregation within major nonwhite areas is concerned. Actually, the data are not unequivocal. In the case of Los Angeles, there are a number of problems of interpretation because of the many peculiarities in the legal city limits. A long series of annexations of territory, and

TABLE 5 Percent with Family Income of $7,000 or More in 1959, by Distance from Central Business District, Nonwhite Families, 24 Selected Cities, 1960[a,b]

Miles	North								Southwest		West		
	New York	Chicago	Detroit	Philadelphia	Cleveland	Indianapolis	Newark	Buffalo	Dallas	Houston	San Francisco	Oakland	Los Angeles
0–1	9.3	12.2	3.3	8.2	11.8	11.4	13.5	7.9	5.5	4.2	29.6	14.3	14.8
1–2			6.7	12.4	10.8	15.2	17.5	12.5		8.2	23.6	15.2	
2–3	12.8	11.8	10.7	15.4	19.1	16.1	33.8	22.1	7.9	19.6	32.8	26.3	19.3
3–4	13.6	16.2	15.7	26.1	29.3	25.9	37.4	32.3	5.5	7.2	26.7	27.3	21.8
4–5	18.8	20.4	21.2	26.2	36.0	46.0			5.0	8.6	40.8	31.0	29.8
5–6	18.8	27.9	23.7	29.8	46.1					10.8	50.5	37.8	34.3
6–7	22.5	26.8	27.3	37.5								27.2	35.6
7–8	15.0	27.7	30.8										24.1
8–9	11.3	41.2											16.3
9–10	–	50.4											29.5
10–11	25.6	45.6											
11–12	40.0	54.6											
12–13	46.9												

200

	Border						South				
Miles	Washington, D.C.	St. Louis	Kansas City	Baltimore	Cincinnati	Louisville	Atlanta	Richmond	New Orleans	Birmingham	Memphis
0-1	12.6	1.8	4.2	7.0	4.7	4.0	5.1	4.0	5.5	2.3	1.9
1-2	19.1	4.1	7.9	11.2	9.6	8.3	8.0	10.9	6.5	8.2	4.2
2-3	24.4	9.4	17.4	21.2	18.1	12.7	10.6	10.4	10.3	10.5	5.4
3-4	35.1	15.7	17.3	27.5	29.1	16.1	14.9	10.4	8.7	8.0	8.0
4-5	41.0	21.4	28.7							7.0	6.7
5-6	28.0									8.2	4.0

aSource: Schnore (1965b, p. 131).
bUnderscoring represents highest percent in column.

the persistence of enclaves like Beverly Hills, would make an analysis of city tracts alone very difficult, and the results wouldn't be very meaningful. But ignoring the city's legal boundaries, as in this study, requires the use of many odd-shaped census tracts. In the Bay Area, we have given separate consideration to San Francisco and Oakland. In any case, the situation can be summed up very briefly: (1) San Francisco reveals the "northern" pattern in only one out of three instances. (2) Oakland's three "deviations" from the same pattern seem almost entirely due to the influence of the University of California at Berkeley, Oakland's "neighbor." The Berkeley ghetto is included in the data for Oakland, and even though tracts with large numbers of students were eliminated, the impact of the university's presence is still quite evident.

One last point: The "nonwhite areas" in metropolitan centers of the Far West are not at all like the "Negro ghettoes" in some other parts of the country. The same thing can be said for Dallas and Houston. For one thing, ethnic minority groups other than Negroes are present in large numbers. In Dallas and Houston, there are substantial numbers of Mexican-Americans, most of whom are white according to census terminology; the areas most heavily occupied by persons of Mexican descent in these two cities happen to overlap the nonwhite areas of concentration rather considerably. The same can be said of Los Angeles, with the added qualification that nonwhite persons of Oriental descent are also present in large numbers; this complicates the question of "class segregation" considerably. Finally, all these groups are well represented in the San Francisco–Oakland Bay Area. This caveat is inserted to prevent possible misunderstandings concerning the implications of the observed patterns in these five cities. . . .

We found a pattern of class segregation *within* a number of nonwhite areas that is very familiar to all students of the American city; it can be summed up as "The higher up the social ladder, the farther out you live." Perhaps even more important, however, is the fact that we found variations.

Is the ghetto, which is itself a manifestation of segregation according to color, also segregated along social class lines? In northern and "border" cities, the socioeconomic status of nonwhite neighborhoods tends to rise regularly with increasing distance from the center of the city. This pattern, however, is not generally observed in southern, southwestern, and western cities, where an alternative configuration appears. Socioeconomic status tends to rise and then to decline with increasing distance from the central business district. Once again, then, important regional variations are observed; cities in all parts of the country do not manifest precisely the same patterns.

A CROSS-SECTIONAL STUDY WITH A FOCUS ON EDUCATIONAL ATTAINMENT AS OF 1960

Of all the cross-sectional studies of 1960 data with which we have been involved, the paper with perhaps the richest research implica-

tions seems to be the one that appeared in *Demography* under the
title "Urban Structure and Suburban Selectivity" (Schnore, 1964).
The elements of "urban structure" examined were such variables as
population size of the urbanized area in 1960; age of the central city,
in terms of decades since reaching 50,000 inhabitants; population
growth, as crudely indexed by proportions of the 1960 population
living in housing built between 1950 and 1960; and annexation experience, as represented by the proportions of the central city's
population living in territory that was annexed between 1950 and
1960.

The "suburban selectivity" that was of interest involved the extent
to which various social strata were dissimilarly distributed between
cities and their suburbs, as the latter were crudely identified as the
outlying portions of 200 urbanized areas wherein a sufficiently large
noncentral population resided. For certain phases of the analysis—to
be stressed below—only 180 areas could be studied. This reduction in
the N was necessary in order to exercise an imperfect, but still useful,
statistical control over varations in color composition between the
cities and their suburbs.

The focus of this paper was a classic problem in ecological analysis;
it dealt with variations in the residential distribution of socioeconomic
strata in urban areas. A large part of the literature dealing with this
topic treats it as a longitudinal problem, i.e., variations over time are
stressed, as in the Burgess theory concerning *The Growth of the City*
(1925). The paper under discussion, however, was largely cross sectional in approach and stressed variations from place to place at a
given point in time, i.e., 1960.

While we continued to work with the gross distinction between
"city" and "suburbs," we turned to a single indicator of socioeconomic status—the number of school years completed by the population age 25 years or older. The earlier study discussed—"The
Socioeconomic Status of Cities and Suburbs" (Schnore, 1963b)—
simply compared the populations in cities and suburbs completing
at least 12 years of schooling. Rather than continuing to work with
this single value, however, we examined the residential distributions
of eight detailed educational classes.

The first basic question posed was: What is the current residential
distribution—city versus suburbs—of each educational class? The procedure is set out in Table 6, where data for males in the four largest
metropolitan areas [Standard Consolidated Areas (SCA's and
SMSA's)] are shown in detail. The fifth column shows the proportion of each detailed educational class that resides in the city, and

TABLE 6   Residential Distribution of Educational Groups in Four Metropolitan Areas, 1960[a]

Males, 25 Years of Age or Older, by Years of School Completed	Number in SMSA or SCA	Number in City	Number in "ring"	Percent in City[b]	Index of Centralization[c]
New York SCA	*4,283,823*	*2,319,679*	*9.964,144*	*54.1*	*100*
None	150,864	110,211	40,653	73.1	135
Grade: 1–4	201,047	126,994	74,053	63.1	117
Grade: 5–6	277,119	162,260	114,859	58.5	108
Grade: 7–8	1,009,038	575,609	433,429	57.0	105
High: 1–3	870,075	468,266	401,809	53.8	99
High: 4	851,210	433,729	417,481	50.9	94
College: 1–3	379,374	188,722	190,652	49.7	92
College: 4 +	545,096	253,888	291,208	46.5	86
Chicago SCA	*1,897,558*	*1,029,007*	*868,551*	*54.2*	*100*
None	36,518	26,963	9,555	73.8	136
Grade: 1–4	99,114	68,796	30,318	69.4	128
Grade: 5–6	117,439	76,651	40,788	65.2	120
Grade: 7–8	455,124	269,211	185,913	59.2	109
High: 1–3	390,603	220,291	170,312	56.3	104
High: 4	402,146	192,772	209,374	47.9	88
College: 1–3	194,801	95,303	99,498	48.9	90
College: 4 +	201,813	79,020	122,793	39.1	72
Philadelphia SMSA	*1,199,583*	*565,652*	*633,931*	*47.1*	*100*
None	26,714	18,238	8,476	68.2	148
Grade: 1–4	61,301	37,554	23,747	61.2	130
Grade: 5–6	94,840	53,525	41,315	56.4	120
Grade: 7–8	288,925	149,809	139,116	51.9	110
High: 1–3	263,492	132,900	130,592	50.4	107
High: 4	244,043	99,418	144,625	40.7	86
College: 1–3	89,414	33,395	56,019	37.3	79
College: 4 +	130,854	40,813	90,041	31.2	66
Los Angeles SMSA	*1,868,644*	*721,264*	*1,147,280*	*38.6*	*100*
None	28,355	15,420	12,935	54.4	141
Grade: 1–4	61,745	28,380	33,365	46.0	119
Grade: 5–6	85,312	37,527	47,785	44.0	114
Grade: 7–8	318,880	118,302	200,578	37.1	96
High: 1–3	377,263	134,431	242,832	35.6	92
High: 4	468,183	172,726	295,457	36.9	96
College: 1–3	286,725	113,146	173,579	39.5	102
College: 4 +	242,081	101,332	140,749	41.9	109

[a]Source: Schnore (1964).
[b]Percent in city shows the proportion of a given educational class in the entire SMSA (or SCA) that resides in the central city.
[c]The index of centralization is the above value for each educational class divided by the proportion for the total male population aged 25 and over.

the last column shows a simple "index of centralization," which consists of the proportion living in the city for each educational class in the metropolitan area in question divided by the proportion living in the city among all males 25 years of age or older in the same area. The resulting ratios can be interpreted as variations around the hypothetical "expected value" of 100 that would obtain if each class exhibited exactly the same balance between city and suburbs. Values above 100 indicate over-representation in the city; values below 100 indicate over-representation in the suburbs.

The last column of Table 6 shows some rather interesting patterns. In the first three instances—New York, Chicago, and Philadelphia—the ratios descend regularly from a high value for those with no formal schooling to a low value for those who have completed 4 years of college or more. This is the precise pattern that one would expect on the basis of contemporary discussions of "the flight of the elite to suburbia," "the loss of city leadership," etc., and we can take it as the "expected" pattern. But observe the deviant pattern presented in the case of Los Angeles; here, we find persons at the top and at the bottom of the educational ladder over-represented in the city itself. (We shall return to the Los Angeles case below.)

The guiding hypothesis was that "suburban selectivity" is a function of "urban structure." In addition to size and regional location, it appeared worthwhile to examine the role of such variables as the age of the city, its color composition, and changes therein, with attention to housing, population growth, and annexation history. Since we are dealing with residential segregation, albeit on a gross scale, color differences are especially deserving of further attention.

Table 7 shows that a number of rather distinctive patterns can be discerned when one examines the residential distribution (city versus suburbs) of the detailed educational classes represented in the census data. Examination of 200 urbanized areas revealed the existence of six detailed types of suburban selectivity, together with the need for recognizing the fact that some areas show no patterned selectivity whatever. The concrete examples shown in Table 7 are the largest areas showing each pattern.

Type "A" (exemplified by Tucson) is perhaps the most interesting of all, since it represents a perfect reversal of the "expected" pattern previously mentioned. In other words, persons with no formal schooling or with very little education are under-represented in the city itself. Those who have completed high school and those who have attended college are slightly over-represented in the city. This means

TABLE 7 Examples of Six Patterns of Residential Distribution of Educational Classes Based on Indexes of Suburbanization for Selected Urbanized Areas, 1960[a]

Pattern of Residential Distribution	1. Highest Educational Classes Over-Represented in the City		2. Both Highest and Lowest Educational Classes Over-Represented in the City	3. Lowest Educational Classes Over-Represented in the City		4. Intermediate Educational Classes Over-Represented in the City	5. No Systematic Variation
Pattern label:	A	B	C	D	E	F	X
Name of area used in example:	Tucson	Albuquerque	Los Angeles	Baltimore	New York	Miami	Memphis
School years completed							
None	90	85	131	128	129	83	98
Grade: 1–4	93	81	113	124	119	137	101
Grade: 5–6	96	88	110	117	111	136	101
Grade: 7–8	99	93	99	104	107	115	101
High: 1–3	100	97	94	98	100	100	100
High: 4	101	103	97	86	91	89	99
College: 1–3	102	106	102	86	87	84	100
College: 4 +	103	110	106	87	84	81	100
Number of areas represented by example shown	14	10	70	23	67	4	12

[a]Source: Schnore (1964).

that the suburbs of Tucson, and those of 13 other areas like it, showed a systematic selection of persons at the *bottom*, rather than at the top, of the educational ladder in 1960, which is the exact reversal of the common image of suburbia.

Type B (ten cases, of which Albuquerque is the largest) is very much like Type A, though there is a minor but systematic tendency in the direction of a reversal at the lower end of the educational ladder. (In later discussions, the Tucson and Albuquerque types will be combined.)

Type C is one with which we are already acquainted; Los Angeles is the largest example. Persons at both extremes are over-represented in the city. While the earlier encounter with this pattern suggested that Los Angeles might be a "deviant" case, Table 7 shows that C is actually the modal type for 1960, for fully 70 out of 200 urbanized areas showed this pattern.

Type D (exemplified by Baltimore) almost achieves the expected pattern, i.e., a systematic decline in index values as one reads down the column, but there is a slight reversal at the upper end of the educational ladder. In subsequent discussions, the Baltimore and New York City types will be combined.

The expected pattern is here labeled E, and it is perfectly illustrated by New York City. The pattern consists of a series of continuously declining values, indicating that the city in 1960 was characterized by an over-concentration of persons with minimal education and that the suburbs of New York were populated by a larger than expected proportion of persons with higher educational standing.

Type F represents only four cases, of which Miami was the largest in 1960. It is basically like Type E, but there is a lower than expected number of persons without formal education in the city itself.

Finally, Memphis (Type X) exemplifies the fact that there were a dozen urbanized areas (out of 200 under study for 1960) that could not be classified as falling into one or other of the six basic types.

Our research was then directed toward discovering those general factors that might underlie the systematic variations observed in suburban selectivity. The search involved examining certain broad characteristics of whole urbanized areas that may be fairly regarded as basic structural features—e.g., location, size, age, and rate of growth. Since our earlier work documented the commonsense observation that the scope of the city's boundaries (and changes therein) will affect city–suburban comparisons, we also looked into this factor as a source of variation in apparent suburban selectivity. More particularly, we tried to deal with the "annexation factor," recognizing that political boundaries are not rigid and impermeable.

There are also a number of reasons for wanting to take account of variations in color composition. For one thing, urbanized areas in the United States vary considerably with respect to the proportion of nonwhites they contain. More important, the residential patterns of whites and nonwhites are known to be highly dissimilar. Finally, whites and nonwhites exhibit substantial differences in terms of educational attainment.

In any case, Table 8 has been prepared to show the associations between selected characteristics of urbanized areas and the patterns revealed by their white populations considered alone. While the same associations are revealed in the table for total and white populations, they are displayed in somewhat sharper form when attention is confined to the white population only; that is, "control" of color seems to bring out even more clearly the operation of the second principle of residential segregation, *viz.*, socioeconomic status.

Perhaps the most intriguing possibility raised by all these materials is suggested by the data related to two variables—size and age of urban areas. This is the basic source of what we shall here call the *"evolutionary hypothesis." The regularities exhibited suggest that cities evolve in a predictable direction, e.g., pattern A through pattern E.* (One of the longitudinal studies taken up below was an attempt to test this hypothesis.)

In the case of size, the larger the area the more likely the appearance of the expected pattern (column 3). Similarly, age appears to be associated with the patterns under examination. The age panel shows that areas with older central cities are more likely to show the "expected" pattern. The first column shows that the "unexpected" patterns (Types A and B) were most frequently found in 1960 in the urbanized areas with the newest central cities, i.e., those that only recently achieved a size of 50,000 or more inhabitants.

The two remaining panels in Table 8 throw further light on the patterns under investigation. Percent in housing units built since 1950 suggests that the rate of recent population growth was at least roughly associated with the type of suburban selectivity. Column 1 indicates that urbanized areas rapidly growing in the 1950's were the most likely to exhibit the "unexpected" pattern, wherein higher status groups are seemingly over-represented in the central city. The proportions set out in the third column, however, do not show the same sort of regularity.

Percent of central city population in area annexed (Table 8) again suggests the importance of annexation. Seven out of every ten cities that failed to annex nearby territory over the last intercensal decade (1950–1960) showed the expected pattern. Conversely, cities that had been very actively annexing surrounding territory of that decade show the unexpected pattern. This may mean nothing more than that they succeeded, more often than not, in annexing "high-status" areas, though we can only speculate on this matter at the moment.

SMITH'S AREAL REFINEMENT OF THE 1960-BASED STUDIES

An important study has been subsequently published by Joel Smith (1970). A few selected quotations from this lengthy and ambitious work will convey the essence of his approach and findings, at least for present purposes (Smith, 1970, p. 421–422, 430–431):

Schnore's findings [for 1960] suggest that ring population superiority is not uniform for all urbanized areas, but is a direct and orderly function of such measurable independent attributes of the central city and total urbanized area as size and age. . . .

In his analysis, Schnore designated as suburbs all that part of the census-defined urbanized area lying outside of central cities and made no distinctions between suburbs and fringes, although he did indicate the possible desirability of such a distinction. We were particularly concerned with the possibilities that (a) earlier generalizations about city–suburb differences might still be valid for central cities and suburbs only; (b) very different patterns might exist for city–fringe differences; and (c) Schnore's data may work out as they do because the proportion of the urban fringe population may increase as the age of urbanized areas decreases. . . .

Our ultimate aim was to retest the hypothesis tested and rejected by Schnore: that suburban populations will show a higher average than central city populations on any measure of socioeconomic status irrespective of size or age of urbanized area. The crucial alteration in the retest is the revised designation of suburbs as only incorporated places.

Smith then proceeded to employ data for incorporated places of 2,500 and over as suburbs, designating the residential area remaining as the "fringe" population. He was able to secure "fairly accurate estimates of fringe and suburb population socioeconomic attributes" (Smith, 1970, p. 432) for 113 urbanized areas. What were his results? Although Smith's work went well beyond our own in many respects, with regard to detailed treatment of additional variables, he did con-

TABLE 8 Patterns of Suburban Selectivity by Selected Characteristics of Urbanized Area, White Population Only, 1960[a]

Selected Characteristics, Urbanized Areas, 1960	1. Highest Educational Class Over-Represented in the City	2. Both Highest and Lowest Classes Over-Represented in the City	3. Lowest Educational Classes Over-Represented in the City	4. Intermediate Educational Classes Over-Represented in the City	5. No. Systematic Variation	Total Number of Areas (equals 100%)
Size of urbanized area						
1,000,000 or more	—	12.5	87.5	—	—	16
500,000–1,000,000	—	27.3	59.1	9.1	4.6	22
250,000–500,000	6.9	27.6	58.6	—	6.9	29
150,000–250,000	15.0	37.5	35.0	5.0	7.5	40
100,000–150,000	20.6	41.2	32.4	—	5.9	34
50,000 –100,000	28.2	46.2	15.4	2.6	7.7	39
Census year in which central city or cities first reached 50,000						
1800–1860	—	14.3	78.6	—	7.1	14
1870–1880	—	13.3	80.0	—	6.7	15
1890–1900	—	22.6	64.5	—	12.9	31
1910–1920	10.9	39.1	43.5	2.2	4.3	46
1930–1940	15.6	53.1	15.6	9.4	6.3	32
1950–1960	38.1	40.5	16.7	2.4	2.4	42

Percent in housing units built since 1950						
40.0 or more	33.3	33.3	20.0	10.0	3.3	30
35.0–39.9	29.2	41.7	25.0	–	4.2	24
30.0–34.9	18.2	31.8	50.0	–	–	22
25.0–29.9	2.9	40.0	51.4	2.9	2.9	35
20.0–24.9	6.8	29.6	50.0	–	13.6	44
Less than 20.0	4.0	36.0	48.0	4.0	8.0	25
Percent of central city population in area annexed 1950–1960						
30.0 or more	43.5	30.4	17.4	4.4	4.4	23
20.0–29.9	23.8	52.4	23.8	–	–	21
10.0–19.9	13.5	40.5	32.4	2.7	10.8	37
5.0–9.9	10.0	45.0	40.0	–	5.0	20
0.1–4.9	10.0	33.3	43.3	3.3	10.0	30
None	2.0	22.5	67.4	4.1	4.1	49

[a]Source: Schnore (1964).

211

clude (1970, p. 449–450) that the retest tended to support our earlier work:

The data have to be taken as confirming Schnore's broadest findings. They also indicate that the total urban area is a city/suburb/fringe mosaic and that there are circumstances when simple inside–outside descriptions of differentiation will hide a more complexly differentiated reality. If, as some observers suspect, urban renewal programs will not substantially raise the status of city populations in the future, it might be suggested that the differentiation that already exists and will develop further in the ring, will become greater than that which urban sociologists in the past have described as characterizing the central city. In dealing with this as a scientific question, size and age may continue to be important and useful variables, but it would seem essential also to introduce other variables, some of which will have additional value and others of which will come somewhat closer to revealing the effective social realities which city size and age may represent.

Smith himself has indicated what some of the "other variables" should be (e.g., the economic base of the city), but an even *more pressing need is to move away from purely cross-sectional inquiries, such as his and ours, and to develop research that is oriented to the study of trends over time.* It is for this reason that we now turn to the results of two longitudinal studies that attempted to get at city–suburban status trends in urbanized areas and metropolitan areas.

City-Suburban Status Changes: Longitudinal Evidence

We have completed and published two studies using longitudinal modes of analysis. Both involve the 1950–1960 intercensal decade, represent attempts to deal with the 1950's, and were designed to avoid the familiar problem of making longitudinal inferences from purely cross-sectional data.

The first longitudinal study to be discussed (Schnore & Jones, 1969) was motivated by curiosity about the results that might be obtained from an examination of education data for the urbanized areas in the United States that were delineated in connection with the 1950 Census of Population. Some of our previous theoretical and empirical work (with 1960 data) suggested that an evolutionary sequence of urban residential patterns might exist. It indicated that an urban area might show a certain pattern of city–suburban status differences when it is relatively small and young but evolve toward another, predictable pattern of differences as it grows and ages.

More specifically, this earlier work suggested that smaller and

younger central cities in the United States tend to be occupied by
the local elite, while their peripheral, suburban areas contain the
lower strata. Second, with growth and the passage of time, however,
this work implied that the central city comes to be the main residential area for both the highest and lowest strata, at least tempo-
rarily, while the broad middle classes are over-represented in the
suburbs. A subsequent stage in this evolutionary process is achieved
when the suburbs have become the semiprivate preserve of both the
upper and middle strata, while the central city is largely given over
to the lowest stratum. In a very rough fashion, of course, this last
stage corresponds to the way in which the various social classes are
arrayed in space according to the original Burgess (1925) zonal hypothesis.

The study reported here was designed as a kind of replication of
the earlier work, "Urban Structure and Suburban Selectivity"
(Schnore, 1964). As noted, that report was a direct follow-up to
"The Socioeconomic Status of Cities and Suburbs," and it considered city–suburban status differences in the same urbanized areas.
It, however, was essentially cross sectional and dealt only with 1960
data. Using Census data on school years completed, it was originally
designed to measure the frequency of essentially *two* types of residential configuration; for the moment, we may simply label them
as the expected and the unexpected. Following the broad implications of the Burgess hypothesis, the expected pattern for United
States urban areas would show a predominance of the lowest social
classes in the central city. Any other pattern or patterns showing
some deviation from that type, whether or not they were perfect
reversals of the expected pattern (as in the classic Latin American
city), would be unexpected.

In the 1964 Schnore study, only five independent variables were
used in the analysis, but they were selected to represent some potentially relevant characteristics of whole cities or urbanized areas. Such
basic features as location, size, age, and rate of growth were examined.

The traditional Census divisions afforded a rough measure of location, though the various divisions differ in many respects insofar as
the characteristics of their constituent urban areas are concerned. As
a result, divisional location is a difficult variable to handle analyti-
cally; it is neither some kind of "pure" locational measure, nor can
it be readily regarded as a "structural" variable. Nevertheless, it
seemed to yield some hints regarding the relation between general
location and patterns of city–suburban status differences.

We have already shown that population size and the age of a city
(as measured here) are correlated with each other (Schnore, 1955),
and we have gone so far as to suggest that they can be important
determinants of a city's social structure (Schnore, 1966). In any
case, these two variables could hardly be neglected in an investigation of characteristics related to "suburban selectivity" as we have
conceived it. Population growth was considered as a third structural
variable of some importance in this work. Since the scope of a city's
political boundaries (and changes therein) will clearly affect *all* types
of city–suburban comparisons, a fourth factor was added as a possible source of variation in suburban selectivity. In the 1964 study,
it was labeled "the annexation factor" and consisted simply of the
percent of the 1960 central city population residing in areas annexed
between 1950 and 1960.

The results of the work with 1960 urbanized areas were previously
shown in Table 7. The three main evolutionary types discussed in
this paper were identified in Schnore (1964). In all, these three types
accounted for 92 percent of the cases under study.

Be that as it may, the really crucial problem with this crude type
of examination is that we are dealing with a set of interdependent
variables. Larger areas usually have older cores; they tend to be
growing somewhat more slowly; and their central cities ordinarily
encounter greater obstacles when attempting to expand their political limits. Smaller areas, on the other hand, are much more frequently
characterized by an opposite set of circumstances. In addition, only
200 cities clearly makes for difficulties if one is using a cross-tabular
mode of analysis; for example, there is literally no possibility of in-
troducing appropriate controls.

What led us to replicate this 1960 work with 1950 data? *Despite
numerous and obvious problems of comparability, it seemed reasonable to expect that the 1950 data would allow at least a few meaningful comparisons with 1960 patterns. First, one might see if the
same or similar cross-sectional associations appeared in the 1950 data.
Second, one might also see what changes occurred in residential distribution patterns and—more important—what direction these changes,
if any, took. The analysis, it seemed to us, might provide some additional evidence for or against an evolutionary view of city–suburban
status differences.*

At the outset, of course, we were faced with the fundamental in-
comparability of the 1950 and 1960 urbanized areas. Urbanized areas
with the same names in 1950 and 1960 are not really the same areas,

and this is so for a variety of reasons. The outer boundaries of all but one urbanized area (Portland, Maine) changed rather substantially between 1950 and 1960. Undergoing the rapid growth created by nationwide trends in migration and natural increase, urbanized areas spread outward during the 1950's as suburban sprawl continued at an accelerated pace. Some grew by only a few square miles, but others expanded by more than 150 square miles. Indeed, the Dallas urbanized area in 1960 was 504 square miles larger than the "same" urbanized area in 1950. But not all of these areal increases reflected "real" suburbanization.

The fact is that the very criteria for inclusion of territory in an urbanized area were changed between the 1950 and 1960 Censuses (U.S. Bureau of the Census, 1962, p. ix; italics added by author).

In 1950, urbanized areas were established in connection with cities having 50,000 inhabitants or more according to the 1940 Census of Population or a later special census prior to 1950. In 1960, urbanized areas were established in connection with cities having 50,000 inhabitants or more according to the 1960 Census.

The boundaries of the urbanized areas for 1960 will not conform to those for 1950, partly because of *relatively minor* changes in the rules used to define the boundaries. The changes in the rules were made in order to simplify the process of defining the boundaries; as a result of the changes, the area classified as urbanized tends to be *somewhat larger* than it would have been under the 1950 rules.

These procedural changes—which were not always "relatively minor" in their effects—had an impact in every part of the country. Actually, the most important change relates to the new *density* criterion that was established for unincorporated territory. In 1950, the minimal density figure was *500 dwelling units* per square mile. In 1960, this was converted to *1,000 persons* per square mile. As a result, the outlying portions of the 1960 urbanized areas contain much more of what is conventionally labeled rural–urban "fringe" territory and do not include only suburbs as they are commonly conceived. (This is the main point of Joel Smith's work so far.)

It is also important to remind ourselves that the core cities of many urbanized areas underwent drastic changes in area between 1950 and 1960. Central city boundaries experienced marked revision between the end of World War II and the 1960 Census. During the Depression and War years, very few cities extended their boundaries; annexations became quite frequent, however, during the post-War period. But annexation was far from uniform in its impact. As a result, the several Census divisions witnessed a wide variety of change. For example, the larger and older cities, most frequently found on the Atlantic seaboard and in the north central region, were those most frequently surrounded by established, already incorporated suburbs. These central cities were thereby forced into an absolute or virtual "freeze" on annexation. Cities in most other parts of the country, however, were in a better position to carry on extensive annexations, and most of them did so quite freely (Schnore, 1962b).

A final point concerns our procedures in this study. We set out to use the same set of rules that were developed for the analysis of the 1960 data. As in the earlier study, "Urban Structure and Suburban Selectivity" (Schnore, 1964), three independent coding judgments were made in order to ensure more objective categorization. The essential purpose of the rules was to identify various types of residential location patterns in 1960. These patterns were based on a set of index values for each area and were derived by dividing the proportion living in the city for each educational class in the urbanized area by the proportion living in the city among the total population 25 years of age or older in the same area. The resulting ratios were interpreted as variations around the hypothetical expected value of 100, which would have appeared if each class had exhibited exactly the same balance between city and suburbs. The overall pattern for each area was examined and independently classified by the three coders working with the 1960 rules.

In order to make the two studies as comparable as possible, the 1960 rules were strictly applied to the 1950 data. The results were extremely disappointing, however, for the rules did not work very well. To be sure, a large number of 1950 areas were easily "typed" according to the 1960 rules. In *45 out of 142 cases*, however, the following difficulties emerged: (a) The three main types—representing the evolutionary stages—did not appear; (b) there were ambiguities that could not be readily resolved by the use of the 1960 rules; (c) there were deviations that were not even hinted at in the 1960 data. We could not help wondering if a more lenient interpretation of the 1960 rules would affect the results. We therefore repeated the procedure, giving more attention to the overall configuration for each area and less attention to the minor deviations within each apparent pattern. [See the appendix to "Urban Structure and Suburban Selectivity" (Schnore, 1964) for the 1960 rules.]

The main objective of the study presently under discussion is to see if there were any *changes* between 1950 and 1960. More importantly, to test the evolutionary hypothesis, the direction of any changes must be known. Thus a cross-tabulation, comparing each urbanized area's 1950 type with its 1960 type (see Table 9), was prepared.

The first notable item in this table is that a large proportion (64 percent) of the areas considered exhibited exactly the same type of residential patterning (or lack of patterning) (italicized diagonal entries) in both 1950 and 1960. Areas of type 1, type 2, and, particularly, type 3 showed the same configurations of residential distribution by educational attainment in 1960 as in 1950. This is hardly surprising, since a single decade is a very short period of time in the history of most cities of the size studied. A number of other areas (27, or 19 percent) moved in the predicted direction; i.e., they appear above the diagonal and represent shifts from type 2 to type 3 and from type 1 to type 2. Why it is that the five areas below the diagonal underwent an evolutionary reversal, or a "devolution," is not entirely clear. (See the positions of Asheville, Greensboro, New Haven, Kalamazoo, and Brockton.) Here, a very close look at each of the cases involved might prove to be helpful, though there are obvious hazards in such *post factum* inquiries. For example, we do not know the particular factors involved in these five instances. Further, some peculiar historical circumstances might well be the crucial factors in these cases; however, we are not aware of them at this time.

Initially, it appears that the results shown in Table 9 for the nine areas exhibited no systematic variation in 1950 and then turned up in the expected category (Table 9, column 3) in 1960. On closer examination and after considering each of the 45 problem cases, a detailed examination of *all* the individual ratios for 1950 was undertaken. This review suggested that still another difference in the Census methods employed at the two dates may be one more reason for the difficulties encountered with the coding rules and those in the cross-sectional findings. The 1950 Census data on education (school years completed by persons 25 and over) were acquired by means of a 20 percent sample, which was then expanded by a constant factor of five to represent the universe. The data we used included a sample-based estimate of how many persons aged 25 and over did not report on their education for one reason or another. In the calculations, this nonresponse was ignored because there was no defensible way to allocate it to the various categories. In the 1960 Census, the education data were again acquired by means of a sample (25 percent), but nonresponses were differentially weighted and automatically allocated to

TABLE 9 Summary of Changes in Type of Suburban Selectivity between 1950 and 1960 for 142 Urbanized Areas[a]

1950 Type	1960 Type					
	1. Highest Educational Classes Over-Represented in City	2. Both Highest and Lowest Educational Classes Over-Represented in City	3. Lowest Educational Classes Over-Represented in City	4. Intermediate Educational Classes Over-Represented in City	5. No Systematic Variation	Total Number of Areas
1. Highest educational classes over-represented in city	9	8	3	–	4	24
2. Both highest and lowest educational classes over-represented in city	2 Asheville Greensboro	30	16	–	2	50
3. Lowest educational classes over-represented in city	–	3 New Haven Kalamazoo Brockton	49	–	–	52
4. Intermediate educational classes over-represented in city	–	–	1	1	1	3
5. No systematic variation	–	3	9	–	1	13
Total number	11	44	78	1	8	142

[a]Source: Schnore and Jones (1969).

218

one or another of the school-year categories in the course of the actual tabulation of the data. For the core cities, we suspect that there was a serious underestimate of the number of those without any formal schooling in the 1950 Census, but there may have been another bias (in the opposite direction) in the handling of the same category in the 1960 Census. In any case, this is another striking instance of noncomparability, offering even more reason for placing limited confidence in the results of this study.

There are two views of these rather ambiguous data. First is the *negative interpretation*. In brief, the 1950 findings do not strongly confirm the idea that an evolutionary trend in socioeconomic residential patterns is or has been under way in urban areas of the United States. It is ture that the expected residential configurations (à la Burgess) were again found to appear most frequently in larger and older cities and that unexpected patterns were displayed in smaller and younger cities as of 1950. Based on the change data (1950–1960) in this analysis, however, the evidence for any evolutionary tendency is far from convincing, to say the least. Many of the problems encountered in this investigation stemmed from the following: changes in the procedures and rules for the delineation of urbanized areas between the 1950 and 1960 Censuses; modifications in the treatment of the sample data on school years completed; and changes in the handling of Census of Housing data relating to the age of physical structures. More important, the complexities of different and ever changing annexation laws and policies, the changing frequency of annexation over the post-War years, and the idiosyncratic factors making for growth (or lack of it) in every urbanized area in the country have posed difficulties that are virtually impossible to overcome in an analysis with limited scope such as this one. Working with such a small number of cases complicates the cross-tabular analysis of every variable, and even a multiple-regression analysis, using dummy variables, does not appear to be very promising.

Urban history is an extremely difficult field of inquiry if one wants to be both quantitative *and* comparative, whether the latter term is taken to mean cross-cultural or not. A case-by-case analysis of changes within each of the 142 areas under study here would be an immense undertaking and would actually lose sight of the original intent of the work—to provide a comparative framework within which a limited number of case studies might be carried out. In other words, the available number is too small for many statistical purposes, yet too large for detailed historical scrutiny.

The results of this study have not added very impressive weight to the work already completed, and in some key respects it casts some doubt on the validity of the longitudinal inferences previously drawn from the cross-sectional 1960 data for urbanized areas. But there is another interpretation, and it should be noted here. A *positive view* was suggested that the original personal conclusions are overly pessimistic. *In fact, it was argued that the evolutionary hypothesis is given a large measure of support.* It can be argued that Table 9—the principal test of the evolutionary hypothesis—does *not* represent a disconfirmation. If the 90 areas that did not change pattern are counted, together with those 27 above the diagonal that shifted in the predicted direction, over 82 percent of the 142 cases under study are consistent with the hypothesis. Moreover, the other cell entries involving types 4 and 5 take care of another 21 instances, or almost 15 percent; again, these can be understood by reference to all of the many procedural changes that were introduced between the 1950 and 1960 Censuses. This leaves only five cases that are *truly* disconfirmations of the evolutionary hypothesis.

THE RESIDENTIAL REDISTRIBUTION OF SOCIOECONOMIC STRATA IN METROPOLITAN AREAS

The last research to be reported in this summary is based on the work of Schnore and Pinkerton (1966). The paper—"The Residential Redistribution of Socioeconomic Strata in Metropolitan Areas"—was longitudinally designed to get at the 1950–1960 trends in the residential location of three broad strata based on the educational measure of class status. The features of the analysis are unique and thus warrant a rather lengthy discussion of its aims, areal units, methods, and results.

This report was an ecological analysis of changes in the spatial distribution of socioeconomic strata within 363 standard metropolitan statistical areas (or substituted units) in the United States. The central hypothesis guiding the study is that certain population subgroups in and around the larger urban areas are shifting their residential locations in predictable directions. Changes in the distribution of educational classes between the central city (or cities) and their surrounding rings from 1950 to 1960 are traced by using Census data. A special feature of the analysis is the inclusion of 163 "quasi-metropolitan areas" centered on cities that had 25,000–50,000 inhabitants in 1960.

The results indicate that residential redistribution according to "social class" is occurring in all these metropolitan areas and that the *pattern* of change varies systematically. Regional differences are pronounced, and, as prior research has suggested, age of the city and population size appear to be important factors. The percent of adults in the high school and college categories in the rings of older and larger metropolitan areas generally increased disproportionately compared to the central cities. A variety of patterns of change, however, occurred among the younger and smaller metropolitan areas.

That men of practical affairs are not entirely clear about urban issues—especially about questions pertaining to cities and suburbs—should come as no great surprise. The plain truth is that the scholarly community is even more confused about the main trends. A recently completed review of the literature demonstrates this confusion in embarrassing detail (Pinkerton, 1969). Most of the difficulties in determining the nature of recent trends in the redistribution of social classes stem from a lack of consensus regarding the appropriate areal units, time intervals, and measures of "social class"; an obtuse reliance on cross-sectional data for testing inherently longitudinal propositions; and a heavy dependence on case studies of individual urban areas, usually larger and older metropolitan complexes.

It is clear that urban studies would benefit by simultaneous attention to three requirements:

1. Studies should be *comprehensive* in scope, that is, the largest possible number of areas should be investigated simultaneously.

2. Investigations should be *comparative* in design, that is, a full range of metropolitan areas by size and different types of areas should be represented.

3. Explicitly *longitudinal* studies should be executed, that is, we should no longer rely on static or cross-sectional information to test ideas that are intrinsically concerned with trends over time.

The "sample" of areas considered in this study is the largest yet examined in any study of this subject. It consists of 200 standard metropolitan statistical areas (or substituted units, as described below) having central cities of 50,000 or more inhabitants in 1960, together with 163 quasi-metropolitan areas, specially devised for this study and centered on cities containing 25,000–50,000 people in 1960. These latter areas had an aggregate population of almost 13.4 million, or about 8 percent of the total population of the United States in 1960.

TABLE 10 Indexes of Disproportionate Change for Three Educational Classes in the Chicago Metropolitan Area, 1950–1960: A Methodological Illustration[a],[b]

Population (Aged 25 and over) by Level of School Completed[c]	1. Percent of City Population, 1950	2. Percent of Ring Population, 1950	3. City-Ring Difference, 1950	4. Percent of City Population, 1960	5. Percent of Ring Population, 1960	6. City-Ring Difference, 1960	7. Indexes of Disproportionate Change, 1950–1960
Grade	46.80	40.35	-6.45	42.92	30.13	-12.79	-6.34
High	39.99	41.41	+1.42	42.80	47.90	+ 5.10	+3.68
College	13.21	18.24	+5.03	14.28	21.97	+ 7.69	+2.66
Total	100.00	100.00		100.00	100.00		

[a]Source: Pinkerton (1965).
[b]The 1950 standard metropolitan area (and its equivalent, the 1960 standard consolidated area) for Chicago and northwestern Indiana.
[c]"Grade" = 0 through 8 years; "High" = 1 to 4 years of high school; "College" = 1 to 4 or more years of college.

222

Standard Metropolitan Statistical Areas   The 200 larger units consist of 1950 standard metropolitan areas, 1960 standard metropolitan
statistical areas, 1950–1960 state economic areas in New England, or
specially created areal substitutions for the foregoing types of units.
We assume that the "rings" of most of these areas provide at least a
fair representation of "suburbia" as the latter is commonly discussed
in the urban literature.

Quasi-Metropolitan Areas   The 163 smaller areas developed for this
study consist mainly of "central cities" between 25,000 and 50,000
inhabitants, together with the countries in which they are located.

Methods   The basic technique employed in this report consists of a
detailed comparison of changes in the relative numbers found in three
broad educational groups in cities and rings between 1950 and 1960.
From these changes, *six exhaustive types or patterns are distinguished.*
The relative frequencies of these patterns are then related to three
selected independent variables—location, population size, and age of
the urban center.

The basic measure of socioeconomic status—educational attainment—has been divided into three classes: those adults who have
completed 0–8 years of grade (elementary) school, those who have
completed 1–4 years of high school, and those who have completed
one or more years of college. Most of the previous studies dealing
with the residential redistribution of social strata have discussed
such changes in terms of two or three classes. The educational data
show heavy clusterings of persons in the categories "grade school:
8" and "high school: 4"; therefore, it is reasonable to believe that
these serve as important breaking points for dividing the population
into "social classes." A three-category classification of the population in the central city and surrounding ring also provides the basis
for showing a wide variety of possible patterns of residential shifts.

Table 10 shows the technique that has been used in this study
for measuring city–ring changes in the location of socioeconomic
strata between 1950 and 1960. The indexes are derived by taking
the differences between the city and ring proportions in each educational class in 1950 and 1960 and then subtracting the results for
1950 from those for 1960. Table 10 has been arranged so that the
indexes of disproportionate change apply to the ring, as has been
the procedure throughout this study. These same figures, however,
with opposite signs, apply to the central city. For example, the in-

dexes for Chicago reveal that between 1950 and 1960 the percent of the ring's adult population in the grade school class decreased disproportionately relative to the changes in the percent of the central city's adult population in that class. In other words, in 1950 the ring's grade school proportion was 6.45 percent lower than that of the city. By 1960, it had become 12.79 percent lower, for a net difference of –6.34 percent.

This technique indicates the extent to which the 1960 educational profiles for city and ring differ from those of 1950. The indexes of change do *not* measure the absolute changes that have occurred in the proportions in the various educational classes. For example, Table 10 reveals that the proportions in both the ring and city high school and college categories increased between 1950 and 1960 and that the proportions in their grade school categories decreased. The fact that both the city and ring experienced increases in the higher educational classes is almost certainly the result of the general upgrading in educational levels that has been occurring for many years throughout the United States. The technique used to derive the indexes of change, however, provides a control on changes of this kind that are common to both the city and ring, because it only reveals how the class structures of the two areas changed in regard to their similarity to each other.

Changes that result from general educational upgrading are not reflected, except for any specific and differential upgrading between the city and ring that has occurred. Some differences in the class structures of the two areas may also be the result of fertility and mortality differences in each class in the ring compared to the same class in the city. Net migration, however, has probably been the most important influence in bringing about changes in the class composition of the city and ring.

Classifying Types of Change: Six Possible Patterns   Using the above technique with a trichotomous classification of educational groups allows the identification of six patterns of disproportionate change. The upper panel in Table 11 shows the six possible patterns of change, viewed from the standpoint of the metropolitan ring. The first pattern of change (1)—or minus, plus, plus—indicates a decrease in the ring's grade school component and increases in its high school and college components. It may be regarded as the expected pattern of change. The remaining five possible types of change are also identified by number and by signs; note that the array is ordered, reading

TABLE 11   Six Possible Patterns of Residential Redistribution of Three Educational Classes, Based on Indexes of Disproportionate Change for the Metropolitan Ring, 1950–1960[a,b]

Type of Pattern	1	2	3	4	5	6	
Grade	–	–	–	+	+	+	
High	+	+	–	+	–	–	
College	+	–	+	–	+	–	Total
Number of metropolitan areas by type	216	100	12	16	9 13.0	10	363
Percent of metropolitan areas by type	29.5	27.5	3.3	4.4	2.5	2.8	100.0

[a] A minus sign (–) indicates a disproportionate decline in the ring; a plus sign (+) indicates a disproportionate increase in the ring.
[b] Source: Schnore & Pinkerton (1966).

from 1 through 6, with 6 appearing as the mirror image of 1, and so on.

The lower panel in Table 11 shows the numbers and proportions of areas found to exhibit each individual pattern. The expected type, previously identified as pattern 1, is found in six out of every ten cases. However, pattern 2 is exhibited by almost three out of every ten areas and thus represents a significant deviant pattern—one in which only the high school group is increasing in the ring, while the grade school and college classes are declining. Finally, over one out of every ten areas is found in one or the other of the four remaining types. These results suggest that the expected pattern—the product of what has been called "the great exodus of the middle and upper classes" from the city—is not nearly so common as one might suppose on the basis of the existing urban literature. What are the correlates of these different patterns?

Independent Variables   The measure of size shown here refers to the aggregate population of the metropolitan area in 1960; i.e., the combined populations of central cities and rings are employed. The measure of "age" is the number of decades that have passed since the central city (or cities) first reached 10,000 inhabitants, as reported in the decennial Census. This indicator seems preferable to others that could be used, such as the date of incorporation or the first date at which the place was reported in the Census.

Table 12 shows the results of the tabulation of variations in pat-

TABLE 12 Patterns of Residential Redistribution of Educational Classes in Metropolitan Areas, 1950-1960, by Size of Metropolitan Area in 1960[a]

	Type of Pattern	1	2	3	4	5	6	
Population Size of	Grade	–	–	–	+	+	+	
Metropolitan Area,	High	+	+	–	+	–	–	Total
1960	College	+	–	+	–	+	–	(= 100%)
Percent distribution by type								
500,000 and over		84	8		8			49
250,000–500,000		82	8		10			49
150,000–250,000		58	27		15			52
100,000–150,000		54	36		10			72
75,000–100,000		51	35		14			49
50,000–75,0000		47	39		14			62
<50,000		40	37		23			30

[a]Source: Schnore & Pinkerton (1966).

tern of social class redistribution by size of the metropolitan area in 1960. It is quite evident that size is a fairly good predictor of patterns of change. At the very least, the proportion of metropolitan areas displaying the expected pattern declines rather markedly as one descends the size scale. Over eight out of every ten very large areas exhibit the expected pattern (type 1), but this fraction falls to half that figure in the very smallest areas (under 50,000 inhabitants). The "deviant" patterns do not fall out in equally clear-cut fashion. It is true that type 2 tends to become increasingly frequent with smaller size, but types 3 to 6 (combined) do not show the same sort of patterned variation. The exceptions to an ordered series are numerous.

Finally, Table 13 exhibits our results according to age of the central city. The format employed is the same as that in the preceding table, and the results are very clear: The older the city, the greater the likelihood that the expected pattern (type 1) will be found in changes occurring between 1950 and 1960. Indeed, almost nine out of every ten of the very oldest places (those that reached 10,000 prior to 1840) reveal the expected patterns; this contrasts sharply with the very newest places, where only one out of every three manifests the type 1 configuration. The progression is quite marked from one age class to the next. Moreover, the relative frequency of the type 2 pattern tends to increase as one reads down the second column, that is, with decreasing age. At the same time, it should be pointed out that there is no such regularity in the appearance of the remaining types (3–6, taken together). Compared to size of the metropolitan area, however, the age of the city appears to be a somewhat more

TABLE 13　Patterns of Residential Redistribution of Educational Classes in Metropolitan Areas, 1950–1960, by Age of Central City or Cities[a]

Census Date at Which Central City or Cities First Reached 10,000 Population	Type of Pattern	1	2	3	4	5	6	
	Grade	–	–	–	+	+	+	
	High	+	+	–	+	–	–	Total
	College	+	–	+	–	+	–	(= 100%)
Percent distribution by type								
1790–1830		87	0		13			15
1840–1850		72	7		21			28
1860–1870		68	27		5			66
1880–1890		62	30		8			94
1900–1910		55	30		15			76
1920–1930		49	35		16			63
1940–1950		33	33		33			21

[a]Source: Schnore & Pinkerton (1966).

effective predictor of the type of change under examination here.

Our goal in this whole enterprise is to determine whether or not there is an "evolutionary sequence" in the redistribution of social classes in American cities (Schnore, 1965b). Although our results tend to contradict some of the assertions in the urban literature, we have found clearly patterned differences in the residential redistribution of socioeconomic strata in 363 metropolitan areas between 1950 and 1960. Age and size have again emerged as apparently important factors. While other variables warrant close attention, these two should certainly continue to be studied in detail.

Conclusions and Recommendations for Future Research

Our conclusions are fairly obvious, from the standpoint of research that is needed immediately. The detailed findings of each of the studies reviewed and summarized in the foregoing sections need not be repeated. This survey of the present state of knowledge is already overly long and perhaps unnecessarily repetitious.

1. Prior research using the 1970 Census data, should be replicated. There is not a single study, of all those reviewed above, that does not merit replication and (hopefully) improvement. Full recourse to computerization of the Census data, if all goes according to official plans, would permit fairly early processing of the data by interested researchers; one need not depend on "handcrafted" treatment of

TABLE 14 Indexes of Centralization for the Detroit Metropolitan Area, 1940-1960[a]

Males, 25+ Years Old, by Years of School Completed	Percent in City			Index of Centralization			Differences in Index		
	1940	1950	1960	1940	1950	1960	1940–1950	1950–1960	1940–1960
None	76.5	73.7	69.3	109.9	116.2	147.7	6.3	31.5	37.8
Grade 1–4	72.1	71.3	64.9	103.6	112.4	138.3	8.8	25.9	34.7
Grade 5–6	71.5	69.3	59.3	102.7	109.3	126.4	6.6	17.1	23.7
Grade 7–8	69.1	62.8	51.4	99.3	98.8	109.5	-0.5	10.7	23.7
High 1–3	69.0	62.2	45.9	99.1	98.1	97.8	-1.0	- 0.3	- 1.3
High 4	70.4	61.2	40.5	101.2	96.5	86.3	-4.7	-10.2	-14.9
College 1–3	69.9	63.3	40.1	100.4	99.8	85.5	-0.6	-14.3	-14.9
College 4+	69.0	59.2	34.9	99.1	93.3	74.4	-5.8	-18.9	-24.7
Total	69.6	63.4	46.9	100.0	100.0	100.0			

[a]Source: Schnore (1964).

228

published tabulations if currently available computer hard- and software are intelligently utilized. There will remain some difficult choices—particularly with respect to areal units and measures of social class standing—but the promise seems great in the continued search for the kind of observed regularities we have been seeking. Such regularities promise to enhance both formal "theories" regarding urban phenomena and policy formulation.

2. There is a need for more longitudinally oriented or historical studies of trends. Early use of 1970 Census materials, when appropriately combined with 1960 data, should permit a far more accurate assessment of trends for the 1960's than we have for the 1950's. The imbalance between cross-sectional and longitudinal studies must be already evident to the reader; it can be seen in the pages devoted to the relatively large number of "snapshot" studies, compared to the two that involve a study of trends in class residence patterns in the 1950's.

3. The simultaneous observation of both color and class segregation should be carried out wherever it is feasible. Many of the foregoing empirical regularities with respect to class, set out in the main body of this paper, may be a function of color differences between cities and suburbs. Table 14, for example, implies a marked class polarization of Detroit city and its metropolitan ring, particularly during the 1950–1960 decade. The very last column, however, suggests that the entire 20-year interval represented in the table was characterized by a distinctly patterned sifting and sorting of the various educational classes between Detroit and its suburbs. Yet, anyone familiar with the metropolitan Detroit situation will recognize that color plays an important role in that area's residential patterns (see Sharp & Schnore, 1962, for a detailed discussion of Detroit, especially pages 182–184).

4. A metropolitan-wide context must be maintained. Although we have opted for use of the urbanized area at many points, it seems clear, from the foregoing reference to Detroit, that much would be gained by a sustained focus on the SMSA and analogous units; this also would include those designated as quasi-metropolitan areas centered on cities of 25,000–50,000 inhabitants. (A number of those that have been delineated on quite arbitrary geographic bases have actually been added to the list of 230 SMSA's recognized in the preliminary 1970 Census reports.) The SMSA is not the ideal areal unit, of course, but it has distinct advantages. For one thing, many series of federal statistics are available for it. For another, it seems

reasonable to assume that the study by Smith, which used urbanized areas, could be profitably extended to cover the SMSA and its areal subparts—including suburbs, rural–urban fringe, and outright rural territory—and to deal with trends over the 1960–1970 intercensal decade.

5. The problem of annexations by metropolitan central cities (and perhaps established suburbs as well) must be confronted directly. These "political" actions, however reasonable from a local standpoint, serve only to confuse the nonlocal researcher or policy-maker. It seems clear that most annexations are decidedly beneficial to the political unit "capturing" the new territory. Table 15 is a clear demonstration of this tendency among those large cities (with 250,000 or more inhabitants in 1960) that annexed substantial territory (3.0 or more square miles) during the 1950's. For all 29 cities concerned, Table 15 shows that the central city median income was raised in each and every instance. In four cases, where unusual income patterns prevailed both before and after the adjustment for annexation, the suburban ring medians were also raised. But in 25 out of 29 cases, as might be expected, the suburban ring lost ground as far as median income was concerned. In any case, it might be desirable to recommend that the U.S. Bureau of the Census make widely available any feasible compilations of data on the characteristics of population in annexed areas.

These five recommendations certainly do not exhaust the problems that might be discussed. Problems of metrics occupy a prominent place in our thinking, based on our own research experience with Census data. Many vexing problems of areal units and measures of social class have yet to be resolved (Schnore, 1967). With respect to the final recommendation concerning annexation, for example, both research and policy goals would be more readily achieved if the U.S. Bureau of the Census were persuaded to publish data on the socio-economic and demographic characteristics, as well as the sheer numbers of persons in areas annexed by larger cities and suburbs. Data on the numbers of inhabitants in areas annexed between 1950 and 1960 was an innovation of the 1960 Census that proved to be very helpful, in a research context, in evaluating the true extent of suburbanization in the 1950's (Schnore, 1962a).

CONCLUDING REMARKS

The major trends of the 1960's by reference to 1960 and 1970 Census data need to be discerned and documented. Preliminary analysis

(Schnore & Klaff, 1971) already indicates that suburbanization continued on a grand scale during the 1960's, though much of it was masked by annexation.

More adequate treatment of segregation by color will be possible if all 1970 Census innovations work as planned. The pioneering work of Taeuber and Taeuber (1965) can be replicated, and even improved. As in their prior work, however, carefully selected case studies of places chosen on a reasoned basis will augment the findings of comparative research.

The promising beginnings in the analysis of characteristics of annexed populations and areas (see Table 15) deserve high priority, but can only be carried out if the proper mix of computer tabulation, adequate research time, and budgetary provisions can be solved.

In conclusion let it be noted that no direct attention has been given to suburbanization of the population at large (Schnore, 1965, Pt. 2), functions and types of individual suburbs (Schnore, 1956, 1957, 1963a), the age–sex structure of cities and suburbs, or segregation according to family type. Two former students, however, are currently engaged in research in the latter areas: James R. Pinkerton, who has already contributed a valuable review of the literature on the topic of this paper (Pinkerton, 1969), is working on the age–sex composition of cities and suburbs, and Avery Mason Guest, who has tested the Burgess hypothesis with available Canadian data (Guest, 1969), has completed his dissertation, *Families and Housing in Cities*; publications will be forthcoming in the near future.

We have also neglected to integrate very valuable lines of research by other teams of investigators, notably Anderson and Egeland (1961), Hoover and Vernon (1962), Nam and Powers (1965), and Goldsmith and his colleagues (Goldsmith & Lee, 1966; Goldsmith & Stockwell, 1969). Some of this work inspired our efforts at many points, while in other cases the scholarly debt would seem to be reversed. A full-scale treatment of the topic, however, would have to take account of the accomplishments of these other investigators.

Acknowledgments

I am grateful to Miss Pat Blair and Mr. Vivian Klaff for assistance in the preparation of this paper. It is dedicated to the memory of my first collaborator, the late Dr. David Wright Varley (1922-1970).

TABLE 15 Summary of the Impact of 1950–1960 Annexation on City–Suburban Median Family Income Comparisons of 29 Large Cities and Their Metropolitan Rings, 1960^a

City	Median Family Income, 1959 ($)					Before and After the Annexation Adjustment	
	Central City without Annexed Area	Central City with Annexed Area	Annexed Area	Metro Ring without Annexed Area	Metro Ring with Annexed Area	Central City Median Income	Metro Ring Median Income
Atlanta	5,029	4,182	6,581	6,320	6,376	+847	− 56
Birmingham, Ala.	4,949	4,826	7,506	5,283	5,398	+123	−115
Cincinnati	5,701	5,673	7,521	6,793	6,803	+ 28	− 10
Columbus, Ohio	5,982	5,789	6,923	7,543	7,354	+193	+189
Dallas	5,976	5,875	6,333	5,844	5,968	+101	−124
Dayton	6,266	6,144	7,034	6,913	6,921	+122	− 8
Denver	6,361	6,185	8,367	6,749	6,876	+176	−127
El Paso	5,211	4,594	5,886	4,758	5,663	+617	−905
Fort Worth	5,484	5,230	6,772	5,794	5,967	+254	−173
Houston	5,902	5,496	6,853	6,430	6,627	+406	−197
Indianapolis	6,106	5,905	7,554	7,786	7,768	+201	+ 18
Kansas City, Mo.	5,906	5,766	7,231	6,631	6,676	+140	− 45
Long Beach	6,570	6,174	8,364	7,237	7,270	+396	− 33
Louisville	5,280	4,934	6,959	6,303	6,416	+346	−113
Memphis	4,915	4,531	6,832	4,849	5,719	+384	−870

Milwaukee	6,664	6,504	7,343	7,776	7,693	+160	+ 83
Nashville	3,816	3,805	4,116	6,364	6,290	+ 11	+ 74
Norfolk	4,894	4,552	5,504	5,229	5,299	+342	− 70
Oklahoma City	5,600	5,467	6,076	5,604	5,730	+133	−126
Omaha	6,315	6,103	7,665	6,036	6,374	+212	−338
Phoenix	6,117	5,365	6,356	5,379	6,001	+752	−622
Portland, Ore.	6,335	6,295	7,615	6,344	6,372	+ 40	− 28
San Antonio	4,691	4,250	6,067	5,424	5,871	+441	−447
San Diego	6,614	6,522	7,216	6,465	6,565	+ 92	−100
Seattle	6,942	6,833	7,469	6,853	6,935	+109	− 82
Tampa	4,667	4,019	5,202	4,395	4,575	+648	−180
Toledo	6,299	6,182	7,739	7,042	7,177	+117	−135
Tulsa	6,229	5,544	7,118	4,958	5,832	+685	−874
Wichita	6,121	5,825	6,728	6,287	6,503	+296	−216

[a]Source: Original calculations by Vivian Klaff from data provided in Miller & Varon (1962).

234

SEGREGATION IN RESIDENTIAL AREAS

References

Ashley, T. L. In *Population trends: Hearings before the Ad Hoc Subcommittee on Urban Growth of the Committee on Banking and Currency, House of Representatives, Ninety-First Congress, Part 1*. Washington, D.C.: U.S. Government Printing Office, 1969.

Anderson, T. R., & Egeland, J. A. Spatial aspects of social area analysis. *American Sociological Review*, 1961, 26, 392–398.

Bureau of the Budget, Executive Office of the President. *Standard metropolitan statistical areas*. Washington, D.C.: U.S. Government Printing Office, 1961.

Burgess, E. W. The growth of the city: An introduction to a research project. In Park, R. E., Burgess, E. W., & McKenzie, R. D. [Eds.], *The city*. Chicago: University of Chicago Press, 1925. Pp. 53–59.

Duncan, O. D., & Duncan, B. *The Negro population of Chicago: A study of residential segregation*. Chicago: University of Chicago Press, 1957.

Goldsmith, H. F., & Lee, S. Y. Socioeconomic status within the older and larger 1960 metropolitan areas. *Rural Sociology*, June 1966, 31, 207–215.

Goldsmith, H. F., & Stockwell, E. G. Interrelationship of occupational selectivity patterns among city, suburban and fringe areas of major metropolitan centers. *Land Economics*, May 1969, 45, 194–205.

Guest, A. M. The applicability of the Burgess zonal hypothesis to urban Canada. *Demography*, August 1969, 6, 271–277.

Hadden, J. K. Use of *ad hoc* Definitions. In E. F. Borgatta & G. Bohrnstedt [Eds.], *Sociological methodology 1969*. San Francisco: Jossey-Bass Inc., Pp. 276–285.

Hoover, E. M., & Vernon, R. *Anatomy of a metropolis*. New York: Doubleday, 1962.

Miller, A. R., & Varnon, B. Adjustment for area comparability of statistics on family income from the 1960 and 1950 censuses of population: Major cities and their standard metropolitan statistical areas. Philadelphia: Population Studies Center, University of Pennsylvania, 1962. (Technical Paper No. 3, Tables 1 and 2)

Nam, C. B., & Powers, M. G. Variations in socioeconomic structure by race, residence, and the life cycle. *American Sociological Review*, February 1965, 30, 97–103.

Palen, J. J., & Schnore, L. F. Color composition and city suburban status differences: A replication and extension. *Land Economics*. February 1965, 41, 87–91.

Pinkerton, J. R. The residential redistribution of socioeconomic strata in metropolitan areas. Unpublished Ph.D. dissertation, University of Wisconsin, Madison. 1965.

Pinkerton, J. R. City–suburban residential patterns by social class: A review of the literature. *Urban Affairs Quarterly*, June 1969, 4, 499–519.

Schnore, L. F. Patterns of decentralization: A study of differential growth in the metropolitan areas of the United States, 1900–1950. Unpublished Ph.D. Dissertation, University of Michigan, Ann Arbor, 1955.

Schnore, L. F. The functions of metropolitan suburbs. *American Journal of Sociology*, March 1956, 61, 453–458.

Schnore, L. F. Satellites and suburbs. *Social Forces*, December 1957, 36, 121–127.

Schnore, L. F. The city as a social organism. *Urban Affairs Quarterly,* 1966, 1, 58–69.

Schnore, L. F. Measuring city–suburban status differences. *Urban Affairs Quarterly,* 1967, 3, 95–108.

Schnore, L. F., & Evenson, P. C. Segregation in southern cities. *American Journal of Sociology,* 1966, 72, 58–67.

Schnore, L. F., & Jones, J. K. O. The evolution of city–suburban types in the course of a decade. *Urban Affairs Quarterly,* 1969, 4, 421–442.

Schnore, L. F., & Klaff, V. Suburbanization in the sixties: A preliminary report. Paper prepared for presentation at the annual meeting of the Population Association of America, Washington, D.C., April 23, 1971.

Schnore, L. F., & Pinkerton, J. R. Residential redistribution of socioeconomic strata in metropolitan areas. *Demography,* 1966, 3, 491–499.

Schnore, L. F., & Varley, D. W. Some concomitants of metropolitan size. *American Sociological Review,* (August), 1955, 20, 408–414.

Sharp, H., & Schnore, L. F. The changing color composition of metropolitan areas. *Land Economics,* (May), 1955, 38, 169–185.

Smith, J. Another look at socioeconomic status distributions in urbanized areas. *Urban Affairs Quarterly,* 1970 (June), 5, 423–453.

Taeuber, K. E., & Taeuber, A. F. *Negroes in cities: Residential segregation and neighborhood change.* Chicago: Aldine, 1965.

U.S. Bureau of the Census. *U.S. census of population: 1960.* Vol. 1. *Characteristics of the population.* Part A. *Number of inhabitants.* Washington, D.C.: U.S. Government Printing Office, 1961.

U.S. Bureau of the Census. *U.S. census of population: 1960. General Social and Economic Characteristics.* Final Report PC(1). Washington, D.C.: U.S. Government Printing Office, 1962.

U.S. Bureau of the Census. *U.S. census of population: 1960.* Vol. 1. *Characteristics of the population.* Part 1. *United States summary.* Washington, D.C.: U.S. Government Printing Office, 1964.

Schnore, L. F. City–suburban income differentials in metropolitan areas. *American Sociological Review,* 1962a, 27, 252–255.

Schnore, L. F. Municipal annexations and the growth of metropolitan areas, 1950–1960. *American Journal of Sociology,* 1962b, 67, 406–417.

Schnore, L. F. The social and economic characteristics of American suburbs. *The Sociological Quarterly,* 1963a, 4, 122–134.

Schnore, L. F. The socioeconomic status of cities and suburbs. *American Sociological Review,* 1963b, 28, 76–85.

Schnore, L. F. Urban structure and suburban selectivity. *Demography,* 1964, 1, 164–176.

Schnore, L. F. On the spatial structure of cities in the two Americas. In P. M. Hauser & L. F. Schnore [Eds.], *The study of urbanization.* New York: John Wiley, 1965a, 347–398.

Schnore, L. F. Social class segregation among nonwhites in metropolitan centers. *Demography,* 1965b, 2, 130–133.

Schnore, L. F. *The urban scene: Human ecology and demography.* New York: Free Press, 1965c.